# THE 7TH PROPERTY

Eric Yakes

Contact the author at yakes.io



Publisher's Cataloging-in-Publication Data

Names: Yakes, Eric, author.
Title: The 7th property : bitcoin and the monetary revolution / Eric Yakes.
Description: Greenwoood Village, CO : Black Poodle Publishing, 2021.
Identifiers: ISBN 978-0-578-90262-3 (paperback) | ISBN 978-0-578-90263-0 (ebook)
Subjects: LCSH: Bitcoin. | Financial instruments. | Money--History. | Monetary policy. | Banks and banking, Central. | BISAC: BUSINESS & ECONOMICS / Bitcoin & Cryptocurrencies. | BUSINESS & ECONOMICS / Money & Monetary Policy. | BUSINESS & ECONOMICS / Banks & Banking.
Classification: LCC HG1710 .Y35 2021 (print) | LCC HG1710 (ebook) | DDC 332.4--dc23.

LCCN: 2021909575

Cover and interior design by CKBooks Publishing
ckbookspublishing.com

Black Poodle Publishing, LLC.
1500 Cherryville Rd
Greenwood Village, CO, 80121

*Dedicated to those who were persistent enough to change my mind and caring enough to change my values.*

# TABLE OF CONTENTS

INTRODUCTION .......... 1

1. THE DIMENSIONS OF MONEY .......... 3

2. THE HISTORY OF DECENTRALIZED MONEY .......... 21

3. THE HISTORY OF CENTRALIZED MONEY .......... 38

4. THE HISTORY OF CENTRAL BANKING .......... 61

5. THE HISTORY OF THE FEDERAL RESERVE .......... 85

6. HOW THE FEDERAL RESERVE WORKS .......... 103

7. THE CYCLE OF CENTRALIZED BANKING .......... 127

8. THE HISTORY OF BITCOIN .......... 156

9. WHAT BITCOIN DOES .......... 173

10. HOW BITCOIN WORKS .......... 202

11. THE RULES OF BITCOIN .......... 225

12. THE BITCOIN ECOSYSTEM .......... 240

13. THE PROPERTIES OF BITCOIN .......... 264

14. THE CRITICISMS OF BITCOIN .......... 283

ACKNOWLEDGMENTS: .......... 311

# INTRODUCTION

I first discovered Bitcoin in 2015 as an undergrad and then wrote a short essay concluding it was a speculative asset with no fundamental value. Though I wish that were not my initial opinion, when applying the economic theory I had learned in school, it was the only logical conclusion I could come to. Over the years, reading about Bitcoin started to consume my spare time. By 2018 I came to the realization that Bitcoin was the next step in the world's monetary evolution. By 2019 I quit my job in private equity and moved into my mom's basement to begin working on this writing.

This 4-year process could have been shorter. It was long because I had to relearn a lot of what I had been taught at university. I started to revisit concepts that I had once questioned. I remember the first time I was taught that interest on US debt was the "risk-free interest rate" because the government could always print more money and can never default. I said to myself, "There is no such thing as risk-free, but what is the risk of printing money?" Within the same year, I was taught that inflation is necessary, and the central bank targets a rate of 2% inflation in our economy. Nobody provided me with a reason as to why inflation was necessary; it was something simply accepted as an encouragement to spending and investment, which make our economy grow. But production of goods and services is what makes an economy grow, right? Isn't there some sort of cost to creating inflation? At the time I did not know enough to conclude that there was a significant cost.

In 2016, a close friend of mine Avinash Patel brought Bitcoin back to my attention. I first invested once I realized it did not need to produce cash flows to have value, but I still saw it as a speculative investment. Now I view Bitcoin as the base layer monetary asset for a new global decentralized financial system.

This book contains the foundational ideas I wish someone had given me back in 2015. I spent thousands of hours researching and synthesizing aspects of monetary economics, central banking, and cryptography. By the end of this book, you will at a minimum consider the possibility that Bitcoin is the new monetary base layer of a new financial system – something which has not occurred for millennia.

This book is intended for those with a background in finance and/or economics, but if you have a more general understanding of business, you can get through it with the occasional google search. Don't be intimidated by the content – if you don't understand something, try to look it up and then keep reading. The first 7 chapters can be challenging but provide the necessary background to understand money and banking – a prerequisite to understanding Bitcoin. If you read this, you will understand Bitcoin well enough to make a decision about its validity for yourself.

# 1. THE DIMENSIONS OF MONEY

What is money?
Why is it used?
Which type of money is best and why?
Who decides this for us?
Is there a way to understand money at a fundamental level so that we can choose for ourselves?
What does it mean when people say money needs to be "backed" by something?

These are important questions that can be expensive to neglect. Money is confusing because it crosses multiple dimensions. Some of these dimensions you have probably heard of, but I have not seen them summarized holistically. Figure 1 is that summary, although it will require some explanation. Briefly study it and move forward with the structure in mind. By the end of this chapter, you will have a mental framework to assess money and determine its merit for yourself.

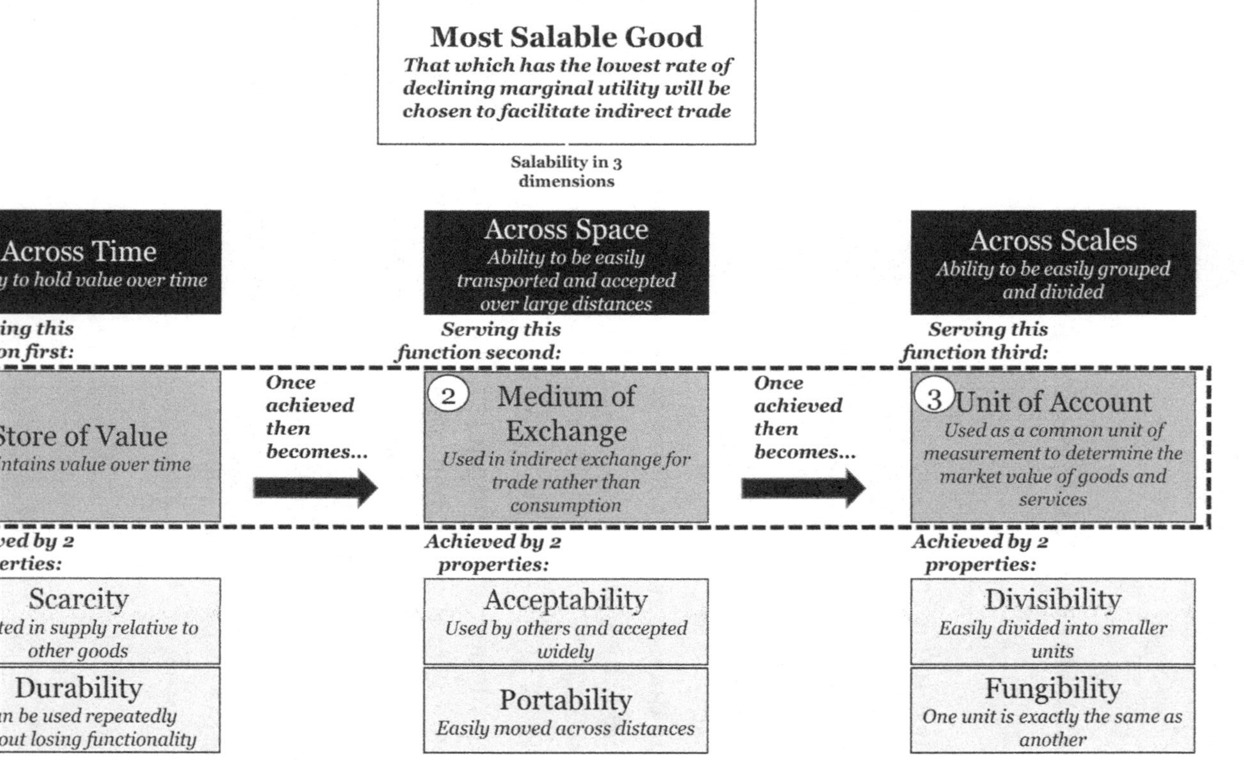


**Figure 1:** the dimensions of money

## The Purpose of Money

If people could create whatever they wanted, whenever they wanted it, there would be no need for trade in a society. But this is not yet possible. Long ago people realized that specializing in a type of production and trading it for their other needs allowed them to consume more than they could otherwise. This is why specialties are called trades. Trade facilitates specialization, which facilitates more efficient means of production and ultimately greater consumption.

Before money, people traded goods through a **barter system** in which one good was exchanged for another. This system works in small groups but becomes more challenging in larger groups, requiring a ***coincidence of interests*** – meaning one must have the good desired in the right **amount**, in the right **location**, and at the right **time, and** that another party desires, and vice versa.

Systems of barter were more prevalent when individuals were organized in small groups (e.g., hunter-gatherer tribes) primarily during the prehistory era of humanity. As groups grew larger, those which utilized forms of money to facilitate transactions and store wealth were able to become more specialized in their productive capacities – allowing more sophisticated forms of organization to emerge and living standards to rise.

***The purpose of money is to facilitate trade, which allows groups to specialize and organize with greater complexity.***

## Defining Money

Barter systems are forms of ***direct trade*** while monetary systems are forms of ***indirect trade***. Goods used in indirect trade are naturally converged upon (i.e., chosen freely through iterations of trade) because they have properties that most people want most often. Goods that maintain these properties are desired because they are most likely to present a coincidence of interest with other parties. In this sense, Money enables a system of ***indirect exchange***.

Carl Menger, in the *The Origins of Money,* defined the relative ability for a good to be sold in a given market at the time and price desired as a good's **salability.**[1] Market participants converge upon the most salable commodity over time, through many transactions.

Consider a producer of apples and a producer of decorative pots. A producer of apples is more likely to have buyers than a producer of decorative pots, but both producers still need to exchange their goods consistently for goods they need. The apple merchant will exchange as many apples as possible for the goods he currently desires. Then, knowing his remaining apples will soon rot, he might attempt to exchange them at a discount with the pots merchant. He does so with the knowledge that he can exchange these pots at a later date as they are more valuable across time. Conversely, the pots merchant might have exchanged his pots for the number of apples he will eat before they rot but then exchange his remaining pots to a salt merchant at a discount because he knows salt is more widely accepted than pots. **The apples merchant is exchanging his surplus to hold its value over time while the pots merchant is exchanging his surplus for a more widely accepted good.** Merchants will continue this process and naturally converge upon a commodity that is **most widely accepted** and **best maintains value over time** to protect themselves from depending on any coincidence of interests in the future. Whichever good is converged upon will eventually be considered money. Buyers and sellers in the market will acquire money not for its inherent utility, but instead for the certainty they can use it to acquire what they desire in the future.

Consider this concept from another perspective. Menger described the ***most salable good*** as that which has the lowest rate of declining marginal utility. A good with high declining marginal utility could be a house – as you only need one, and each incremental house purchased provides much less benefit than the initial house purchased. A good with medium declining marginal utility could be electricity – the first unit to the $n^{th}$ provides similar utility up until you've powered everything you need. A good with low declining marginal utility is one in which each consecutive unit consumed provides nearly equal benefit to the prior unit. Whatever good this is will naturally become money and therefore the most salable.[2] Money is the good that you can't get enough of.

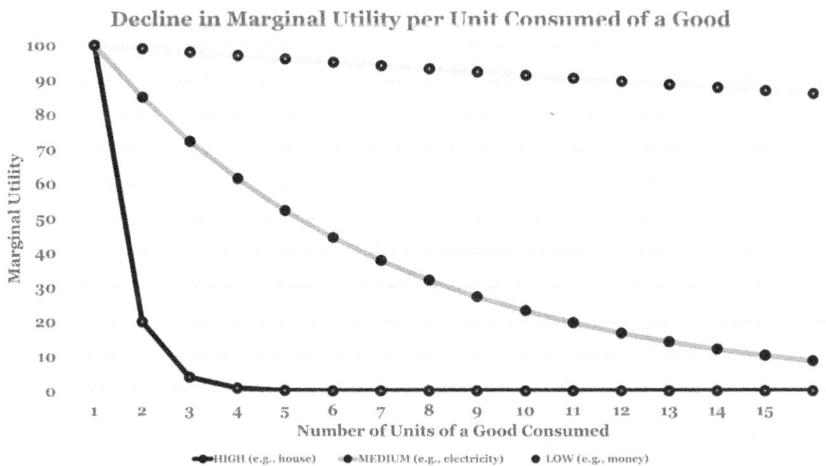


**Figure 2:** example of declining marginal utility

We've now defined the first aspect of our monetary dimensions table:

| **Most Salable Good** |
|---|
| ***That which has the lowest rate of declining marginal utility will be chosen to facilitate indirect trade*** |

**Figure 3:** most salable good definition

Saifedean Ammous precisely defines a good's salability across three dimensions[3] which solve three different types of coincidence:

1. **Salability across Time** – Ability to hold value over time, removing the coincidence of timing.
   - (Pots are relatively better than apples for this purpose.)
2. **Salability across Space** – Ability to be easily transported, removing the coincidence of location.
   - (Digital money is relatively better than physical money for this purpose.)
3. **Salability across Scales** – Ability to be easily grouped and divided, removing the coincidence of amount.
   - (Water is relatively better than a house for this purpose.)

**Most Salable Good**

***That which has the lowest rate of declining marginal utility will be chosen to facilitate indirect trade***

**Salability in 3 dimensions**

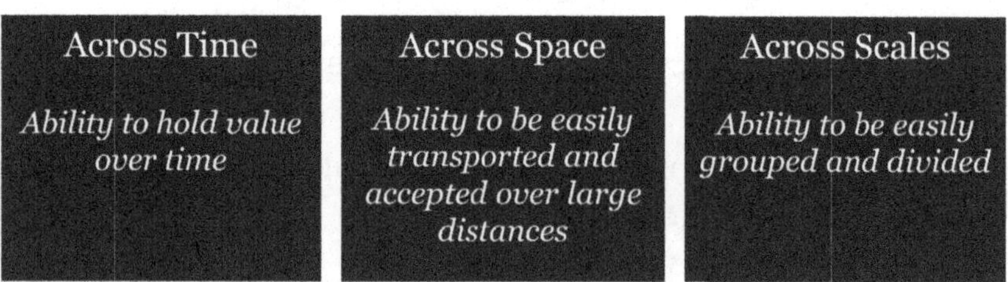


**Figure 4:** the dimensions of salability

***In a free market, the most salable good will be chosen as money. Salability can be broken into three dimensions: time, space, and scales.***

## Defining Monetary Value

Thus far we've discussed how a good maintains **monetary value.** This is not to be confused with a good's **market value. Think of this as a good's utility for trade vs. its utility for consumption.** Market value is derived from a good's consumption value, while monetary value is derived from a good's monetary properties.

Consider an example where you want to sell your car and you find 2 people interested in buying it. One person, Jim, has always wanted this type of car and offers $20,000. The other person, Joe, is a car dealer and offers you $15,000. Jim is paying you more because he wants to use the car, while Joe is paying you less because he plans to turn around and trade it to someone else for $20,000. Therefore, your car's utility for trade is valued at $15,000, while its utility for consumption is valued at $20,000. **The good that has equal trade and consumption value is money.** Nobody will trade you a discount for money because it is the most tradeable good. Thus, monetary value is distinguished from market value as it reduces the implicit economic cost of trade ($20,000 - $15,000).

The market value of a good exists without a monetary medium. A monetary medium cannot exist without underlying goods and services that have market value. In this sense, **a monetary good obtains its value by enabling the trade of goods** which have market value and need to be exchanged across space, time, and scales. The better the form of money used, the lower the costs of transacting, and the greater the ability to transfer, store, and measure wealth.

***The monetary value of a good is obtained by its ability to enable trade and is completely separate from the good's market value for consumption.***

## How People Choose Money

People commonly think of something as valuable if it can be utilized in some form of consumption (i.e., you can eat it, wear it, live in it, etc.). However, money is not something that needs to be consumed to have value. This doesn't mean money can't also have consumption utility, and in fact, it did for most of history until paper was adopted. **Paper money was never naturally chosen as money, it was enforced.** Before money was enforced, participants in a market chose their form of money by its utility for the purpose of trade.

In a free market, the good most sought through indirect exchange will become the medium of exchange (or monetary medium or money) over time. This is how organized groups eventually began using precious metals, which had little consumption utility at the time, because they had relatively better properties to facilitate trade.

The process of convergence increases exponentially due to **network effects** – as more market participants use a common medium, it becomes increasingly likely that other participants will use it. This effect can be seen today in the growth of social media platforms, with individuals naturally converging upon a few platforms despite the fact that many of them exist with relatively homogenous functionality. Similarly, societies converge upon a monetary medium, assuming no barriers exist, because it is more beneficial to an individual to transact in a money which he/she knows is going to be the most widely accepted.

However, this assumes that there are no barriers to usage. For example, country-specific currencies are used because of government enforcement. Looking back in history, we see that multiple metals were used for coins within a country. Looking back farther, people converged upon many different goods before the world was integrated and societies were simply not aware of each other's currency. **These barriers were either the product of information opacity, sovereign coercion, or monetary utility tradeoffs.**

Information opacity has been reduced to a great extent by the internet. But sovereign coercion still exists, and as a consequence most people aren't aware of any monetary utility tradeoffs (because we don't choose our money). If money were not forced upon us, society would have to choose between different tradeoffs of different monetary mediums in a market environment. Tradeoffs do exist, and I am not aware of private alternatives that have found a way to traverse across them (more on this later). Similarly, we maintain a variety of different social networks because they specialize in various tradeoffs. You can't have a social network that is both professional and candid, so we have created separate networks for each. The benefit of these various tradeoffs is the competitive environment that results, protecting us from natural monopolies. If the world could choose its money, I believe similar principles would apply.

***In a perfect world, there would be one form of money. In the real world, there are many.***

Once a monetary medium achieves the critical mass necessary to reach wide acceptance, participants will begin to use it as a **unit of account** – that is, as a common form of price measurement for all goods and services within a market. This function is more relevant as a market becomes large and pricing in a common unit reduces the complexity of economic comparison.

As a society grows, the process of exchange becomes more complex as people become more specialized in producing goods and services. A greater need emerges to efficiently exchange over longer periods of time and greater distances. Stated differently, **the more people specialize, the greater the need for trade, the**

**greater the implicit costs of trade, and the greater the value maintained from trading most efficiently.**

Further, barter transactions (direct exchanges) do not scale well due to the exponential complexity of pricing. If $n$ is the number of products, then $n^2$ is the number of prices that must exist. That is a lot of prices, and people would spend a lot of time trying to compare them. Money is beneficial because it acts as a common unit of account to decrease this complexity. If there are $n$ products, then there are $n$ prices. The existence of a common unit of account allows for more complex economic assessment, increasing the transparency of information, reducing price arbitrage, and ultimately creating a more efficient market.

The evolution of a good's transition to becoming a monetary medium can be roughly summarized as follows. First, it must have properties that **store value,** in that one can reasonably assume its market demand will not deteriorate over time. As more market participants realize a certain good stores value, they can then exchange it between themselves for this property, even though it may not be widely accepted yet. As more of this exchange occurs, the knowledge of it being widely accepted becomes a self-fulfilling prophecy, and its use as a **medium of exchange** becomes more frequent. Once it is accepted at a large enough scale as a medium of exchange, participants using it as a medium will begin to commonly quote the prices of their goods and services in amounts of the good – until finally it becomes a common **unit of account**.

## The 3 Functions of Money:

1. **Store of value** – maintains its value over time.
2. **Medium of exchange** – is used in indirect exchange for the purpose of exchanging it again, rather than consuming it.
3. **Unit of account** – is used as a common unit of measurement to determine the market value of goods and services.

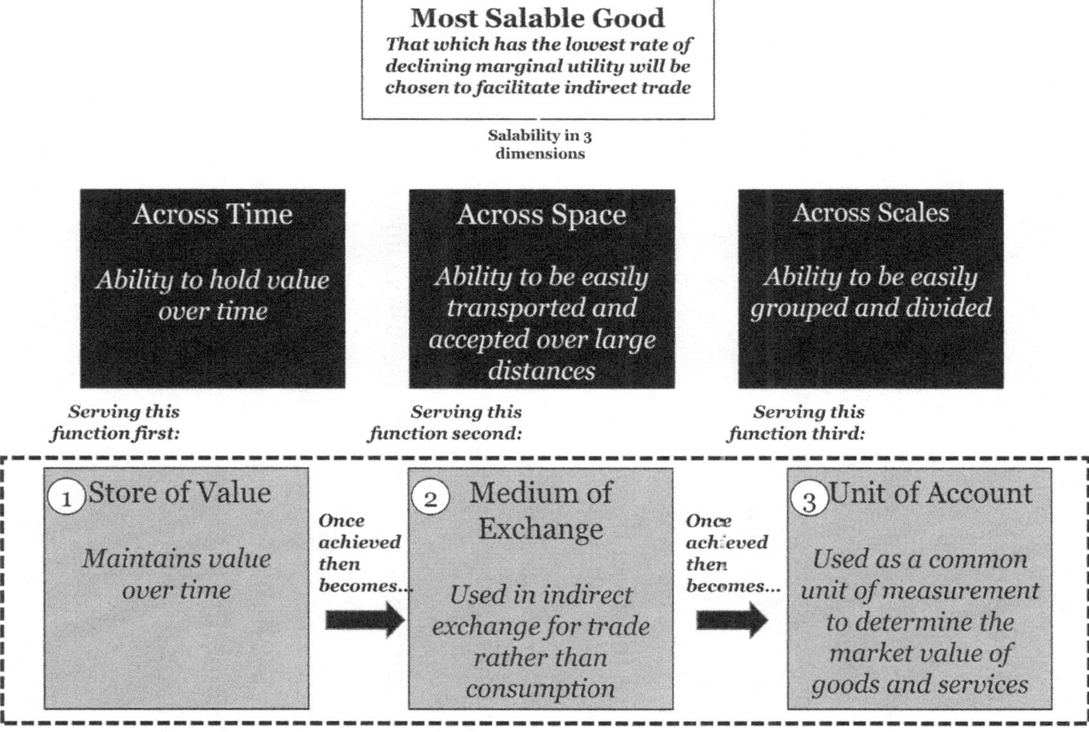


**Figure 5:** the functions of money

***Market participants naturally converge upon a good as a monetary medium that best stores wealth through time, is most widely accepted across space, and is adopted as a unit of account.***

## The 6 Properties of Money

The monetary medium chosen by societies has differed by availability and evolved as new materials and technology emerged which better fulfill the properties sought in a monetary medium. **What is consistent across history is that goods chosen as money have maintained certain properties that enable monetary functionality.**

There are 6 monetary properties that determine a good's merit for fulfilling the desired functionality as money:

1. **Scarcity** – is limited in its supply relative to other goods.
2. **Durability** – can be used repeatedly without losing its functionality.
3. **Acceptability** – it is used by others and thus accepted widely in a group.
4. **Portability** – capable of being moved across distances.
5. **Divisibility** – can be divided into smaller units of value.
6. **Fungibility** – one unit is viewed as exactly the same as (and thus interchangeable with) another unit.

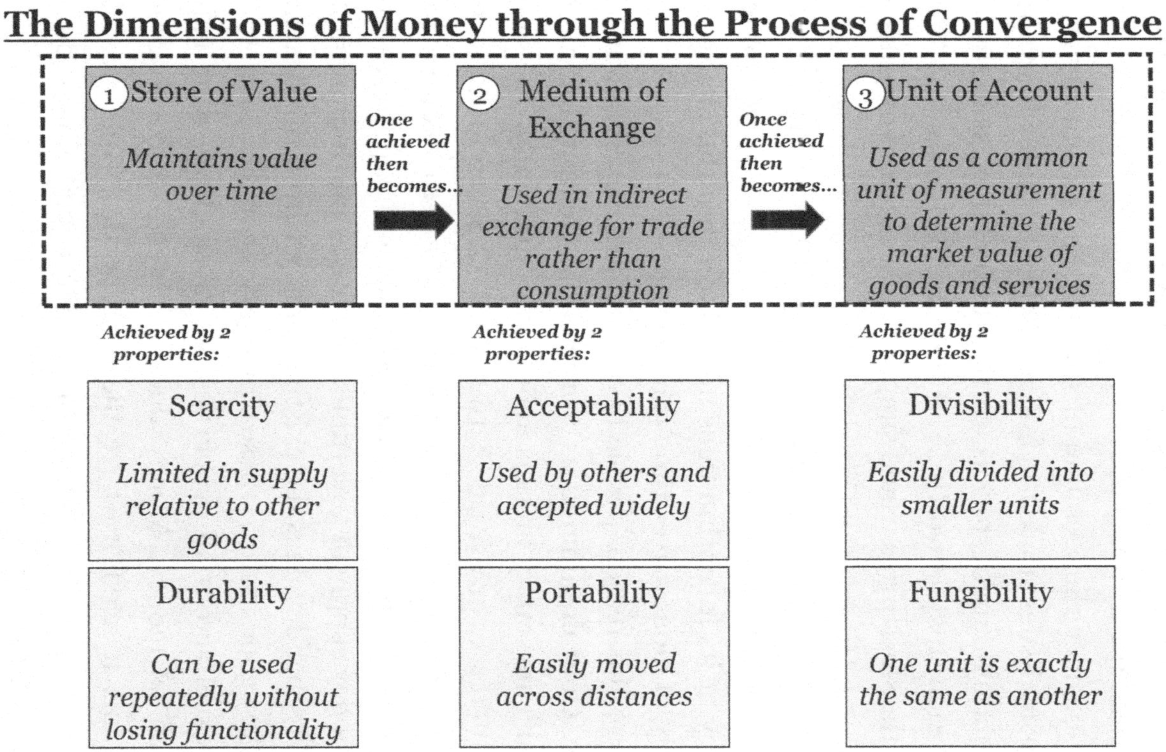

**The Dimensions of Money through the Process of Convergence**

1 Store of Value

*Maintains value over time*

*Once achieved then becomes...*

2 Medium of Exchange

*Used in indirect exchange for trade rather than consumption*

*Once achieved then becomes...*

3 Unit of Account

*Used as a common unit of measurement to determine the market value of goods and services*

*Achieved by 2 properties:*

Scarcity

*Limited in supply relative to other goods*

Durability

*Can be used repeatedly without losing functionality*

*Achieved by 2 properties:*

Acceptability

*Used by others and accepted widely*

Portability

*Easily moved across distances*

*Achieved by 2 properties:*

Divisibility

*Easily divided into smaller units*

Fungibility

*One unit is exactly the same as another*

**Figure 6:** the properties of money

Let's quickly expand on the property of scarcity, as it is arguably the most important property of money. For goods with low declining marginal utility, a scarce good is one that has a limited increase in supply. **The rate of increase of supply is more important than the initial supply.**

Consider the example of the stock of a company. When a company issues stock, the initial number of shares is arbitrary. If the total amount of stock is worth $100 and they issue 100 shares, then each stock is worth $1. If they decided to issue 200 shares, then the stock price would simply be 50 cents and no value is lost or gained. However, if the company issued 100 shares and then a year later decided to issue 100 more, all the existing stockholders would have their stock value diluted by 50%. **The amount of money at its inception does not matter, but the change in the supply of money over time is important.**

For this reason, people have sought money that was hard to make. **Gold dominated as a monetary medium for millennia because its supply increased only very gradually.** The supply of gold increases on average between 1.5 – 2.5% annually, so people are certain the supply won't drastically increase, causing prices to drastically rise, and reduce their purchasing power. However, the money supply of government increases much more rapidly, a tragedy that devalues the existing money within the system.

Any good that has these 6 properties could be money. Goods that excel across all properties are most likely to be naturally chosen as money. Money does not need to be "backed" by anything; it needs to have these properties. Gold was chosen because it has these properties, while paper money does not. Thus, paper money needed to be "backed" by gold so that it could maintain monetary properties while also being more efficient for use in trade. That is where the term "backed" comes from and it was only necessary because enforced paper money needed to be backed by something that actually had monetary properties. When people say that money is "backed by the government," it means nothing. Actually, it means less than nothing, but I will explain this in a later chapter.

## Money Across All Dimensions

Let's recap the dimensions of money and how they can be used to conceive whether or not a good will be converged upon as a monetary medium.

For a good to become money in a free market it must be the most salable good. Salability can be thought of in 3 dimensions: time, space, and scale. A good must excel in certain properties to be considered salable in a respective dimension. For example, if a good is the most salable across time, then it will be the best store of value. If a good is the most salable across space, then it will be the best medium of exchange. If a good is the most salable across scale, it will be the best unit of account. Some goods can be highly salable in one dimension while not at all in another. The good that is the most salable across all three will eventually become money through the process of convergence. Spend time analyzing figure 7 to grasp this theory.

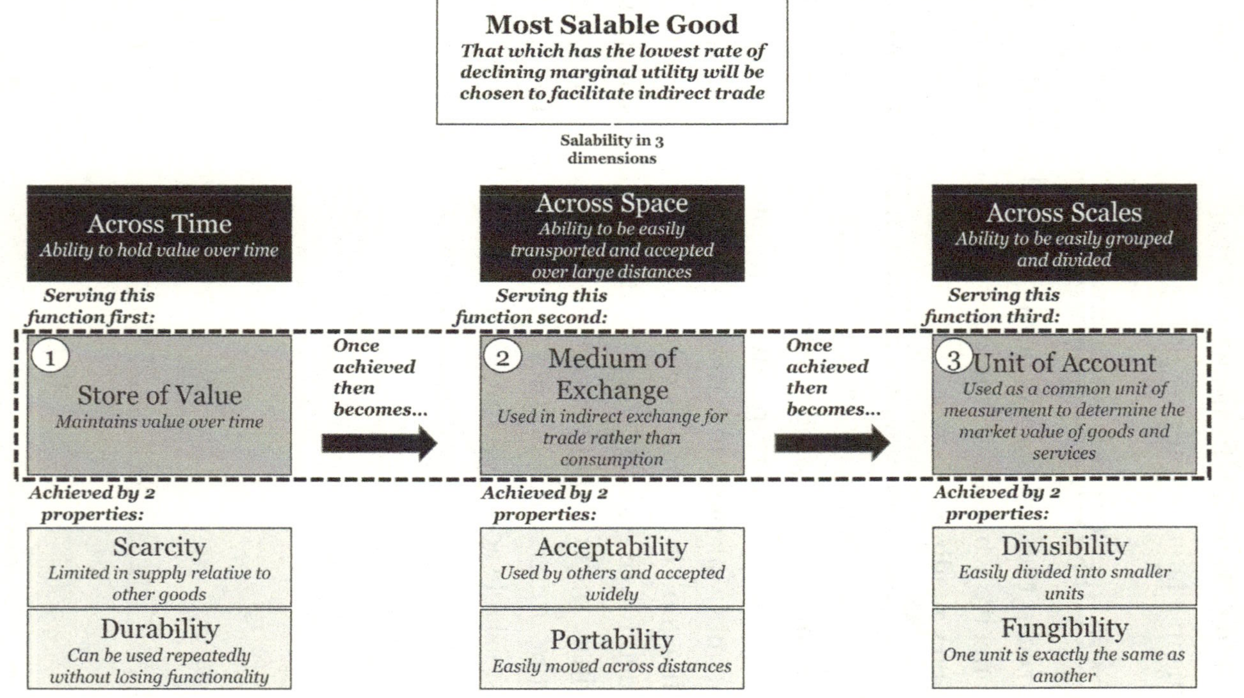


**Figure 7:** the dimensions of money, note that these properties mapped to each function are not mutually exclusive but intended to describe the most salient properties of that function.

## Conclusion

Money emerged as a solution to complex trade within barter systems. Goods that emerge as money maintain properties that create monetary value, not to be confused with market value for consumption. Money is defined as the most salable good across the dimension of time, space, and scales. There are 6 defined properties that enable money to serve its function in those dimensions. Money's function is to be a store of value across time, a medium of exchange across space, and a unit of account across scales. Money does not need to be backed by anything. Money needs to have these properties. Anything that does not have these properties is not money and needs to be backed by something that does.

We now have an understanding of money at a fundamental level that will enable us to compare and contrast its varying forms throughout history. However, this understanding is only true under the assumption that individuals are free to choose money. In a free society without information asymmetries, constituents should naturally utilize a common medium of exchange through adoption motivated by its merit. However, as our monetary systems have been monopolized, we lack perfect information and are subject to moral hazard by the agents who define our money. Societies subject to a fiat monetary system are transacting in a monetary medium that benefits the agents of the system at the cost of the participants, most of whom assume the agents to be acting in good faith. Fiat money means money by decree and not by merit. In the next 2 chapters, we will review the evolution of money to illuminate just how these problems emerged.

## References

1. *The Origins of Money*, Carl Menger, 3-4
2. *Grundsätze der Volkswirtschaftlehre,* Carl Menger
3. *The Bitcoin Standard*, Saifedean Ammous, 4

# 2. THE HISTORY OF DECENTRALIZED MONEY

*Sometimes I put on a ski mask and dress in old clothes, go out on the streets and beg for quarters* – *Mike Tyson*

## The Evolutionary Role of Money

Cooperation of a species based on trust is paramount to achieving mutually beneficial outcomes. The late evolutionary geneticist John Maynard Smith posited that certain genes evolved to provide strategic thinking in competitive environments that required trust for organisms to organize. Economist John Nash (the subject of the movie *A Beautiful Mind*) later defined this behavior in what is famously known the **Nash Equilibrium.**[1]

A common representation of the Nash Equilibrium is the **prisoner's dilemma** where 2 prisoners are separated and not allowed to communicate with one another. If both cooperate by staying silent, the total years served is 2 (1 year for each prisoner). If one of them betrays the other, the total years served is 3 but the betrayer serves none. If both betray each other the total years served is 4.

| Prisoner A \ Prisoner B | Stays Silent (cooperates) | Betrays (defects) |
|---|---|---|
| Stays Silent (cooperates) | Each serves 1 year | Prisoner A: 3 years<br>Prisoner B: goes free |
| Betrays (defects) | Prisoner A: goes free<br>Prisoner B: 3 years | Each serves 2 years |

**Figure 8:** the prisoners dilemma

**Nash defined a conflict of interest between the individual and the group.** The discovery of this conflict of interest fundamentally impacted the study of game theory. There is evidence that genetic evolution of strategic thinking towards Nash equilibria was a catalyst to complex forms of organization grounded in trust.[1]

Zoologist Richard Dawkins in *The Selfish Gene* suggests:

> *Many of our psychological characteristics–envy, guilt, gratitude, sympathy etc. – have been shaped by natural selection for improved ability to cheat, to detect cheats, and to avoid being thought to be a cheat* [2]

Without trust in an agreement, one must assume the other party will not fulfill their end of the agreement and will thus choose to avoid agreements in the future. It is a requirement for cooperation between parties to create trust and provide value to each other. For species that struggled to establish this cooperation, the cheaters were rewarded at the cost of the more trusting party. However, for species that **could establish cooperation**, there were significant gains through more sophisticated organization.

***The best cheaters survived as individuals, while the best "trusters" survived as groups.***

The essence of the ability to organize in groups, through cooperation, requires trust between parties in a transaction of **delayed reciprocal altruism**. Put simply, if you are to do someone a favor, you either need to have it returned immediately or be able to trust that the other party will one day reciprocate.

**Figure 9:** *if you scratch my back, I'll scratch yours*

Without a form of money, this process is challenging, as it requires a **coincidence of interests** to execute a mutually beneficial agreement – meaning that both parties must happen to have and be willing to trade something that is mutually desirable simultaneously. If this is not the case, one party must trust in delayed reciprocal altruism. There are high costs to initially develop this trust and a still higher risk of loss once that trust is established, making this type of cooperation unlikely. **It was out of the necessity to remove trust from transactions that humanity's ancestors began using primitive forms of money.**

***For our ancestors, organizing in groups was challenging because it required trust. Money naturally emerged to eliminate the need for that trust.***

## Primitive Money

Prior to the establishment of modern forms of money, civilizations used a variety of rare collectibles. The earliest known evidence consists of artifacts dated back to 75,000 B.P. in modern day South Africa – with later evidence found in Europe, Asia, Kenya, Spain, and Australia. Typically, these rare collectibles were shells or bones artistically manufactured as beads on a string (which allowed for divisibility through splitting or combining them), but they also came in other forms such as furs, flints, axes, and other items.[1]

Humans were differentiated from their immediate ancestors by the use of primitive forms of money. Dawkins states that "*Money is a formal token of delayed reciprocal altruism.*"[2] Interestingly, he stated this as a passing comment while focusing on the evolution of cooperation – but it is an astute observation.

Money, or rare collectibles in the prehistory era, eliminated the need for delayed reciprocal altruism by removing the requirement of a coincidence of interests. One party can agree to provide a product or service and the other party, who may not have a product or service that is desired by the provider at the time, can instead trade money in return. **Money provides immediate reciprocation for the product or service, eliminating the need for trust that it will be provided in the future.**

There is evidence that this impacted our evolutionary path significantly. Neanderthals were stronger and had thicker bones than their early Homo Sapien successors, giving them a form of biological advantage. However, evidence suggests that Homo Sapiens lived in more concentrated groups than Neanderthals and used primitive forms of money, while Neanderthals did not. It is reasonable to argue that money allowed Homo Sapiens to organize and ultimately eclipse Neanderthals.[2]

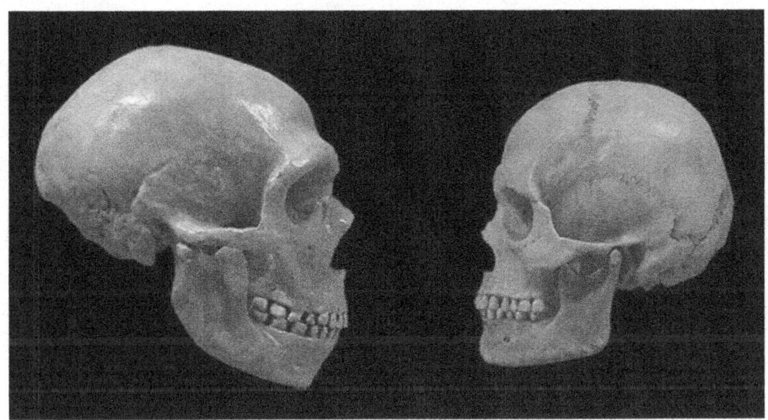

**Figure 10:** Neanderthal skull (left) Homo Sapian skull (right)

In a hunter-gatherer tribe, you cannot pass down slaughtered prey to your infant, as it will rot before they are capable of consuming it. But using precious collectibles, value can be stored over time. Rare collectibles could be passed down so the children could trade the collectibles and consume the product of their trade. The establishment of collectibles as primitive forms of money made humans the first animals to pass material wealth on to their kin in the next generation, thereby achieving large gains to their growth and productivity. Evidence indicates that by 40,000 B.P. these collectibles had matured to the point where they no longer had physical utility (like a blade) but were manufactured purely for their monetary properties.[1]

Referring back to the properties of money, primitive forms of money required a minimum of three properties to function sufficiently:

1. **Security from loss and theft** – Primarily meaning you could carry it with you and hide it easily (portability)

2. **Difficult to produce** – The effort to create money would be costly, thus making it scarce.
3. **Simple to measure through observation** – Allowing amounts of it to be easily added or subtracted, creating divisibility.

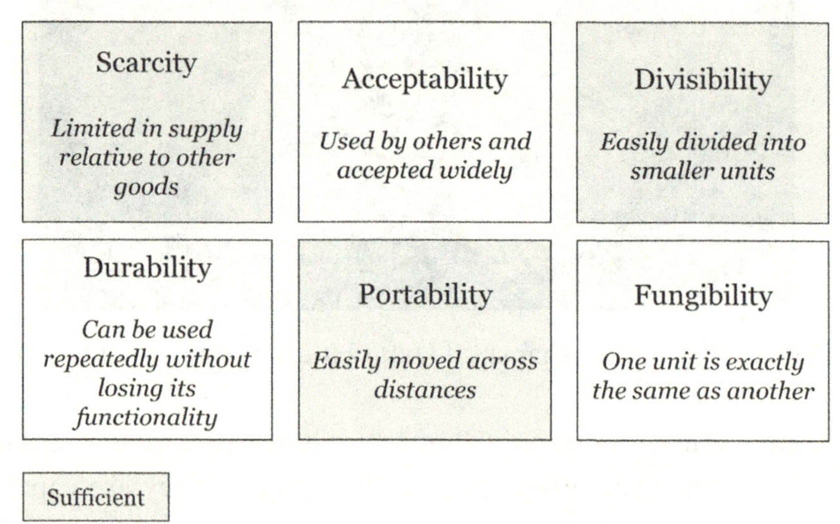


**Figure 11:** the monetary properties of primitive money

## Decentralized Production

Recall from chapter 1 that money is the most salable good which has the lowest declining marginal utility. Put simply, you can't have enough of it. From this perspective, **money is fundamentally different from all other goods because it is the most desirable (most salable) of them all, simply because you can trade it for whatever you want.**

This distinction has a major implication for its production. **By its nature, money creates a conflict of interest between the producers of money and those who they trade it to, more so than any other good.** The producers have an incentive to retain as much of it as they can. This conflict of interest incentivized the producers of primitive money to decrease its homogeneity as much as possible without being detected. **This was prevented by decentralized production and verification.**

For example, a single producer could be responsible for producing 10 bead necklaces in a tribe of 10 people, 1 for each person. He then could privately make 11 necklaces with slightly smaller bead sizes, keep 2 for himself, and give everyone else the 1 they expected to receive. This would effectively give him more money by diluting the value of everyone else's necklace. Nobody else is producing the necklaces and are thus unable to verify the homogeneity of each individual necklace. To everyone else, a necklace is a necklace, and they all look pretty similar.

Economic theory supports this argument. **Information asymmetry** between a principal and agent results in **moral hazard**. Known as the **agency problem**, when you elect an agent to provide a service or good for you who also has a conflict of interest, they will prioritize their interests above yours (moral hazard). **This principal applies to money more so than any other good because it is the most marketable good.**

If anyone can create money, this significantly reduces information asymmetries. Everyone is generally aware of the creation process and what constitutes good money. This makes verifying homogeneity easy as they trade between one another (e.g., Do these beads have the weight, size, color, texture, pattern I'm used to making?). Deception becomes significantly harder, thus significantly reducing moral hazard. Despite the inefficiencies of decentralized production of money, it materially benefited localized groups for most of history. As will be seen, once production started to centralize, moral hazard soon followed.

***The production of money is more subject to moral hazard than any other good. Decentralized production of primitive money enabled verification at the necessary cost of efficiency.***

An extreme example of this are the Rai stones of Yap Island (part of present-day Micronesia) This money was effectively a collection of very heavy stones kept in a public area on the island for all to see. They were brought from other islands and were difficult to procure, making it costly to increase the supply. When the owner of a stone wanted to exchange it, he/she would announce it publicly to the islanders. This public awareness provided security that a stone would not be stolen. Under this system, ownership was verified by achieving public consensus, materially reducing the risk of theft.

This innovative monetary system worked for centuries until foreigners with more modern means of production began quarrying more stones and transporting them to the island for trade. This drastically increased the supply, and the monetary system crumbled.

**Figure 12:** *Rai Stone on Yap Island*

## Precious Metals

Prior to the adoption of precious metals, various forms of money were used in primitive societies, including cattle, salt, seashells, stones, beads, flint, furs, and others. Like the monetary system of gold and silver to come, that of cattle and salt. This was the antiquity **dual monetary system.** Dual monetary systems are necessary when tradeoffs of monetary properties exist between 2 forms of money. Cattle were portable and could be transported and sold easily to areas in which they were scarce. However, cattle were not divisible at the point of sale. Large transactions over greater space were conducted in cattle while small immediate transactions were conducted in salt. Interestingly, the words pecuniary and salary are derived from the Latin *pecus* (cattle) and *sal* (salt).[3]

As societies progressed, developing more sophisticated forms of manufacturing and resource extraction, commodity production grew. Precious metals (e.g., silver, and gold) were converged upon and ultimately adopted as money by societies as they carried superior monetary properties to previous forms of money. The dawn of monetary precious metals can be traced to the Neolithic era in the Middle East and Europe. Certain kinds of jewelry became more standardized, an intermediate step between the primitive collectibles and precious coins. This purer form of money evolved into precious metals that lacked uniformity, until the emergence of the Lydians about 700 B.C. in Anatolia (modern Turkey).

**Measuring Scarcity:** At this point, it is necessary to describe a common measurement of scarcity that can be used as a relative point of comparison – **the stock to flow ratio**. The delineation of a stock and flow variable dates to the work of Fisher and Irving in 1896 and is conceptually applied across the fields of finance, accounting, and economics.[9] Stock is the accumulated amount of some asset at a point in time, and flow is the increase in that asset over a period (typically a year). The stock/flow ratio is a metric to show the amount of time in which it will take for the current stock to double in amount. The higher the ratio, the longer it takes for the asset's stock to double and the scarcer the asset. This is particularly helpful when assessing the relative degree of scarcity in commodities. Today the stock to flow ratios of gold and silver are roughly 60 and 10 years, respectively. The scarcity of the precious metals, gold in particular, is the primary reason that societies converged upon them. Gold's high scarcity relative to silver made it the ultimate standard of value.

Before systems of standard coinage were created, merchants priced their goods in the weight of the metal. Customers would pull out an ingot of gold and chop off little pieces until the weight was sufficient. This was costly, as small amounts were lost in the process. Out of necessity, gold was used for larger transactions over greater space, as it was more valuable per unit weight than other metals. Silver was used for smaller, immediate transactions, as it was less valuable per unit weight, making it less costly to divide (i.e., more divisible). This dual monetary system is known as **bimetallism**.

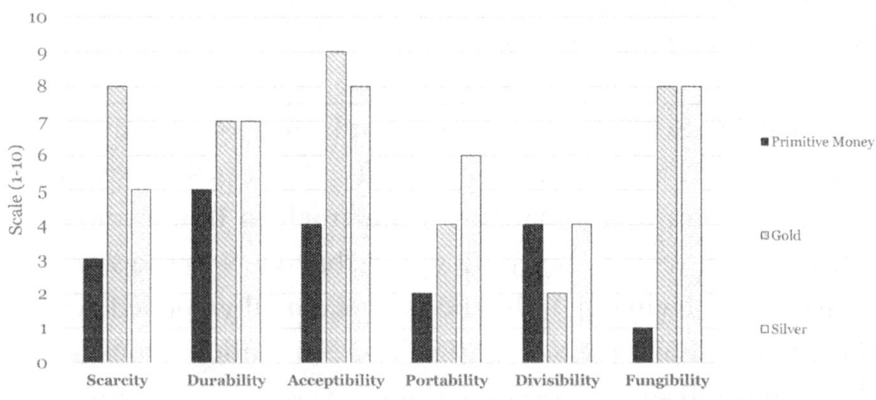


**Figure 13:** comparison of monetary media. Gold and silver properties shown prior to coinage systems.

## Centralization of Production

As adoption of gold and silver grew, there was a transition from sale per unit of weight to a minting system. This system emerged as merchants who cast coins would stamp the weight on top. People started to value coins by count instead of weight. This was an important development as it **required trust in the weight per coin**. The minting of metals for the purpose of **coinage** was monopolized by governments to ensure weight. The Kings of Lydia (700 B.C.) were the first major issuers of coins, according to the archeological and historical record.[1]

Regarding the production of money, Menger states: "*All these measures [taken by the state] nevertheless have not first made money of the precious metals, but have only perfected them in their function as money.*"[4]

Centralized manufacturing increased fungibility as well as public confidence that the money was in fact genuine. By centralizing production, the burden of verification is removed, so long as you trust your government.

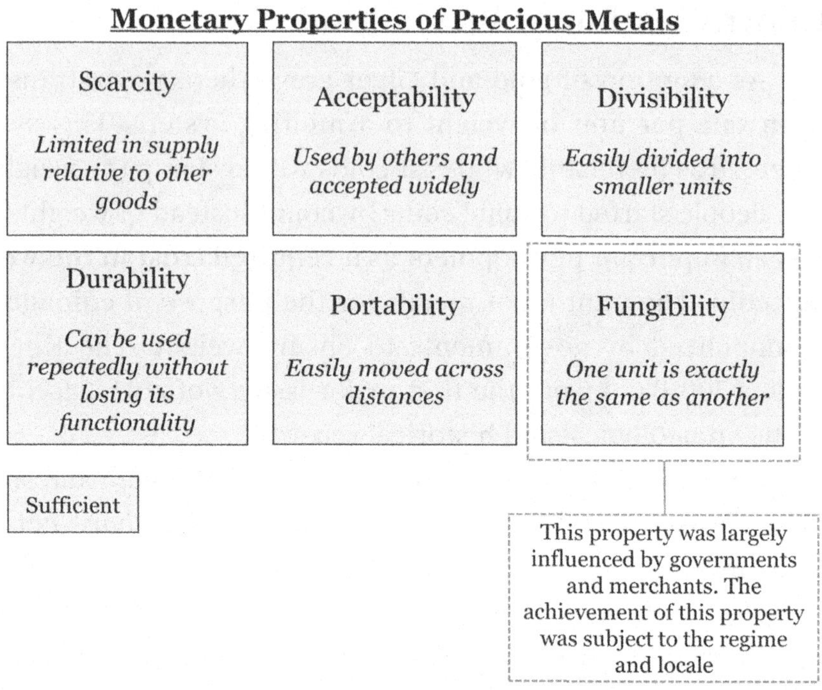


**Figure 14:** monetary properties of precious metals

Some government monies flourished while these systems were in their infancy. In Ancient Greece, the **drachma** was used as the de facto monetary unit due to the dependability of its silver content. This coinage remained as a standard for centuries even after the fall of Athens. The **solidus** was used under the Byzantine Empire, and the dependability of its content was proven by its wide acceptance, including in places where it became known as the **bezant**. This was largely due to the strict Byzantine laws against **coin clipping** and counterfeiting, both of which were punishable by the cutting off of a hand. The empire flourished for 800 years without becoming insolvent.[5]

**Coin clipping** was the primary form of **currency debasement** during the precious metal era. It began with merchants shaving off small amounts of each coin they handled. Government treasuries applied the same practice to the coins they received in taxes. Save up enough clippings and you can mint them into new coins. Eventually, governments turned to diluting their coins by melting them down and combining them with a more abundant, non-precious metal. They would use the diluted coins to pay their expenses under the pretense that the value was the same and use their new coins to purchase even more goods. This process is simply a form of wealth redistribution by exchanging less money for more goods. It allowed governments to produce nothing and exchange it for something. As the general population then held an increased number of diluted coins, prices began to rise. **The reduction in purchasing power of the population due to price increases is an indirect method of taxation.** Governments maintained the pretense that it was the stamp on the coin that gave it its value, in an attempt to convince people that neither weight nor contents, but only count, mattered. They still do this today by stating our money is backed by the government. Here Lincoln's dictum applies that you can fool all of the people some of the time and some of the people all of the time but not all of the people all of the time.

**Figure 15:** unclipped coin (left) clipped coin (right) (image from Wikipedia)[10]

The Roman Republic and Empire was fraught with monetary debasement and controls. Driven by the need to finance their lavish spending on the military and various luxuries, coin clipping when minting their currency became a common practice. In fact, the origin of the word "mint" is from the Roman temple of Moneta where currency was manufactured. Juno Moneta was the personification of money in Roman culture. This is how the English words "Money" and "Monetary" came to be.

In the late republic and early empire, the standard roman coin was the silver **denarius**. Its value had been gradually reduced prior to Diocletian, as emperors issued tin-plated copper coins and still called them denarii. **Gresham's law**, which states that as bad money is introduced into circulation, people will naturally begin to hoard good money, became the norm (you can see this playing out today in Treasury Secretary Steven Mnuchin's tweet[6]). People hoarded their gold and silver as best they could. During the period ending with Claudius Victorinus in 270 A.D., the silver content of the denarius fell to one five-thousandth of its original level, and at this point the monetary system had lost its bearings. Trade was reduced to barter, and economic activity collapsed, nearly destroying the middle class.[6]

When Diocletian assumed the throne in 284 A.D., the prices of commodities and wages had reached all-time highs. De Moribus Persecutorum, a surviving source, blames government spending on armed forces and the commensurate increase in taxation; Diocletian blamed the merchants (the most common scapegoat in centuries to come). The classical historian Roland Kent in the *University of Pennsylvania Law Review* echoes this sentiment, naming inherited economic instability and lavish spending to be the sources which caused economic collapse and destructive taxation. Most likely, the salient cause was the debasement of the currency (more on this later).[7]

Aware of the existing deterioration of the empire, Diocletian took a variety of measures to restore order. He reorganized the government structure with emperors in both east and west, devised an in-kind system of taxation (making the lower class into serfs), and attempted to reform prices, wages, and the currency. By issuing a new denarius copper coin, Diocletian expected to achieve price stability but instead only caused prices to rise even higher. He was forced to either cut costs or continue issuing more coins, and despite being aware of his predecessors' actions, he chose the latter. He believed that he could quell the inflation by simultaneously fixing prices and suspending the freedom of the people to decide what the currency was worth. The famous edict of A.D. 301 was the result, and it was all-pervasive – fixing all commodity prices, with the death penalty for anyone who sold goods above those fixed prices.[6]

In less than 4 years after the currency reform, the price of gold in terms of the denarius had risen 250%.[7] By A.D. 305 there was a return to more fiscal irresponsibility, and the process of currency debasement began again – producing a 2000% rise in the price of denarius/gold by the end of the century.[7] The historian of Rome M. Rostovtzeff explained this experiment:

> *As a general measure intended to last, it was certain to do great harm and to cause terrible bloodshed, without bringing any relief. Diocletian shared the pernicious belief of the ancient world in the omnipotence of the state, a belief which many modern theorists continue to share with him and with it.*[7]

**Figure 16:** the silver denarius eventually fully diluted into copper

Successive emperors continued the same practices with attempts to control wages and preventing workers from leaving their professions unless they could find a willing replacement. The controls implemented by the Empire were simply no longer economically sound for producers of goods. Naturally, they tried whatever they could to defect from the oppressive system. Prior to the Empire's demise, many workers had dispersed to lands outside of Roman control. The descendants of those who were able to hold onto their gold throughout this period became feudal lords, while those without became serfs.[8] The wealth of Europe evaporated out of the hands of the many and into the hands of the few, who owned whatever sound money that was left.

## Conclusion

Money was an evolutionary catalyst toward complex organization, as it removed the need for trust in many aspects of cooperation. Primitive forms of money were largely produced in a decentralized manner, mitigating the risk of moral hazard.

Precious metals emerged due to their superior monetary properties. As societies centralized production through the minting of coinage, they were widely subject to moral hazard. These systems were the "antiquity" of modern monetary policy.

The title of this chapter is *The History of Decentralized Money*. "Decentralized Money" refers to the decentralized production and storage of money. In this chapter I have described the centralization of monetary production by governments, but the people of these societies still largely maintained sovereignty over physical storage of their money. The consequences of the next advancement in monetary storage is strikingly parallel to the previous one, but with a significantly greater impact.

## References

1. *Shelling out: The Origins of Money,* Nick Szabo
2. *The Selfish Gene*, Richard Dawkins, 169
3. *Whither Gold?*, Antal Fekete, 16
4. *The Origins of Money,* Carl Menger, 51-52
5. *The Creature from Jekyll Island*, G. Edward Griffin, 152
6. https://twitter.com/stevenmnuchin1/status/1293258850548817921?s=20
7. *Forty Centuries of Wage and Price Controls: How Not to Fight Inflation*, Robert L. Schuettinger and Eamonn F. Butler, 21 - 25
8. *The Bitcoin Standard: The Decentralized Alternative to Central Banking,* Saifedean Ammous, 22
9. *What is Capital?*, Irving Fisher, 514
10. https://en.wikipedia.org/wiki/Methods_of_coin_debasement

# 3. THE HISTORY OF CENTRALIZED MONEY

*When Jesus comes back, these crazy, greedy, capitalistic men are gonna kill him again* – *Mike Tyson*

## Government Appropriation

After the fall of the Roman Empire, Europe entered a period of economic disarray under the feudal system. Until the latter half of the Middle Ages, people largely stored money in whatever form they could, typically in their home or in a hiding place. Bank-like services existed, but these were rare and largely only for the very wealthy. In effect **the storage of money was widely decentralized.** Banks of deposit predominantly emerged in early Greece and later spread throughout Europe. Subsequently, a major evolution in money occurred with the birth of modern banking in England.

As people accumulated wealth, they needed a place to safely store it. Historically, the two most common places for safekeeping were temples and monasteries. In England monasteries were often used until Henry VIII dissolved them in the 16th century. The only options left were government mints. The London Mint was the most popular until Charles I (17th century) appropriated money deposited there.[1] The **centralization of storage** in government mints lead to **government appropriation**. The people of

England were now out of options for safe storage; the time was ripe for a new method to emerge.

The **goldsmiths of London** handled large amounts of precious metals in their dealings and owned large storage vaults. Demand grew to use the excess space in their vaults to store gold in exchange for a fee. The goldsmiths in turn would provide a receipt to their customers, which allowed them to redeem their gold upon request. This practice was the dawn of custodial services, the most basic function of modern private banking. Jongchul Kim has stated: "*The historical event that allowed goldsmiths to become the biggest deposit-takers in London was Charles I's appropriation of cash deposited in the London Mint.*"[2] Physically storing their gold in vaults did not protect gold depositors from appropriation. What was effective in preventing appropriation was the practice of loaning deposited gold to borrowers. Goldsmiths would issue loans to new borrowers while still offering to their depositors the right of withdrawal on demand. This innovation kept the gold in the vaults, while creating **simultaneous ownership claims on the same money**. This made it harder for the Crown to appropriate funds by eliciting greater opposition if it attempted to do so. This protection was legally similar to modern day trust schemes. It also made appropriation more economically destructive **as more money would be tied to any amounts taken.**[1]

***The accumulation of wealth led to centralized storage of money, which was later appropriated by the government. People responded by storing their money with goldsmiths, which gave rise to the services of modern banking.***

## Derivative Money

It was also the birth of what I will define as **derivative money**. Derivative money is any sort of legally enforceable document (paper receipt) that grants the owner redemption of a defined amount of money. The paper receipt itself is useless as money, as it does not possess the necessary monetary properties. Its value is derived from the certainty that the money backing it is physically stored safely, and is accessible for withdrawal on demand by holders. Note that this definition is parallel to, but not to be confused with, derivatives – contracts that derive their value from underlying securities, not money.

Paper receipts were portable, divisible, and fungible. As the practice of using paper receipts grew, it became more accepted. Paper receipts were sufficiently durable, albeit less so than gold. However, they were not scarce, which is why people needed to be certain receipts could be redeemed in something that was. **The key point is that paper receipts must be redeemable in real money, and on demand, to have value.**

At first only the owner could personally redeem the receipt's value. It became **common for receipt holders to endorse their receipts to a third party,** and this practice was eventually ratified under The Promissory Notes Act of 1704. This was the **start of our modern checking system.**

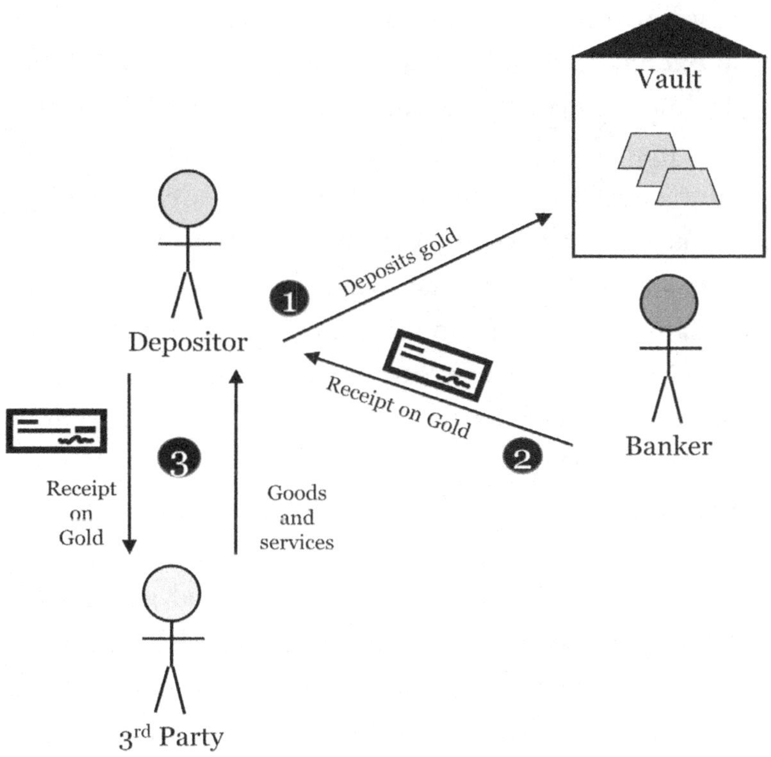


**Figure 17:** the beginning of derivative money

There were three major advancements from the 15th to 19th centuries that expanded the adoption of derivative money:

1. **The Printing Press** – Economized paper receipts and increased uniformity as handwriting was now obsolete for this purpose.
2. **Double-Entry Bookkeeping** – Allowed the accumulation of capital under contracts.
3. **The Telegraph** – Allowed for communication over wide distances, increasing portability.

**These inventions eventually removed the necessity of physical exchange of gold.** With each invention, the adoption of derivative money grew, increasing the ability to trade. Eventually nations formalized the use of derivative money. After failing to implement a system of notes that were not redeemable for gold, Britain was the first to implement a **gold standard** by which government-issued notes that were fully redeemable in gold. The standard was held from 1717 until its suspension in 1797, during the Napoleonic wars. Suspension of the gold standard was to become commonplace for redeemable sovereign currencies during wartime. (More on this later.)

The gold standard was definitely adopted in England in 1821, which marked the beginning of the end for bimetallism. The monetary properties of silver were diminished given the superior properties of derivative money. Redeemable paper primarily required that whatever was backing it be scarce, and silver was relatively less scarce than gold. Further, redeemable paper had superior portability and divisibility to silver. Despite the inferior monetary properties of silver, elected officials would attempt its resurrection before the end of the century (just as the Romans tried to tell people tin was as good as silver).

***The centralization of storage and technological advances spawned the next evolution of money into paper derivatives.***

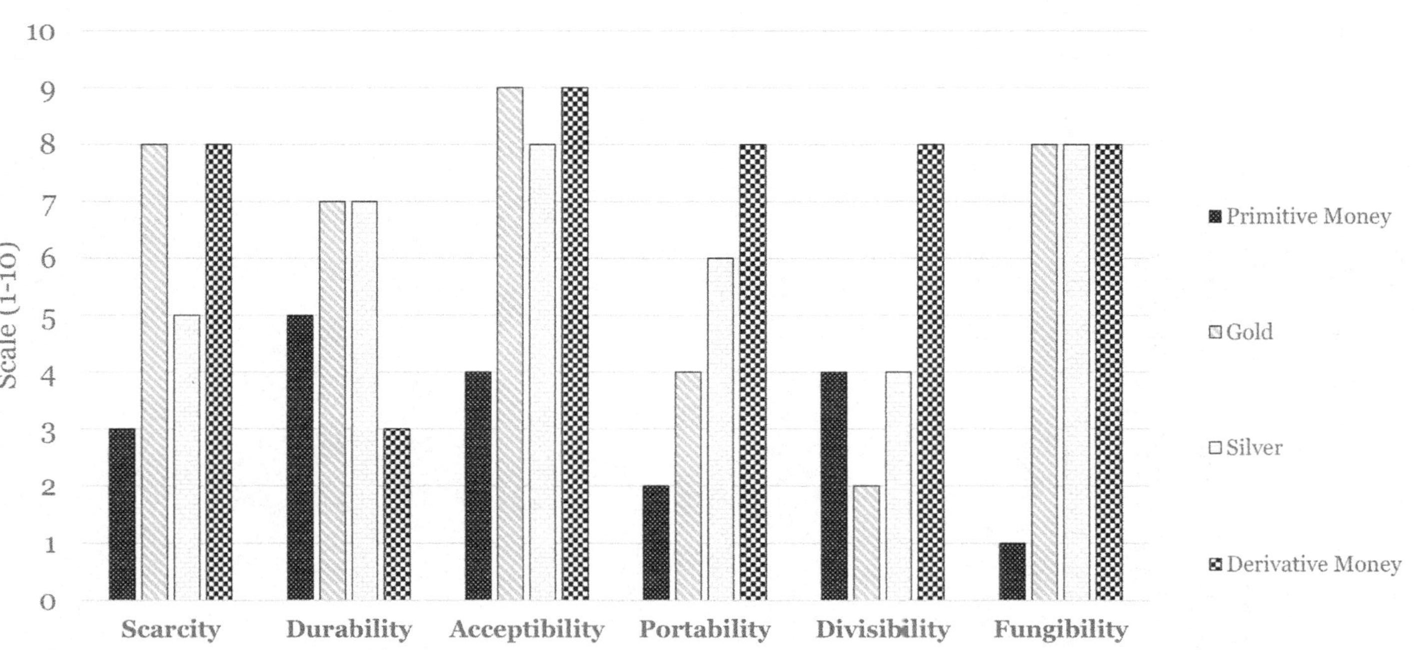


**Figure 18:** comparison of derivative money to prior forms of money

## Fractional Reserve Banking

While this new system created greater efficiencies for trade, people did not realize the risk in giving a third party control over their money. The use of receipts for money was fine so long as one receipt redeemed one unit of money. However, goldsmiths were handing out debt receipts on the same gold as they had issued redeemable paper receipts to depositors. Effectively, one unit of gold had a claim from the depositor and a claim from the borrower. The goldsmith was collecting a storage fee from the depositor and interest from the borrower on the same money.

The Figure 19 depiction is how one would expect this system to have worked:

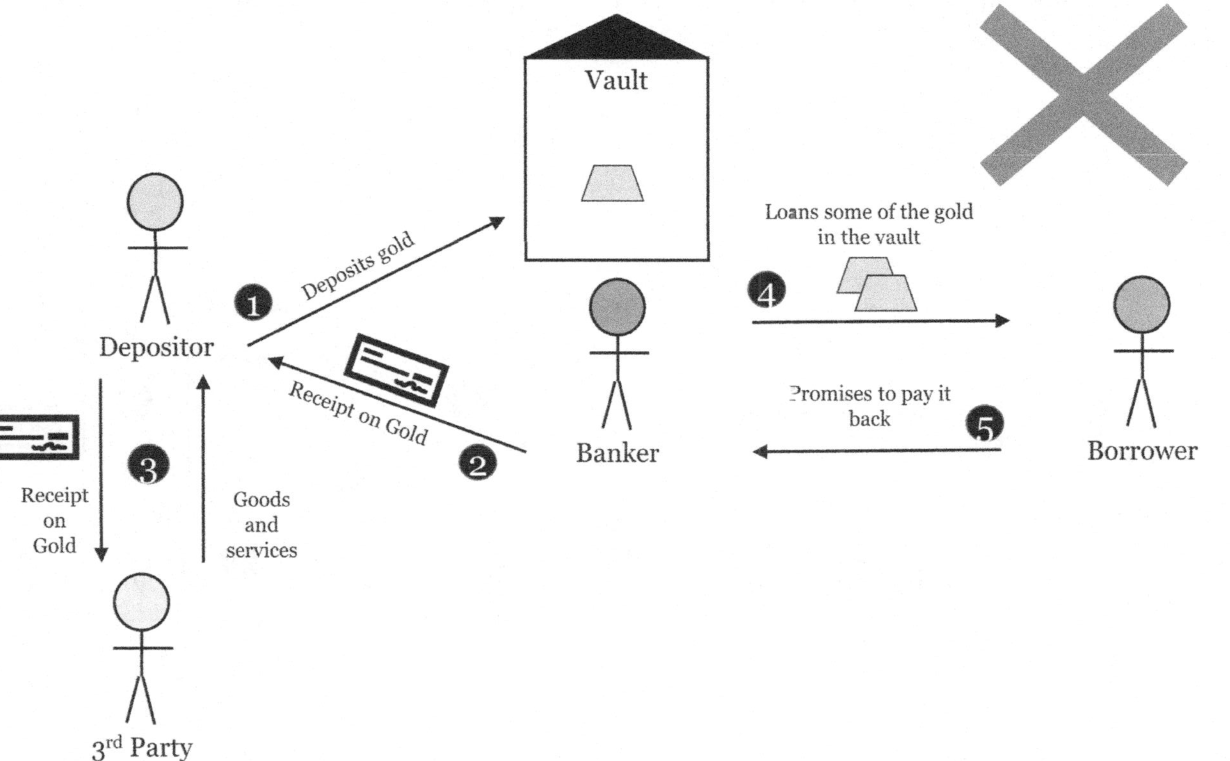


**Figure 19:** the intuitive way the goldsmith banker fractional reserve system would have worked. It, in fact, did not work this way

This is how it actually went:

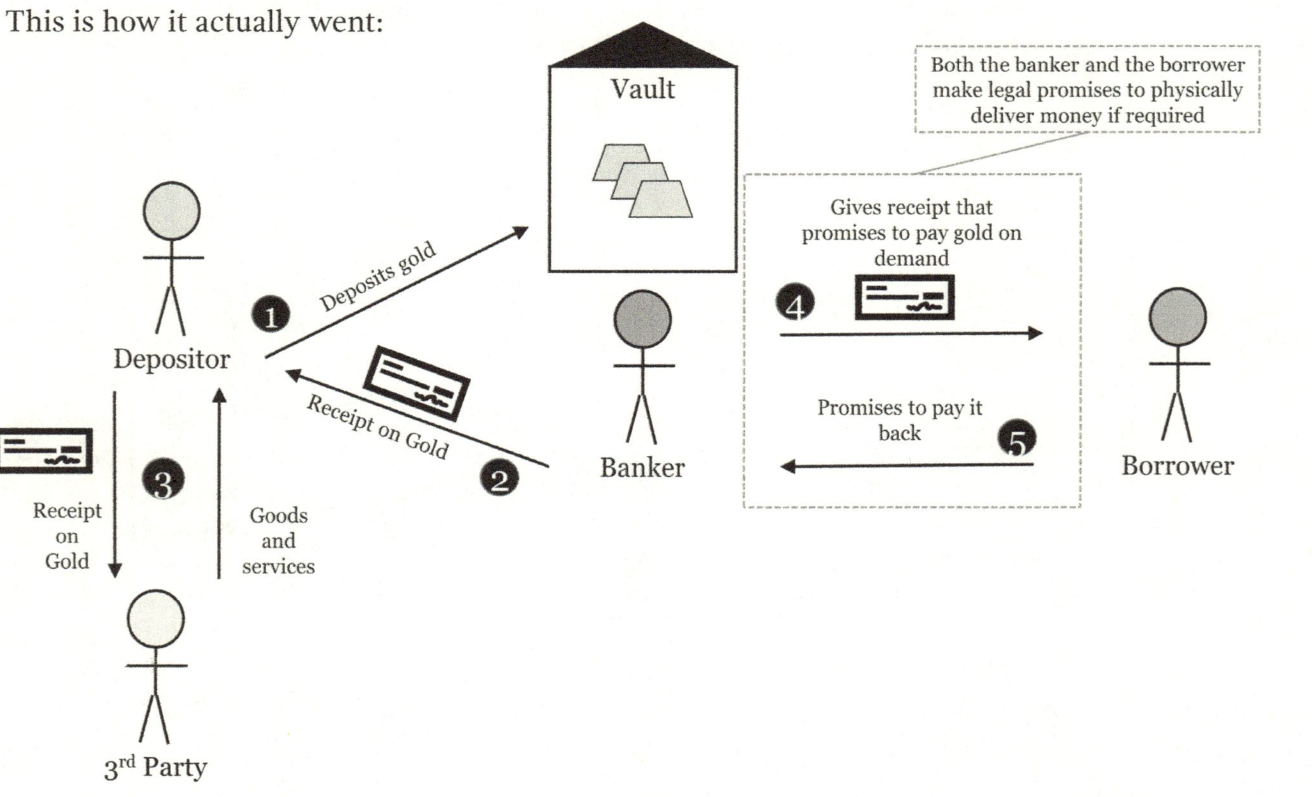


**Figure 20:** how the goldsmith banker fractional reserve system actually worked

This system is confusing, and it should be, because the logic is circular. Kim of Songang University provides an explanation:

> *The bankers issued the notes to those who came to borrow money, mainly those who brought bills of exchange to discount them. Here these debtors to the bankers became the first holders of the notes. But because the bankers' notes were bankers' promises to pay, the bankers became debtors to the holders of the notes as well. This mutual indebtedness made the trustworthiness of the bankers' notes depend on the trustworthiness of the persons to whom the bankers' debts were loaned.* [3]

So the bankers made a loan to somebody but didn't physically give them money. Instead, they gave them a piece of paper that was based on a *promise to pay*. On the other end, through the action of depositing, the depositors of the gold transferred authority to the goldsmith-bankers, allowing them to lend their funds. Kim continues:

> *Goldsmith-bankers' deposit-taking was self-contradictory because it was simultaneously a loan contract and not a loan contract. Because deposits were repaid on demand, the ownership of deposits practically remained in the hands of depositors. But bankers lent deposits at their own discretion and in their own names, and they attained and retained the ownership title of the loans. Here the ownership of deposits was transferred from depositors to bankers because a person – in this case, the goldsmith-banker – could lend property in his or her name only when he or she had ownership of it. How could ownership of the thing simultaneously be transferred and not transferred?* [4]

If the borrower didn't return the money, they were in default to the goldsmith. If the borrower requested physical delivery of his loan, the goldsmith was legally required to deliver. Goldsmiths could make these loans because the depositors transferred to them authority to lend their gold. Why would depositors voluntarily agree to this? Ultimately, it was because **it was better than the risk of appropriation from the government.** This system created a multitude of claims on the same money, which made legal ownership tenuous.

What is more, the goldsmiths were lending out more than they actually had in the vaults, maintaining a **fractional reserve**. This meant that gold was held in amounts that generally ranged from 10% to 66% of the amount they were lending.[5] If all of the depositors and none of the borrowers requested their money back, it **would be** there. If all of the borrowers and none of the depositors demanded physical delivery, then the gold **wouldn't be** there. In reality, both borrowers and depositors could request physical delivery at any time. The percentage of gold held relative to claims on the gold was much lower than 10% to 66%, because there were multiple claims on each unit of money. The loser in this game was whoever was holding their piece of paper last.

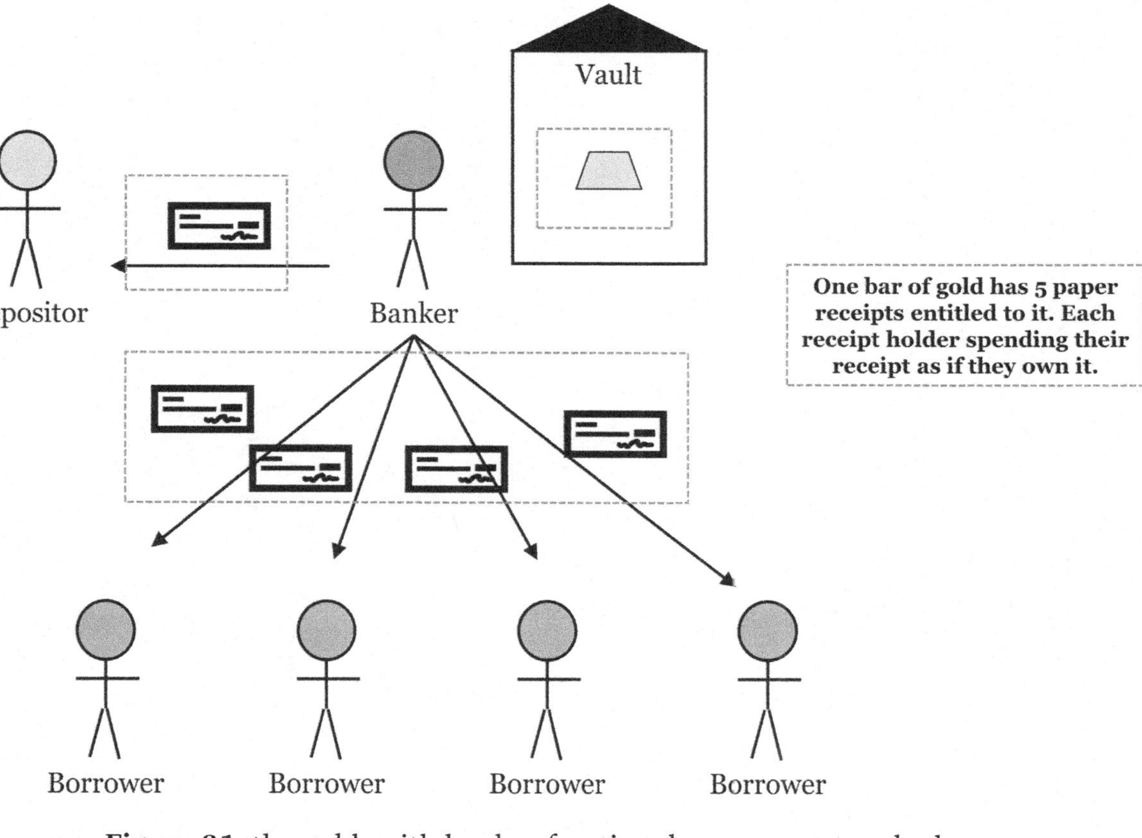


**Figure 21:** the goldsmith banker fractional reserve system had many claims to each unit of gold

The same money was being used in multiple places at the same time. This is how fractional reserve banking expands the money supply, by lending out the money of another person who is also using it himself. In modern banking this is referred to as the **money multiplier.** If the borrower takes the money and does not repay it, then the banker or depositor loses. In modern times, the taxpayer has become the loser, but it should always be the bank. This is why many people hate bankers – they privatize their profits and socialize their losses.

History shows us that this system did not end well. Kim states:

> *However, this seemingly secure scheme was, in fact, insecure. Illiquidity in the form of bank-runs and other liquidity crunches could easily be caused by external agitation or the defaults of goldsmith-bankers' large debtors...Charles II defaulted in 1672 on the money that goldsmith-bankers loaned him. This default, called the Stop of the Exchequer, resulted in the failure of many London goldsmith-bankers and made their notes unacceptable during the 1670s.* [6]

***Fractional reserve notes lost all of their value when the government defaulted on its debt.***

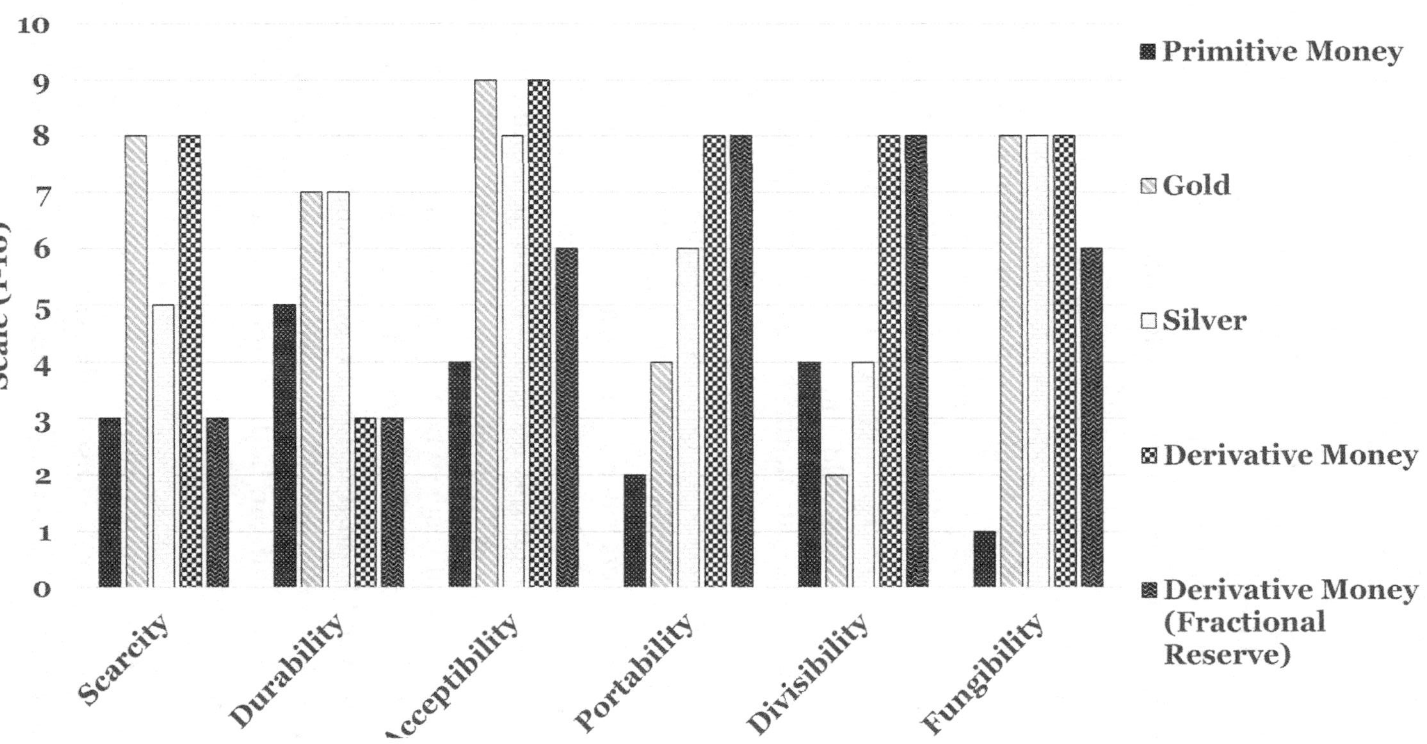


**Figure 22:** comparison of fractional reserve derivative money to prior forms of money. Derivative money is fully redeemable while derivate Money (Fractional Reserve) is not.

The limiting factor of this system was that the goldsmiths were not able to lend infinite amounts of money since the borrowers still had a legal claim on physical delivery of gold. What was eventually reasoned by bankers and government alike is that if you could remove the requirement to have gold in the vaults and simply issue paper that is irredeemable, there would be no limitation to the amount you could loan.

## Fiat Money

The **Stop of the Exchequer** was a major event in the early history of banking in England. With the growth in **fractional reserve derivative money**, the concept of **creating money out of debt** took form. The Stop of the Exchequer was a repudiation of debt owed to the goldsmith-bankers by the government. By using the court system, the bankers attempted to fight to get their money back. In 1694, the **Bank of England** was created as a mechanism to pay the government's debt and to finance war. Parliament granted the bank the privilege of issuing **bank notes,** which were purely **fiat money**. Fiat money is that which is declared "legal tender" by a government. **Legal tender simply means money that has no reserve balance, and one is legally required to use it in some form** (typically for paying taxes). While fractional reserve banking was backed by gold to at least some degree, fiat was backed by nothing at all. So **the problems that emerged from fractional reserve banking were solved by further exacerbating the underlying issue.** This is the money we use today and can be best understood by the words of the Federal Reserve:

> *Currency cannot be redeemed, or exchanged, for Treasury gold or any other asset used as backing. The question of just what assets 'back' Federal Reserve notes has little but bookkeeping significance*[7]

Notably, the notes issued by the Bank of England were rejected by the market and replaced in the exchequer *bill* of 1696. The notes created were fully redeemable in gold. The Bank of England's first attempt at a modern fiat system was a failure (it lasted less than 2 years) but created the blueprint for the practice of modern central banking today.

***The Bank of England was created to repay government debt in pure fiat money, created out of debt. The Bank of England failed at this and England subsequently moved to a gold standard.***

## Centralization of Storage

To recap, as wealth grew, people centralized its storage with the government, and the government eventually appropriated it. The market responded by storing money in a private banking system that developed a complex and contradictory legal structure as protection. This protection came with significant risk, and as a result, fiat money was created. As is commonly said today, this fiat money was money created out of nothing. However, it wasn't just nothing – it was debt – which is less than nothing (a negative value). Antal Fekete illustrated this idea for modern times in one of my favorite essays, *Whither Gold?*:

> *Previously, in the world's most developed countries, money (and hence credit) was tied to a positive value: the value of a well-defined quantity of a good of well-defined quality. In 1971* [in the United States] *this tie was cut. Ever since, money has been tied not to positive but to negative values – the value of debt instruments.* [8]

As we have examined monetary evolution in this chapter and its predecessors, a pattern has begun to emerge. Recall that primitive forms of money were produced in a decentralized, time-consuming, and publicly verifiable manner. During the era of precious metals, governments began manufacturing standardized coins and providing assurance of authenticity, which saved users the timely process of verifying the validity of the coins. In this step of monetary evolution, **people traded trust for efficiency**.

Governments assumed the role of protecting the consumer from coin clipping by monopolizing money and punishing coin clipping severely. Along with many other examples, the Roman Empire used its control of the coinage to do precisely what it was supposed to prevent.

Fast forward a millennium and the pattern continues. Individuals centralized their storage into government mints. They trusted that the government would safeguard this money as promised. Governments appropriated their wealth. People then moved their storage to the vaults of goldsmiths and derivative money was born. By using their receipts as money, they **traded trust for efficiency**. The goldsmiths took advantage of this through **fractional reserve banking**. When these fractional reserve institutions failed, the government once again had a solution by creating fiat money, doing precisely what they were supposed to prevent.

***The exchange of trust for new benefits came at an increasingly high cost with each step of monetary evolution.***

## The 7th Property

The centralized production of money inevitably leads to debasement (inflation). The centralized storage of money inevitably leads to unsustainable fractional reserve banking (more on this in the next chapter). In modern times these concepts have become not only normal but legally required. The government makes paper money at the mint, and you must keep your money in a bank for all practical purposes.

Today, the production and storage of money is to some degree decentralized, but this degree is insufficient and increasingly so. As a result, our money has become highly mutable. Early forms of money maintained some degree of **immutability** because they were produced and stored in a decentralized manner. **The decentralized production and storage of money enables immutability.**

Recall that there are 6 monetary properties, and centralization gradually reduced the immutability of money over time. Immutability, however, is not characterized as a monetary property. Thus, **ideal money should have a 7$^{th}$ property of immutability which is enabled by the decentralization of production and storage.** In figure 23 I append this property to the graphic of monetary dimensions from chapter 1:

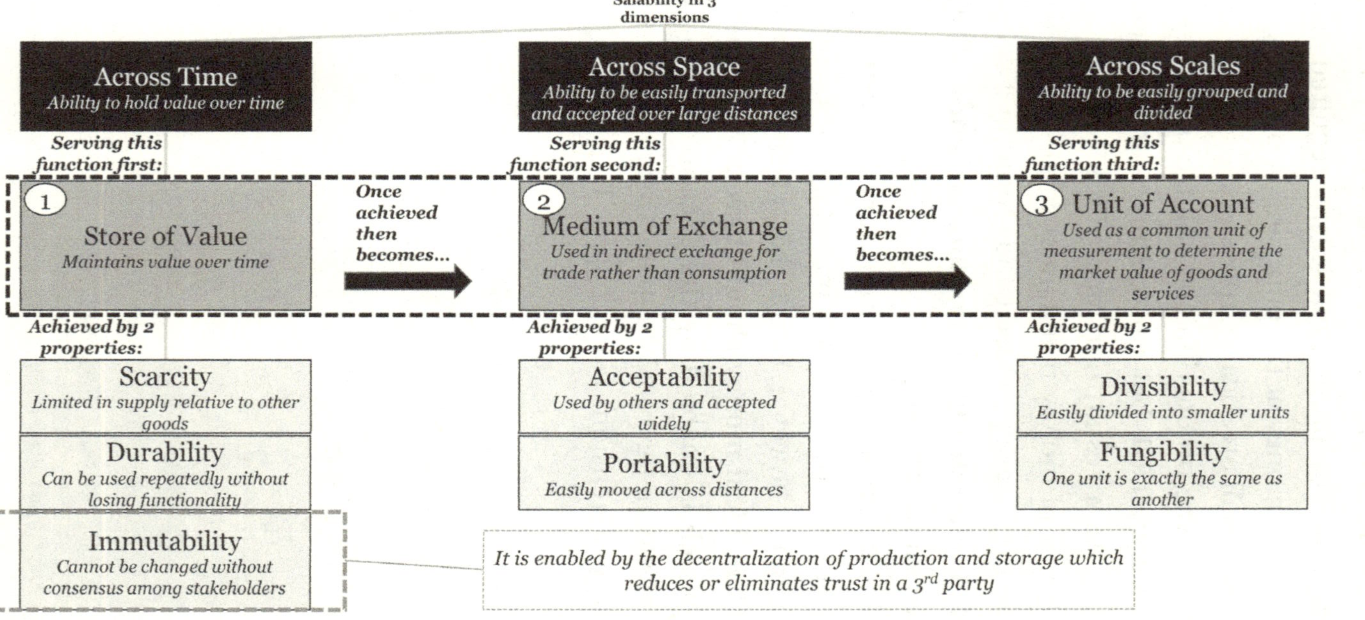


**Figure 23:** immutability through decentralized production and storage as a 7th property of money

A form of money which has the necessary characteristics to be produced and stored in a decentralized manner is the next step in the evolution of money. Decentralization eliminates the **need** to trust in a third party who has a conflict of interest, which in turn leads to moral hazard. In all prior forms of money, immutability came at the cost of efficiency – money was expensive to procure and costly to validate. **In the digital age, there is opportunity for innovation but also the risk of even greater moral hazard.**

An interesting property of software is that it is almost infinitely replicable. If you create something once, you can create it repeatedly at practically no cost. Further, the creators of software can control it from anywhere in the world over a network. This means that digital money controlled by a government could be controlled from anywhere in the world and deleted or created at a moment's notice. Today, most people in developed countries have accounts at banks, and a lot of those banks have accounts at the Fed. So this form of control exists to some degree. However, if a central bank issued a digital US dollar, this would mean that every citizen and institution using it would have an account at the Fed. This would be an incredibly powerful position for an institution. For more on this look up CBDCs (central bank digital currencies).

Digital money will reach an inflection point at which people will need to decide if they will trade trust for efficiency once again. It is my goal to convince enough people that they should not.

Figure 24 highlights the historical trend in the property of immutability:

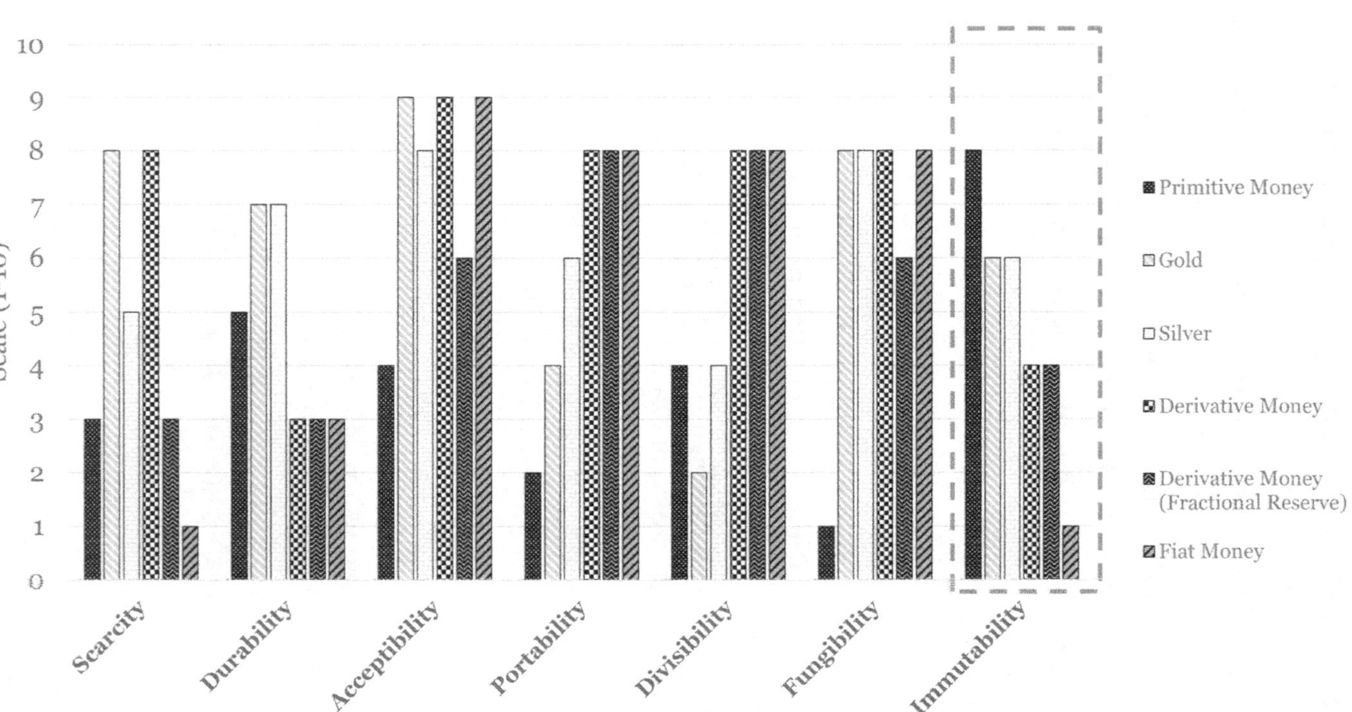


**Figure 24:** fiat money comparison to prior forms, with emphasis on the 7th property of immutability

## Conclusion

Through the monetary evolution of coinage, the production of money became increasingly centralized. In the subsequent evolution, storage was centralized as well. Sacrificing the decentralization of money was at a far greater cost than that which was gained. From this view, an ideal property of monetary value should be immutability, which is achieved by decentralized production and storage – **the 7th property**. If society can reclaim this property without trading away efficiency, that will be the next key evolutionary step in the development of money. The question of how this will happen is soon to arise – but before that we need to understand how the banking system evolved and where it is today.

This concludes the history of money. Changes and advances that occurred after the 18th century did not change the properties of money but rather the system of banking itself. It is important to return to history again to gain a wider view of the cause-and-effect relationships that emerged from the partnership between governments and the banking system. This discussion will bring us to the present, which is still tightly bound to the past.

## References

1. *How Modern Bank Originated: The London Goldsmith-Bankers' Institutionalization of Trust*, Jongchul Kim, 27
2. *How Modern Bank Originated: The London Goldsmith-Bankers' Institutionalization of Trust*, Jongchul Kim, 28
3. *How Modern Bank Originated: The London Goldsmith-Bankers' Institutionalization of Trust*, Jongchul Kim, 13
4. *How Modern Bank Originated: The London Goldsmith-Bankers' Institutionalization of Trust*, Jongchul Kim, 16-17
5. *Essai sur la nature du commerce en general*, Richard Cantillon, 299-303
6. *How Modern Bank Originated: The London Goldsmith-Bankers' Institutionalization of Trust*, Jongchul Kim, 15-16
7. *I Bet You Thought*, David H. Friedman
8. *Whither Gold?*, Antal Fekete, 1

# 4. THE HISTORY OF CENTRAL BANKING

*I'm just happy I'm not a phony.* – *Mike Tyson*

This chapter is long and packed with information. It illuminates a consistent pattern throughout history, showing how central banks emerge and the boom-and-bust cycles they create in our economy. This pattern is a popular topic of debate, and the purpose of this chapter is to provide you with the facts that have guided my perspective. The modern narrative is that central banks are used to reduce economic volatility, but history shows otherwise.

## The Emergence of Banking

The evolution of banking in England was the blueprint for the US banking system. However, depository institutions and lending existed centuries before this. Depository banking can be traced back to early Greece and was concurrent with the development of coinage. Subsequently, it emerged in a variety of places such as India, Egypt, Syria, and Spain. Generally, it is the banking system of Venice that is considered the cradle of modern banking.[1]

The Bank of Venice was the first national bank established within Europe. In 1361 the Venetian Senate passed a law forbidding bankers to engage in commercial pursuits. Their books and stockpiles were required to be open for public inspection, reducing the temptation to pursue risky lending practices. By

1524 a body of bank examiners had been created which required physical settlement in coins rather than by check. Despite these precautions, the house of *Pisano and Tiepolo* was lending against its reserves and was unable to issue refunds to depositors in 1584. The government took control at that point and established the *Banco della Piazza del Rialto*. It was not allowed to make any loans or profit from credit issuance. **It was required to profit solely from the fees received from coin storage, currency exchange, and handling transfer payments.**[1] In effect, it functioned as a custodian that cleared checks. **The bank enjoyed years of prosperity as the center of Venetian commerce, with its fully-backed derivative money trading widely across borders.**

As the memory of banking abuses faded with time, the Venetian Senate once again allowed the extension of credit through fractional reserves. **The politicians, not willing to face citizens with a request for tax increases, decided to create a bank that would create the money they needed and then"lend" it to them.** In 1619 the *Banco del Giro* was formed, and within two decades this bank had absorbed *Banco Della Piazza del Rialto*.

Banks emerged throughout Europe during the 15th and 16th centuries. All of them followed the practice of fractional reserve banking.[2]

The expansion of banking beyond that of a depository institution was emerging in Europe. Fractional reserve lending, for reasons stated in chapter 3, was too profitable to be ignored. Governments noticed this and discovered there was a role they could play. While profitable for a period, fractional reserve lending was a fragile system that collapsed under extreme circumstances (if there was a bank run, the money was not there). Governments realized that the claim on physically-backed money by the holders of the paper ultimately left the system vulnerable. However, if this claim could be eliminated, the scheme could continue with the consequences of failure falling upon the value of the paper itself.

## The Centralization of Banking

The system of central banking was ultimately born as a mechanism to create money backed by debt to finance government expenses. In return, the banks were (generally speaking) given a monopoly to issue notes that were decreed by the government to be **legal tender**. This partnership was a solution to the recurring issue of credit contractions, which were all too familiar under a fractional reserve system. Stated differently, **if people traded money that could not be redeemed, then there could not be a run on the banks**. However, full-scale implementation of this system is a long story of failure by governments. The Bank of England's first attempt was a drastic failure. The USA failed with three central banks before establishing one that printed pure fiat money with no legal reserve. With each failure of fiat money, there was a return to some form of gold standard (note that adherence to a gold standard is an on and off proposition for many countries/banks throughout history).

As we review this history, note the general pattern in the emergence of and outcome from establishing a central bank:

- **Emergence**
    - There is a need to finance government expenditures, often due to war.
    - The bank is created to print money and lend it to the government.
    - For this money to be accepted, the government must confer some type of legal status upon it (legal tender) or provide assurance that it is backed by real money.

- **Outcome**
  - The bank issues paper money far beyond the amount in its vaults.
  - Once this is public knowledge, people demand their deposits, which are not there.
  - The debased currency results in rapid inflation.
  - The government attempts to fight inflation by mandating price controls.
  - As prices are artificially low, people stop producing, and the economy suffers from shortages in the supply of goods.
  - Further economic dislocations occur, resulting in wealth inequality, political discontent/extremism, civil disobedience, or regime change.

The pioneer of central banking was the Sveriges Riksbank of Sweden in 1668, as a response to the collapse of the Bank of Stockholm, which had issued too many notes on too few deposits. The Riksbank was not given permission to issue bank notes (paper backed by nothing) until 1701. However, this right was not granted to it exclusively until the end of the 19th century, meaning other private banks could also issue notes. Sweden had a history of relatively sound banking practices, and **its paper money was backed by gold in some form until 1931,** when it experienced its most severe recession in history. Today, Sveriges Riksbank is the oldest surviving bank in Sweden.

While the Riksbank was the first, the Bank of England was the template for modern central banking. It was created in 1694 amid financial disarray and war with France. Prior to this point numerous bank charters had been granted in England, and the issuance of fractional money led them all to fail. W.A. Shaw, in *Theory and Principles of Central Banking,* states: "*Disaster after disaster had to come upon the country....* [because] *of the indifference of the state to these mere private paper tokens."* [3]

The Bank of England, the government's creator of debt-based money, was favored and **saved multiple times from insolvency through acts of Parliament.**

The Bank of England assisted the government in paying off its debts by printing money and lending it to the government (paying off debt with more debt). In return it was granted the right to print bank notes, which were pure **fiat money** (not backed by any monetary medium). Despite being declared **legal tender** (legally required to be used in some form) these notes were rejected by the market, as failures resulting from this type of money were still a recent memory. **Subsequently, the bank issued exchequer bills in 1696 – bills fully redeemable in gold.**

***The Bank of England failed to implement a fiat monetary system because the public rejected the fiat money.***

In 1707 the Bank of England was given the responsibility of managing its own currency. **The bank transitioned back to bank notes of fractional money,** which gradually replaced existing bills by the middle of the 18th century.

In 1797 the Bank could no longer meet demand for physical delivery of its fractional reserves. **Parliament intervened** and authorized the bank **to suspend payment in specie** (i.e., forbidding people to redeem the gold backing their paper money). Prior to the government suspending payment in specie, the bank was required to redeem payments in gold. **By force of law, the Bank was now exempt from having to honor its contract to return gold deposits.**[23]

In 1815 **price controls were implemented** by the government in response to high inflation (i.e., the famous CornLaws). England went into a **deep depression and riots ensued.**[4]

In 1821 England returned to a gold standard, creating a period of deflation and recession. However, the reserves were still fractional, and the central bank mechanism still existed. Note that the term gold standard is loosely defined. That is, a central bank could maintain reserves in full or just partially.

By 1825, another crisis began in England, resulting in 64 bank failures. The convention of a **"lender of last resort"** was established – meaning the central bank could choose to freely lend to banks if they were at risk of insolvency. A former governor from the Bank of England referred to this as "*the most mischievous doctrine ever breathed in the monetary or banking world.*"[5]

***The Bank of England's fractional reserve system resulted in a run on the banks, inflation, price controls, recession, and social unrest.***

Shortly after the establishment of the Bank of England, the Bank of France was established. France had accumulated a significant amount of debt from the wars of Louis XIV and needed a solution. John Law convinced the king to establish the bank and decree that all taxes and revenues be paid in its notes. In 1716 it was chartered as a private bank and then nationalized two years later. With its legal tender status, the bank, like many others before it, began to issue more notes than it had in reserves. Wild speculation ensued in the famous Mississippi Bubble. The result was a run on the banks in 1720 with roughly 50% inflation of the currency. The term banking came to be associated with fraud, and France did not establish a central bank for another half-century.

In 1776 the Bank of France's successor was born, once again out of the need to finance war. By 1793 inflation was rampant. During that year, the revolutionary government of the new

French Republic attempted many experiments in price and wage controls designed to quell inflation. The most notable of these was called the Law of Maximum. Artificially low prices resulted in massive food shortages. Farmers kept their produce away from markets as best they could, as it was not economic for them to trade at such low prices. Ironically, France was one of the richest agricultural countries in Europe. A historian on the subject states:

> *Her food problem in that year was not one of production but rather of distribution. A constant series of decrees and regulations, each one designed to remedy the defects of the last, had the effect of leading the bread basket of Europe to the brink of starvation* [6]

Popular uprisings took place, and in 1794 price controls were officially repealed. Robespierre – an influential figure of the French Revolution – stated while being carried to his execution: "*There goes the dirty Maximum!*" [6]

***The Bank of France's fractional reserve system resulted in a run on the banks, inflation, price controls, recession, and social unrest.***

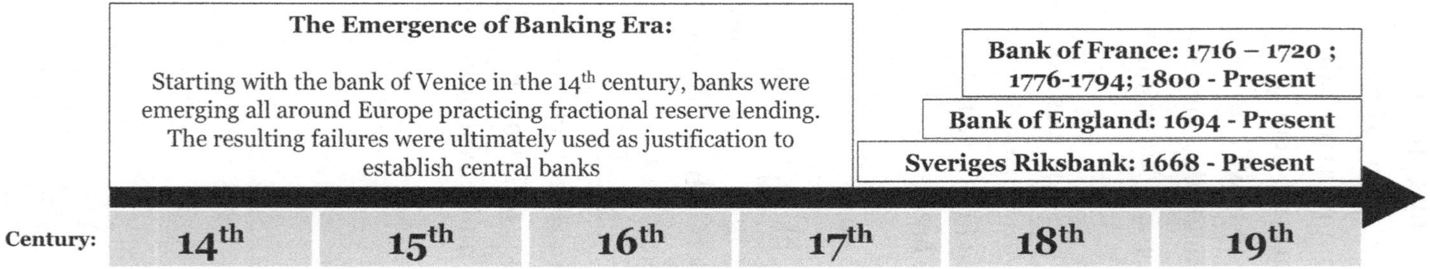

**The Emergence of Banking Era:**

Starting with the bank of Venice in the 14th century, banks were emerging all around Europe practicing fractional reserve lending. The resulting failures were ultimately used as justification to establish central banks

**Bank of France: 1716 – 1720 ; 1776-1794; 1800 - Present**

**Bank of England: 1694 - Present**

**Sveriges Riksbank: 1668 - Present**

**Century:** **14th** **15th** **16th** **17th** **18th** **19th**

**Figure 25:** timeline of major European central banks

## Central Banking in the United States

Thus far we have examined the major banking institutions of Europe that created the template for the modern system of central banking. The USA later adopted similar banking practices and eventually became a pure fiat system with no legal reserve requirement. Keep in mind the pattern of cause-and-effect relationships stated earlier. This pattern is important to understand what occurred in the first 3 US central banks as well as in the 4th, which still exists today.

From 1690 to 1764 the American colonies had their first experience with pure fiat money. Prices rose drastically and legal tender laws were enacted to force acceptance. By 1750 Connecticut had inflation of 80%, Carolinas 900%, Massachusetts 1000%, and Rhode Island 2300%.[24] The British Parliament had to intervene and stop fiat production. The forced use of fiat caused everyone to hoard their real coins (Gresham's Law), and now that paper money was worthless, people used their coins again. Prices adjusted back to reality, and prosperity ensued up until the Revolution.[7]

In 1775 one of the first acts of the Continental Congress was to authorize the printing of paper money, the **Continental**. Just before the revolutionary war, the colonial money supply stood at roughly $12 million. By 1780 it was roughly $227 million, a ~2000% increase.[8] Commodity prices had risen 480%. In response the government implemented price controls and legal-tender laws, while blaming "unpatriotic speculators" for the inflation (recall Diocletian blamed the merchants). After Washington's army nearly starved to death at Valley Forge, the Continental Congress eliminated the price controls.[9]

Thomas Jefferson gave us his thoughts on the matter:

*Every one, through whose hands a bill passed, lost on that bill what it lost in value during the time it was in his hands. This was a real tax on him; and in this way the people of the United States actually contributed those sixty-six millions of dollars during the war, and by a mode of taxation the most oppressive of all because the most unequal of all.* [10]

With the price controls removed, inflation spiked. There immediately followed a period of deflation, resulting in the destruction of businesses.[8] The Continental was directly issued by the government and was backed by nothing. As the Constitution had yet to be written, direct issuance of fiat was lawful. Toward the end of the war, a *de facto* central bank was established.

***Colonial fiat money resulted in inflation, price controls, shortages, and social unrest.***

The **Bank of North America**, the first US central bank, was chartered in 1782 before the Constitution was written. Alexander Hamilton was its primary proponent in Congress. It maintained a fractional reserve and issued paper notes in excess of actual deposits, although the notes were not declared legal tender. It also did not have the power to directly issue the nation's money. Effectively, it loaned money to the government to finance the Revolutionary War but was terminated upon the war's end.

**Figure 26:** the Bank of North America

In 1787 came the Constitutional Convention. At the time there was intense debate over what future monetary policy should be. Three months prior to the Constitutional Convention, George Washington voiced his rejection of fiat money:

> *The necessity arising from a want of specie is represented as greater than it really is. I contend that it is by the substance, not the shadow of thing, we are to be benefited. The wisdom of man, in my humble opinion, cannot at this time devise a plan by which the credit of paper money would be long supported; consequently, depreciation keeps pace with the quantity of the emission, and the articles for which it is exchanged rise in a greater ratio than the sinking value of the money. Wherein, then, is the farmer, the planter, the artisan benefited? An evil great is the door it immediately opens for speculation, by which the least designing and perhaps most valuable part of the community are preyed upon by the more knowing and crafty of speculators* [11]

## Wealth Inequality from Inflation:

Washington was aware of the wealth inequality that is created from fiat monetary expansion. This phenomenon was observed by economist Richard Cantillon and is known as the **Cantillon Effect**. He proposed that rising prices occur in different sectors of an economy at different times. The first sectors to receive newly created money can spend it before prices have risen, while each subsequent holder of the money must spend it with prices having already risen.

This is analogous to the Roman government's coin clipping. The government first spent their coin clippings before prices rose, while agricultural laborers spent it after prices had risen. Today those who receive the money first are the largest banks. This money goes out in loans to, mostly, companies. Eventually, it is the wage earners who receive it from those companies. The banks trade the new money while prices are still low, and the wage earners trade it after prices have risen.

Another way to think about this is that those who are furthest removed from interaction with financial institutions end up worst off. This group is typically the poorest in a society. Thus, the ultimate impact on society is a wealth transfer to the wealthy. Poor people become poorer, while the wealthy get wealthier, resulting in the crippling or destruction of the middle class.

Here is a clip of Fed chairman Jerome Powell dancing around this question.[25]

And here is a chart of wealth inequality in the US since it transformed to a pure fiat system in 1971. (More on this later.)

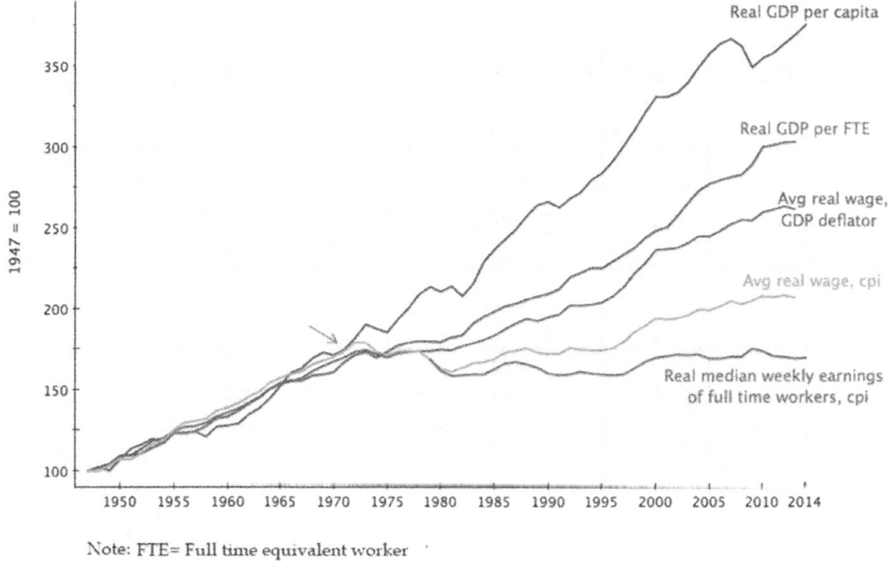


**Figure 27:** inequality started to expand materially in 1971 (image source is wtfhappenedin1971.com)[28]

Back to history. Washington's sentiment was shared widely among those who influenced our constitution:

- Oliver Ellsworth: "*This is a favorable moment to shut and bar the door against paper money. The mischief of the various experiments which have been made are now fresh in the public mind and have excited the disgust of all the respectable parts of America.*" [12]
- George Mason: "*They may pass a law to issue paper money, but twenty laws will not make the people receive it. Paper money is founded upon fraud and knavery.*" [12]
- James Wilson: "*It will have the most salutary influence on the credit of the United States to remove the possibility of paper money.*" [12]
- George Reed (on allowing the government to issue paper

money): *"Would be as alarming as the mark of the beast in Revelation"* [12]

- Thomas Paine: *"The punishment of a member who should move for such a law ought to be death."* [12]

The defenders of sound money ultimately won under the Constitution Article I, sections 8 and 10:

- *"Congress shall have the power...To borrow money...to coin money, regulate the value thereof, and of foreign coin, and fix the standard of weights and measures; ...and to provide for the punishment of counterfeiting"*
- *"No state shall... Coin money; emit bills of credit; [or] make anything but gold and silver coin a tender in payment of debts"*

Congress was given the power to coin money but not to create it (in today's terms, print it). This congressional power is easy to interpret for coins but not for paper money. These 2 sections of the constitution are the subject of intense legal debate concerning their interpretation. Money was to be created privately and coined by the government. This fact was made explicit in the Coinage Act of 1792. In this act, the dollar was defined to have a fixed content of silver that it was fully redeemable in. In the words of Washington:

> *We may one day become a great commercial and flourishing nation. But if in the pursuit of the means we should unfortunately stumble again on unfunded paper money or any similar species of fraud, we shall assuredly give a fatal stab to our national credit in its infancy.*[13]

Prior to the Coinage Act, Alexander Hamilton was at work establishing a new central bank. His rationale for the bank was that it would create a stable currency and a lower cost of debt, making it easier for the economy to flourish.[14] Hamilton also had ties to English banking interests that wanted to establish a presence in the USA. Note that similar to politicians today, Hamilton had flipped-flopped from his prior statements praising sound money. Thomas Jefferson led the side against the establishment of a central bank, and there was a year of intense debate.

- Jefferson:
  - *"A private central bank issuing the public currency is a greater menace to the liberties of the people than a standing army."* [15]
  - *"We must not let our rulers load us with perpetual debt."* [16]
- Hamilton:
  - *"No society could succeed which did not unite the interest and credit of rich individuals with those of the state."* [17]
  - *"A national debt, if it is not excessive, will be to us a national blessing."* [18]

Hamilton won. In 1791 the First Bank of the United States was granted a twenty-year charter. **This occurred because the Constitution allowed the federal government to *borrow* money.** By establishing a bank that was quasi-private, that bank could create paper money and lend it to the federal government. While technically it could lend to anyone, it had a mandated maximum rate of interest of 6%. This made it impractical to lend to anyone besides the government and institutions with pristine credit.[19]

Jefferson was troubled about the matter:

*I wish it were possible to obtain a single amendment to our constitution. I would be willing to depend on that alone for the reduction of the administration of our government to the general principle of the Constitution; I mean an additional article, taking from the federal government their power of borrowing.*[20]

**Figure 28:** the First Bank of the United States

The First Bank of the United States was remarkably like the Bank of North America. It was granted a monopoly on the issuance of bank notes. These were not enforced as legal tender, but they could be used to pay taxes, making them attractive to some people. It was the official depository of federal funds and was always required to redeem its notes in gold or silver upon demand. However, it was not required to keep full amounts in gold or silver needed to pay its note obligations. So the bank maintained a fractional reserve. Over the next five years, the dollar inflated by 72%.[19]

***The first central bank was established as a private institution to intentionally circumvent the constitutional limitation on printing money that the Founding Fathers had been in favor of.***

The bank's charter was up for renewal in 1811 but was defeated by one vote in both house and senate, and so it closed its doors. After this state-chartered banks assumed the ability to print notes. As the War of 1812 broke out, the state banks were needed to finance it. By 1814 the banks of the nation (except for New England) were insolvent[26], and the dollar had inflated by 66% as the federal debt rose from $45 million to $127 million.[27] The federal government refused to redeem its obligations to keep the banks solvent. When the public found out and demanded their deposits, riots ensued, and the banks had to hire guards for protection.

***Wartime money printing resulted in inflation, bank failure, and social unrest.***

To solve the problems created by the state banks, the USA created another central bank. **Just as Britain established the Bank of England to fix its fractional reserve problem with goldsmith-bankers, the USA established the Second Bank of the United States to fix its fractional reserve problems with state banks.** It was chartered in 1816 under President Madison and was identical to its predecessor. What was different this time around was the competitive dynamic existing between this new bank and the existing state banks.

**Figure 29:** the Second Bank of the United States

When the Second Bank of the United States began operations, it was competing for market share with the existing state banks. Established under the pretense of generating tax revenue, the states imposed heavy taxation upon any bank operating within their borders that was chartered outside of the state. The central bank didn't like this, and it resulted in a lawsuit that went all the way to the Supreme Court.

The case, McCulloch v. Maryland, was novel for this time and important for the establishment of federal power. Maryland argued the central bank was unconstitutional, as the Constitution did not give the federal government power to charter a bank. McCulloch argued that a central bank was "necessary and proper" for Congress to carry out its other powers that are given to it under the Constitution. This was a strong defense, as it was easy to manipulate the term "necessary and proper" under Article I Section 8.

What is interesting is the focus of the argument. The question should have been whether it was within congressional power to issue bills of credit, either directly **or indirectly**. The bank was creating money, and most of it was being used to finance the government. Further, the government was granting the bank a national monopoly and enforcing it with governmental power. Without the federal government, the central bank could not exist.

The Supreme Court ruled unanimously in favor of McCulloch. As a result, the concept of a nationally chartered bank operating separately from the federal government was firmly established.

In 1818 the central bank was in danger of failing, so it called in much of its credit, causing the Panic of 1819. Historian William Gouge observed, *"The Bank was saved, and the people were ruined."* The bank's charter was up for renewal in 1836, and a political battle arose between President Andrew Jackson and the bank's chairman, Nicholas Biddle. Jackson wanted to end the bank and was paying for government expenses in gold while campaigning for reelection. **The bank's chairman was fraudulently advancing payments to congressmen and accommodating important members of the press.** Jackson began draining federal deposits from the bank, and Biddle responded by deliberately creating a credit contraction, which he then blamed on Jackson's decision.

In 1836 the bank charter was suspended; it was restructured as a state bank, and **chairman Biddle was arrested and charged with fraud.** That is the end of the story of the last US central bank before the Federal Reserve was created.

***The second central bank of the US ended in fraud, with the chairman deliberately creating an economic contraction.***

When the Civil War broke out in 1861, the nation faced financial risks along with it. The government financed the war **by unconstitutionally imposing an income tax,** selling war bonds, and printing fiat money (the famous greenback). How did they print fiat, given the Constitution? Lincoln ignored the Constitution in many respects during the Civil War. There is no better time to take away freedom than during a crisis, especially war.

**Figure 30:** the greenback

During the war, the National Banking Act of 1863 was passed to establish a group of nationally chartered banks. It was marketed honestly as a wartime measure. For the remainder of the 19th century, the US banking system existed as a distributed group of national banks. By the end of the Civil War, the Northern money supply had increased 138%, and greenbacks were inflated by 65%.[21] In the South, the commodity price index had risen by 9,200%. All occurred despite mandated price controls. Riots and looting ensued, particularly in the former confederate states.[22]

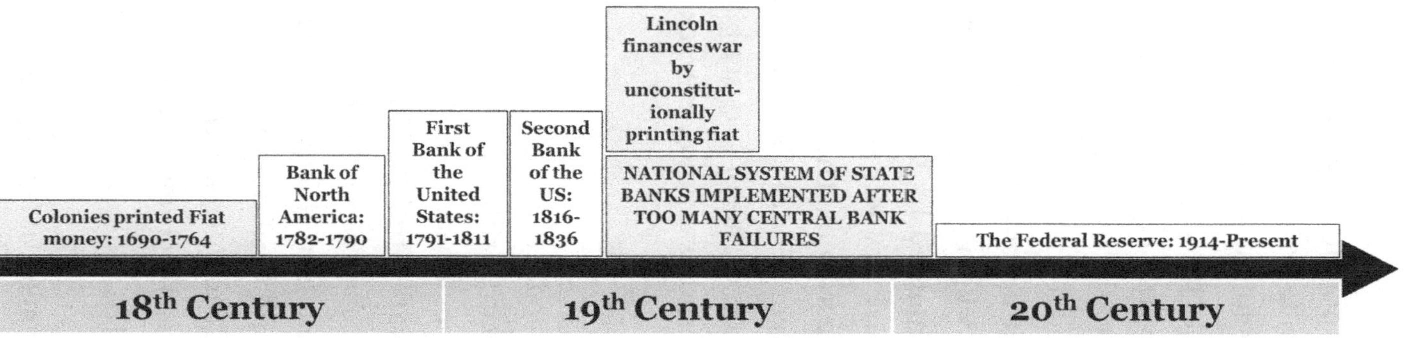


**Figure 31:** a timeline of US central banking

## Conclusion

Formal banking practices can be traced back to 14th century Venice. Modern banking practices emerged in 16th century Europe, and central banking followed soon thereafter. History shows a pattern of boom-and-bust cycles driven by the partnership between banks and governments. Maintaining a gold standard was the thorn in the side of the fractional reserve banking system, and governments replaced it with pure fiat systems. The USA opened and closed three central banks before the creation of the Federal Reserve, the last of which was closed in part due to politically motivated fraud committed by the bank's chairman. The latter half of the 19th century saw war inflation and the establishment of a national banking system. These events set the stage for the Federal Reserve System we are subject to today. The next chapter will be the last piece of history, describing how the Federal Reserve came about and examining its track record.

## References:

1. *The Creature from Jekyll Island: A Second Look at the Federal Reserve*, G. Edward Griffin, 171
2. *The Creature from Jekyll Island: A Second Look at the Federal Reserve*, G. Edward Griffin, 172
3. *Theory and Principles of Central Banking*, W.A. Shaw, 32
4. *The Creature from Jekyll Island: A Second Look at the Federal Reserve*, G. Edward Griffin, 181
5. *The History of Central Banks*, The Economist, April 27, 2017
6. *Forty Centuries of Wage and Price Controls: How Not to Fight Inflation*, Robert L. Schuettinger and Eamonn F. Butler, 45–47
7. *The Creature from Jekyll Island: A Second Look at the Federal Reserve*, G. Edward Griffin, 310 – 311

8. *The Creature from Jekyll Island: A Second Look at the Federal Reserve*, G. Edward Griffin, 161 - 163
9. *Forty Centuries of Wage and Price Controls: How Not to Fight Inflation*, Robert L. Schuettinger and Eamonn F. Butler, 38 – 41
10. *Thomas Jefferson*, Observations on the Article Etats-Unis Prepared for the Encyclopedia, June 22, 1786, 165
11. *Washington to Stone, 16 February 1787*, Quoted by Bancroft, 231-32
12. *A Plea for the Constitution*, George Bancroft, 30; 40-43
13. *A Treatise On Monetary Reform*, quoted by Louis Bassio, 5
14. *The History of Central Banks*, The Economist, April 27, 2017
15. *The Writings of Thomas Jefferson*, New York: G.P. Putnam & Sons, Vol. X, 31
16. *The Basic Writings of Thomas Jefferson*, Willey Book Company, 749
17. *The Age of Jackson*, Quoted by Arthur M. Schlesinger, Jr., 6-7
18. *The Global Debt Crisis: America's Growing Involvement*, John H. Makin, 246
19. *The Creature from Jekyll Island: A Second Look at the Federal Reserve*, G. Edward Griffin, 331 - 332
20. *The Continuing Tax Rebellion Old Greenwich, Letter to John Taylor, November 26, 1789,* Quoted by Martin A. Larson, xii
21. *The Creature from Jekyll Island: A Second Look at the Federal Reserve*, G. Edward Griffin, 388
22. *Forty Centuries of Wage and Price Controls: How Not to Fight Inflation*, Robert L. Schuettinger and Eamonn F. Butler, 51 – 52
23. *William Pitt, The Bank Of England, And The 1797 Suspension Of Specie Payments: Central Bank War Finance During The Napoleonic Wars,* Scott N. Duryea, 6
24. *The Case for Gold,* Ron Paul and Lewis Lehrman, 25

25. Jerome Powell discusses monetary policy at 51:40: https://www.youtube.com/watch?v=ehI0wxxEilc
26. *The Mystery of Banking*, Murray N. Rothbard, 198 – 199
27. *The Creature from Jekyll Island: A Second Look at the Federal Reserve*, G. Edward Griffin, 338
28. https://wtfhappenedin1971.com/

# 5. THE HISTORY OF THE FEDERAL RESERVE

*In America, we're really good at blowing things up but not so good in knowing where the pieces land.* – *Mike Tyson*

A system of boundless fractional reserve banking necessarily requires that either:

1. Derivative money be replaced by money that is not redeemable in anything (i.e., fiat money).
2. Bank failures and bailouts, which have gone on since the 17th century, continue.

The story of the 20th century reveals how governments finally achieved a pure fiat form of money. As their control over the banking system expanded, the idea that money could be backed by debt became more feasible in the mind of the public until it became status quo. Today, most people do not understand why money is the way it is, its purpose, or what properties it should have. It was not always this way. **Politicians used to campaign with a stance on central banking.**

As we cover the remainder of US central banking history, we will focus on the major events that brought our monetary and banking system to its present state.

## The Federal Reserve

At the beginning of the 20th century the US was operating under a system of national banks, which functioned much in the same way as a central bank. The Panic of 1907 is commonly said to have occurred as the result of the inability of the banking system to "provide liquidity." The system didn't have a "lender of last resort," or a bank to print money and lend it to banks that had extended credit beyond their reserves. Of course, fractional reserve banking was never publicized as being the crux of the issue.

Interestingly, growth in private markets was decreasing centralization of banking during this time. In the 1880s most banks were national banks. By 1913 non-national banks controlled 57% of the nation's deposits, and this number was growing. Between 1900 and 1910, 71% of American corporate growth was funded by profits, making the industry organically less dependent on banks for debt.[1]

However, the banking powers did not like this newfound competition. Just as in any industry, the leaders of banking did not want increased competition and consumer independence. Today, the idea of financing through organic profits is rare and the assumption of debt is a foregone conclusion. How did we end up in a debt-ridden society?

In November 1910 there was a meeting of 7 men at the exclusive Jekyll Island Club off the coast of Georgia. This group included Senator Nelson Aldrich, Treasury Secretary A. Piatt Andrew, and five of the most prominent bankers on wall street: Benjamin Strong, Henry Davison, Arthur Shelton, Frank Vanderlip, Charles D. Norton, and Paul Warburg. An article in the *New York Times* on May 3, 1931 stated: "One-sixth of the total wealth of the world was represented by members of the Jekyll Island Club."

The Jekyll Island team knew it had to **sway public opinion** in favor of a new central bank. On top of a variety of other measures, the banks all contributed **$5 million to a "special educational fund"** much of which found its way into **Princeton, Harvard, and the University of Chicago**. Around this time the new study of economics was becoming an acceptable field. Professors were open to and willing to create politically convenient research in exchange for grants and favors. The fund created the National Citizens League under chairman James Laughlin of the University of Chicago. Rockefeller (a major banking interest) had donated $50 million to their endowment. Effectively, a public think tank financed by bankers was established.

On December 23, 1913, the Federal Reserve Act was passed, establishing the Federal Reserve. Importantly, the words "central" or "bank" were replaced with terms like "federal" and "reserve," despite it being a quasi-private institution. This was done to avoid public outcry from those who remembered the many past failures of central banking. Although the initial goal of the Federal Reserve was to provide financial stability to the system, **it has presided over the following economic recessions since inception: 1921, 1929, 1937, 1945, 1949, 1954, 1957, 1960, 1969, 1975, 1981, 1987, 1990, 2001, 2007, 2020.** Recessions were a pattern. Further, since the Fed's inception, the purchasing power of the dollar has fallen 96%.

On this matter Nobel laureate economist Milton Friedman stated:

> *Throughout its history, the Fed has proclaimed that it was using its powers to promote economic stability. But the record does not support this claim. On the contrary, the Fed has been a major source of instability.* [2]

**The Federal Reserve has failed in its objective (to promote economic stability), yet it continues to conduct experiments**

**on the largest economy in an integrated global financial system.** On the other hand, if its stated objective had been to centralize control of the banking system, then it has been a complete success. One year after the act was passed, Aldrich was quoted in *The Independent*, stating:

> *Before the passage of this Act, the New York bankers could only dominate the reserves of New York. Now we are able to dominate the bank reserves of the entire country.* [3]

The Federal Reserve is a system of 12 private banks across the country, all governed under a board of officials chosen by the government. At this time, it operated under a gold standard, but its mandated powers were vague. The Federal Reserve Act had been amended 195 times before the end of the century.[4] There were 2 key developments that impacted the ability of the Fed to implement its mandate:

1. **The Definition of Reserves:** generally speaking, reserves are actual money stored in a vault. What changed over time was that **private banks could reclassify loans they made as reserves.** All private banks have an account at the Fed that has a reserve stash of cash. Now, once those banks made a loan to a business, the Fed allowed them to classify the value of that loan as a reserve in their account. Before reserves were just money, but now reserves included debt. For accounting purposes, they were classified as the same thing.
2. **Controlling interest rates:** The Fed created a tool called the **discount window** that allowed them to (a) expand the money supply and (b) lower interest rates. The Fed would loan money to banks at an interest rate it chose, and the banks then took this money and loaned it to somebody else. Now that it had been loaned out, the banks could reclassify

the loan as a reserve, allowing them to loan more. By the Fed lending money to banks at a "discount rate" (hence discount window), banks make a profit by lending the same money at a higher rate. The lower the discount rate the Fed charged, the lower the interest rate the banks needed to charge, and the lower interest rates in the economy generally would be. This effect made borrowing money much easier and played a key role in international markets.

## Defining the Gold Standard:

Gold standard means the dollar is redeemable, from the government, for some fixed amount of gold. Before World War I, most countries were on some form of this standard. More precisely, they had gold coins circulating as money alongside paper notes that were fractionally backed by some amount of gold in banks. The less gold you had backing the paper notes, the less valuable they were.

**Figure 32:** 5 dollar bill redeemable in gold

During the war, many countries stopped circulating physical gold coins and instead kept them as reserves to support the value of their paper notes. Under the **international gold standard,** currencies were fixed in terms of gold and thus their relative value could be derived from their weight in gold. However, if a country departed from maintaining the ratio of paper to gold, it's currency would lose value relative to other currencies that did not do this.

For example, if 1 US dollar bought 2 ounces of gold and 1 British pound bought 2 ounces of gold, then the exchange rate between the currencies would be **one to one (i.e., one dollar could buy one pound)**. So, all countries, if they maintained their gold standard, would maintain a *parity* of exchange between one another, using gold as the common denominator. Consider if Britain printed twice as many notes and 1 pound now bought 1 ounce of gold. That would mean **1 dollar now bought 2 pounds**. The exchange rate would have changed, and parity would no longer exist.

## World War I

At the beginning of the war nearly all the countries engaged went off the gold standard by suspending payments in specie (i.e., suspending the ability to redeem paper for coin) and instituting embargoes on gold exports by private citizens. Countries financed the war by exporting gold, borrowing from foreign countries, or printing money. This resulted in material devaluations of their currencies that would be realized after the war, as gold left the country while more paper currency was being printed.

A novel development over the prior 50 years was that a global monetary system had emerged in which countries attempted to maintain parity in exchange rates. This was important because changes in currency exchange affected whether money flowed in or out of a country.

As all countries were printing money, all of them were devaluing. Depending on how much printing each did, the parity of exchange would shift one way or the other.

If exchange parity reached the **gold export point**, this meant that it was profitable to ship gold to the country with the stronger currency and sell it there (because you would get more valuable currency for it). Indeed, governments began restricting private citizens from doing so during the war.

The British wanted to import goods and at the same time maintain the value of their currency. **They could not continue exporting their gold indefinitely without risking the loss of their monetary dominance**. From January 1916 to March 1919, they attempted to peg the exchange rate of the pound to the dollar at $4.76 through the assistance of J.P. Morgan acting as agent of the British Treasury.[5] They did this by paying in paper (as opposed to gold) and simply stated that their currency was still worth $4.76. However, they were changing the ratio of paper to gold, thus devaluing their currency.

After the war, countries did not want to reveal that their currencies had been materially devalued. As Britain was the *de jure* reserve currency of the time, other countries waited until it had stabilized before deciding what to do with their own currencies. If countries were to return to a gold standard, then the devaluation of the currency would subject their respective economies to a major contraction. **Britain needed gold reserves, and the USA had them.** The Fed attempted to support the British pound by executing policy that effectively made the US a gold exporter. By maintaining artificially low interest rates via the discount window, the USA was a gold exporter in every month from June 1919 to March 1920.

**By lowering interest rates, the Fed encouraged people from abroad to borrow dollars**. The borrowers then invested that money domestically at a higher rate. This phenomenon effectively moved money outside of the US. This meant that low interest rates in the US were moving gold outside the country, devaluing the US currency.

**This concept was the defining factor behind the inflation-**

**ary monetary policy of the 1920s.** With the inflationary pressures that ensued from this policy and a need to maintain the gold standard, the Fed increased interest rates from 1.25% to 6%, causing the depression of 1921.[5]

Economists blame this depression on adherence to the gold standard, while neglecting the fact that artificially lowering and then spiking interest rates created the issue in the first place.

The US maintained this interest rate policy until the mid-1920s, causing gold to flow back into the country. While the dollar was the de facto gold standard reserve currency, much of Europe was still tied to the pound.

To assist Britain as it prepared to restore the gold standard, the Fed lowered interest rates once again, increasing its debt by roughly 57%.[5] Britain was able to return to a gold standard in 1925. As credit expansion ensued in the US, the Fed slightly raised rates for a short time, but by July 1927 the central banks needed to support the pound, and the US once again lowered interest rates. By the end of the year, Federal Reserve bank credit had expanded by 93%.[5]

Let's recap this interaction between countries. Each country is faced with a tradeoff between international and domestic interests when maintaining a gold standard. They need reserves to exist at some mandated percentage of the notes they have printed. When they lower interest rates, borrowing gold becomes cheaper. Countries from abroad then borrow gold and invest it in their own countries, moving gold abroad. Paper currency is devalued when the gold backing it leaves the country, all else being equal. **To attract gold back, a country must raise interest rates.** Higher interest rates mean people borrow less. Credit then contracts and causes a recession. Many economists have blamed the gold standard for this problem (i.e., if they did not have to maintain reserves, then they would not have to raise rates). This logic ignores the first order issue that reserves need to be maintained for money to properly serve its function. If you do not hold yourself to a diet, then you may avoid breaking your diet, but you will still get fat.

Read this table by column from left to right:

| Category | Baseline | Decrease Interest Rates | Increase Interest Rates |
|---|---|---|---|
| **Paper Notes** | 100 | 100 | 100 |
| **Gold** | 50 | 25 | 100 |
| **Paper/Gold** | $2 | $4 (currency is devalued) | $1 (currency increases in value) |
| **US Domestic Interests** | Na | Good: increased lending and economic expansion | Bad: decreased lending and economic contraction |
| **US International Interests** | Na | Bad: gold leaves the country, currency is devalued, monetary dominance decreases | Good: gold comes in from abroad, currency strengthens, monetary dominance increases |

**Figure 33:** the impact of interest rate policy on domestic and international interests

***A gold standard forced countries to adhere to a trade-off: you can either have low interest rates and a booming economy, or you can have gold reserves backing your money and steady growth. You cannot have both. However, governments do not like trade-offs.***

## The Great Depression

After an induced recession, the US dollar was the *de facto* gold standard currency, and Britain was losing its formerly unchallenged supremacy.

The monetary situation in Europe was weak as many banks did not hold the necessary amount of reserves. Eventually, investors got scared, starting with a run on the banks in Austria. European banks seeking safety began to demand gold, and despite

Britain's restrictive monetary policy, gold rapidly flowed out of the country.

By September 1931 Britain abandoned the gold standard once again. At this point the USA was strongly conflicted between its domestic objective of maintaining a strong economy and the international objective of maintain a strong currency. The USA prioritized its international objective and increased interest rates.

Following the stock market crash of 1929, the US money supply decreased by one third – spiraling the country into the greatest depression in history by 1931. By 1933 over 5,000 banks had failed, the stock market had lost 80% of its value, and 12 million people were unemployed.[5] There was an internal run on banks by people demanding gold redemption. The Federal Reserve and every state suspended banking operations. Once banks reopened, President Franklin D. Roosevelt issued an executive order prohibiting banks from redeeming gold and requiring gold to be returned to the Federal Reserve banks.

***The USA raised interest rates to gain international monetary dominance while Britain was struggling. But this came at a cost to the US domestic economy.***

What is most interesting is that the USA did not need to suspend the gold standard at all. The legally mandated reserve ratio was 35%. Prior to FDR confiscating citizens' gold, it stood at 51%, after which it increased to 61%.[5] Leland Crabbe of the Federal Reserve stated in an article from 1989:

> *Restoration of the gold standard did not involve insurmountable problems: Legislative initiatives were rebuilding confidence in the banking system; notes were returning to deposit accounts; the gold reserve ratio was recovering; and the dollar was clinging near the gold export point throughout the period. Had it so*

> *desired, the Roosevelt Administration could have preserved gold parity...The United States suspended the gold standard not out of necessity but out of a change of attitude.* [5]

In 1934 Congress passed the Gold Reserve Act, transferring the title of gold from the Federal Reserve to the US government, prohibiting gold coinage, and banning it from circulation. Prior to this, under Executive Order 6102, the government had coerced people to exchange gold with the US treasury at $20.67 per ounce. After the Act, the Treasury changed the price to $35 per ounce – the price at which it sold on the international market. With all gold nationalized, the US government profited to the tune of $3 billion from buying gold from citizens at $20 and selling it internationally at $35.

The USA now held the citizens' gold and had materially devalued the dollar. This forced European countries to abandon the gold standard and devalue their currencies or suffer through deflation.[5] Competitive devaluation was the expedient choice; one that a government can always be counted on to make.

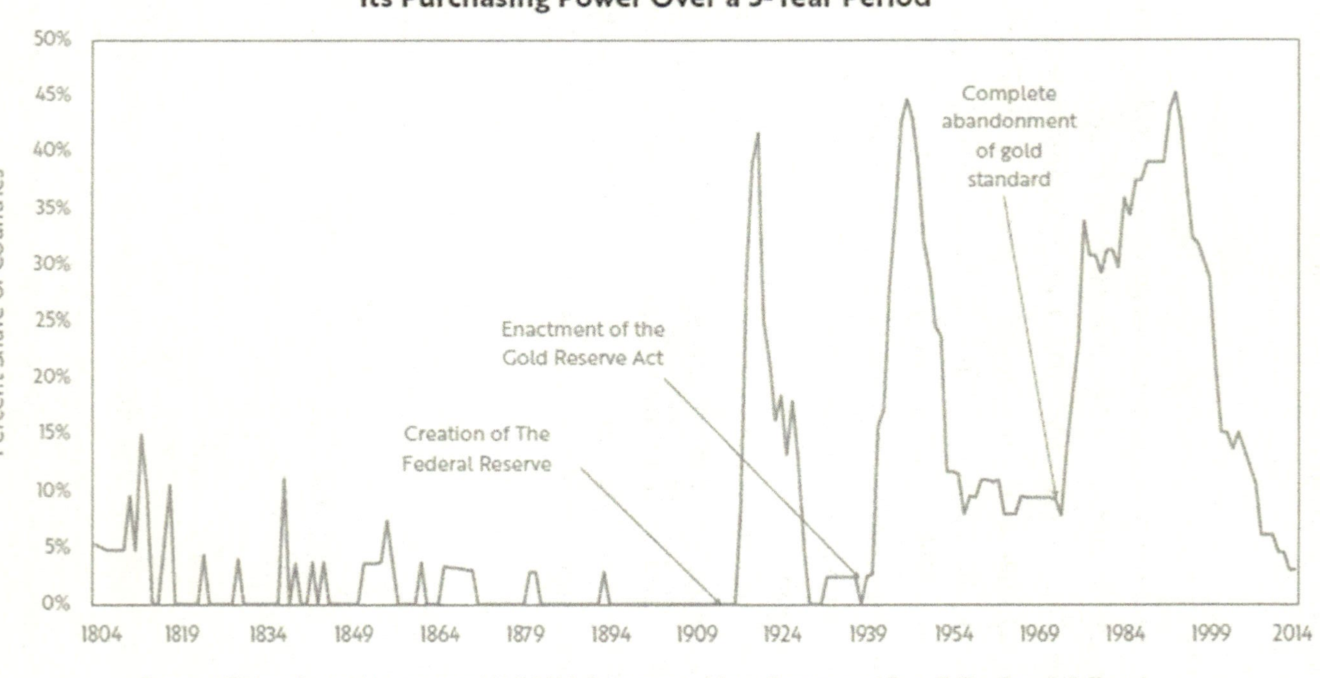


**Figure 34:** frequent worldwide currency devaluations since the inception of the federal reserve (image source from Lyn Alden from Ark Management report)[8]

The USA was left controlling the international monetary regime with the dollar as the *de facto* world reserve currency. Meanwhile, citizens at home were suffering from the greatest depression in history. Prior to the crash, debt levels had reached a historical peak.

Monetary policy and credit expansion from the 1920s had caused a rise in wages and prices, and once the Fed contracted credit, prices began to deflate. When the party was over, prices needed to correct to their natural state.

## The Bretton Woods Conference

In 1937 another recession famously hit called the "Roosevelt Recession," resulting from a cut in government spending. Prior to the spending cut, the economy had become materially dependent on government spending. Once the cut was made, there was a void in the economy that needed to be replaced. People were upset, and Roosevelt couldn't garner Congressional support for more New Deal programs. After Americans returned from World War II, in the years 1945-1948, the economy entered a period of prosperity. This was despite a 75% cut in government spending during this period.[6]

However, this cut in spending occurred largely because the war ran the largest fiscal deficit in history. So returning to normal just meant not running a massive deficit.

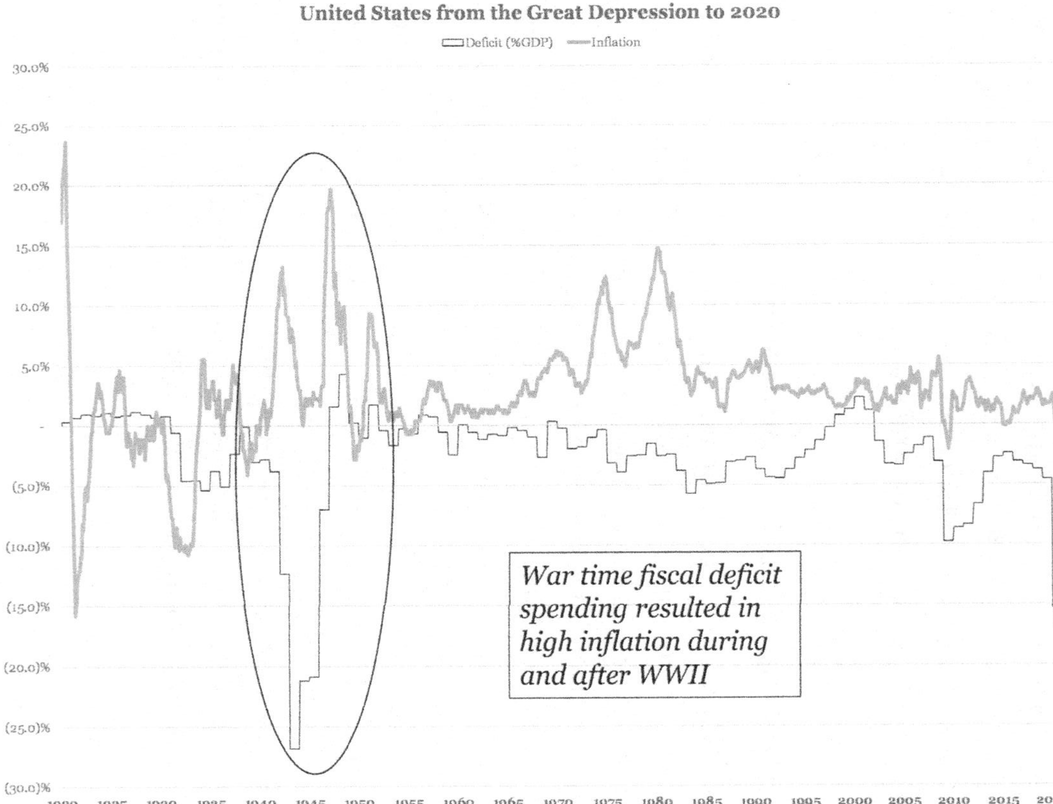


**Figure 35:** the United States fiscal deficit and inflation

Americans were still not allowed to own gold, but the US government would redeem gold for dollars at the international level. This was a gold standard but not in the original sense of the term; governments were still printing money and failing to maintain parity of exchange rates. But the United States wanted to give the gold standard another try. It summoned the relevant developed countries to the Bretton Woods conference in 1944. The USA was in the driver's seat because it possessed the most sound monetary policy and strongest military power.

Bretton Woods established the IMF (International Monetary Fund) and the World Bank. The attendees of the Bretton Woods meeting intended to use these organizations to eliminate the tradeoff between their international and domestic interests. In actuality, these organizations further centralized trade and monetary systems and did not permit the members to have both booming economies and international exchange parity. Put simply, centralizing international trade and monetary policy was their attempt to have their cake and eat it, too. The stated intention of the newly-created institutions was to manage trade policy and move money to countries experiencing significant deficits. **The US dollar was established as the de jure world reserve currency**, and all countries could convert dollars into gold at the price of $35 per ounce. As I write these words, the same amount of gold today trades at $2,000.

Robert Schuettinger and Eamonn Butler in *Forty Centuries of Wage and Price Controls* state:

> *Major nations met in New Hampshire in 1944 to develop a new system of international currency exchange, which fixed parities up to a certain point, but which never really worked. The gold exchange system was revived and gold became the foundation of the new economic system. Each nation would hold its reserves in gold, which could be freely converted into dollars. The parities of*

*other currencies were fixed, but devaluation was possible within a narrow range of ten percent, or more if there was agreement from the international monetary fund.* [7]

This system created major disequilibria and alarming flows of gold from the United States. Foreign countries responded by devaluing their currency against the dollar. France was the first to object to the system by calling the USA reserve currency status "America's exorbitant privilege." In 1966 $14 billion was held by non-US central banks, while only $3.2 billion of gold was backing it. By 1971 the US money supply increased by 10% and, West Germany left the system. Other nations began to demand redemption of their dollars for gold. Congress released a report recommending dollar devaluation for protection against "foreign price-gougers." Then Switzerland left the system. The objective of Bretton Woods was "to promote exchange stability and exchange arrangements and to avoid competitive exchange depreciation," but the system ultimately produced the opposite.[7] **The system was replaced *de facto* with pure fiat currency in 1971, which is generally referred to as the Nixon Shock. Announced as a temporary measure, this ended the convertibility of the dollar into gold** and imposed wage and price controls for good measure. This temporary measure of pure fiat currency remains in place today.

**Figure 36:** a fiat 5-dollar bill no longer backed by anything and decreed legal tender

## Conclusion

The Federal Reserve was created by some the wealthiest men in the world just prior to World War I. This required a carefully managed campaign of persuasion and the enlisting of support from academia, given the fraud committed by prior central banks. Created as a private institution to encourage economic stability, it has since presided over 16 economic recessions. The USA prioritized international monetary objectives over domestic objectives, inducing the Great Depression. With the USA controlling the de facto reserve currency, the US government confiscated gold from its citizens at $20.67 per ounce and sold it on the international market at $35. The immediate post-World War II period was highly inflationary due to the enormous fiscal deficit stimulus needed to finance the war. The Bretton Woods conference established the dollar as the world's *de jure* reserve currency and created organizations that attempted to maintain parity between global exchange rates. Competitive devaluation ensued, and the system eventually failed, as the USA could not maintain a gold standard. Announced as a temporary measure in 1971, the Nixon Shock ended the US dollar's convertibility into gold. This was the beginning of the pure fiat system we have today. Just how the Federal Reserve operates in this way is the subject of the next chapter.

## References

1. *The Creature from Jekyll Island: A Second Look at the Federal Reserve*, G. Edward Griffin, 433
2. *An Economist's Protests: Columns in Political Economy,* Milton Friedman, 65
3. *The Creature from Jekyll Island: A Second Look at the Federal Reserve*, G. Edward Griffin, 20
4. *The Creature from Jekyll Island: A Second Look at the Federal Reserve*, G. Edward Griffin, 472
5. *The International Gold Standard and U.S. Monetary Policy from World War I to the New Deal*, Leland Crabbe of the Fed eral Reserve, 425 – 439
6. *The Bitcoin Standard: The Decentralized Alternative to Central Banking,* Saifedean Ammous, 49 – 51
7. *Forty Centuries of Wage and Price Controls: How Not to Fight Inflation*, Robert L. Schuettinger and Eamonn F. Butler, 105
8. https://www.lynalden.com/fiscal-and-monetary-policy/

# 6. HOW THE FEDERAL RESERVE WORKS

*Our money is bait money, and bait money is not to be used.*
*– Mike Tyson*

## Structure & Responsibilities

The Federal Reserve remains one of the least known and most powerful economic entities worldwide. There are 12 Federal Reserve banks throughout the country: Atlanta, Boston, Chicago, Cleveland, Dallas, Kansas City, Minneapolis, New York, Philadelphia, Richmond, San Francisco, St. Louis. In addition to these 12 banks, the Federal Reserve system has its headquarters in Washington, DC.

Governance of the Federal Reserve System is split between 2 separate boards:

1. **The Federal Reserve Board of Governors** is comprised of 7 officials appointed by the President for 14-year staggered terms, subject to a vote from the Senate. The chairman of the board is appointed for a 4-year term and is the most powerful position in the system. This board governs the entire system and makes policy decisions.
2. **The Federal Open Market Committee (FOMC)** is a second governing body comprised of all 7 governing board members, 4 regional bank presidents, and the New York regional branch president. It meets every 6 weeks at the systems

headquarters in DC and is responsible for conducting the Fed's open market operations. The president of the New York Fed is always on the FOMC as market interventions are conducted through her/his office.

**The legal status of the Fed is "quasi-private"[4] as it is owned both privately and publicly.** The private owners of the Fed are the commercial banks that participate in the system. They own all the stock but only receive small (1%) annual distributions from the Feds profits. The remaining 99% goes to the US Treasury, which was ~$55 billion in 2019, making it **the most profitable "company" in the world.**[2] Calling this "stock" is a misnomer, because the owners are not entitled to the profits. Economically, it appears the US Treasury owns the Fed – but who controls it?

Control of the Fed rests with the board members. Elected officials in the branches of government have no *de jure* control over the board members other than the power to appoint them. But they do have control over the existence of the system itself. The governing board is selected purely by the president with Senate confirmation, and nearly all profits are distributed to the US Treasury. For all practical purposes, the US government appears to own the Fed.

| | Governance | Ownership |
|---|---|---|
| **Public Company** | Board members selected by stockholders | Stockholders receive profits |
| **Private Company** | Board members selected by stockholders | Stockholders receive profits |
| **Federal Reserve** | Board members selected by the Government | Government receives 99% of profits |

**Figure 37:** comparison of public and private companies to the Federal Reserve

**The independence of the Federal Reserve is controversial,** and recall that the president of the Second Bank of the United States was charged with fraud by the means of deliberately creating an economic contraction to serve private interests.

The official mandate of the Fed is to "promote effectively the goals of maximum employment, stable prices, and moderate long term interest rates." Having multiple goals can be traced back to the 1940s and has long been recognized to create conflicting interests.

To summarize, the Federal Reserve System executes its policy decisions through 12 separate banks. These banks are governed by the Federal Reserve Board of Governors. Policy decisions related to the purchase of bonds in the open market are determined by a separate board, the FOMC. The US Government elects the Fed's governing board and receives 99% of its profits. The Fed states it is neither private nor public, but it is owned by the government. It is certainly not independent. The multiple goals of its mandate are patently conflicting.

## Functions

The Fed has the following roles and responsibilities:

1. **Asset Purchaser.** Purchases assets in secondary markets for all different types of debt, including federal, state, corporate, real estate, student, and auto. As of September 2020 the Fed owns ~23,000 different securities[5] and is **the world's largest investor**.
2. **Loans to commercial banks.** This is the original function of a central bank, i.e., being a "lender of last resort" to create money and lend it to banks when large numbers of depositors attempt to withdraw their deposits simultaneously.
3. **Banker to commercial banks.** Banks can apply for membership in the Federal Reserve System and as members

own stock in the Fed and must maintain a mandated level of reserves. When a commercial member bank has "reserves," these are assets held at the Fed that are deemed appropriate to be called reserves.

4. **Banker to the federal government.** Tax revenues and deposits from the US Treasury are held at the Fed.
5. **Other services:**
    - Issuer of currency
    - Processor of checks
    - Supervisor of banks

The Fed's February 2021 balance sheet (Figure 38) shows just how significant its asset purchasing functions have become. The Fed currently holds nearly $7.2 trillion of asset purchases, of which there is $4.8 trillion in US treasury debt and $2 trillion in mortgage debt. Loans are relatively minor at $52 billion. The box with dashes illustrates $86 billion in asset purchases specifically related to COVID-19 monetary policy tools.

**5. Consolidated Statement of Condition of All Federal Reserve Banks**

Millions of dollars

| Assets, liabilities, and capital | Eliminations from consolidation | Wednesday Feb 10, 2021 |
|---|---|---|
| *Assets* | | |
| Gold certificate account | | 11,037 |
| Special drawing rights certificate account | | 5,200 |
| Coin | | 1,565 |
| Securities, unamortized premiums and discounts, repurchase agreements, and loans | | 7,263,935 |
| Securities held outright[1] | | 6,871,038 |
| U.S. Treasury securities | | 4,798,901 |
| Bills[2] | | 326,044 |
| Notes and bonds, nominal[2] | | 4,109,172 |
| Notes and bonds, inflation-indexed[2] | | 320,422 |
| Inflation compensation[3] | | 43,263 |
| Federal agency debt securities[2] | | 2,347 |
| Mortgage-backed securities[4] | | 2,069,790 |
| Unamortized premiums on securities held outright[5] | | 346,211 |
| Unamortized discounts on securities held outright[5] | | -6,492 |
| Repurchase agreements[6] | | 800 |
| Loans[7] | | 52,378 |
| Net portfolio holdings of Commercial Paper Funding Facility II LLC[8] | | 8,558 |
| Net portfolio holdings of Corporate Credit Facilities LLC[8] | | 26,274 |
| Net portfolio holdings of MS Facilities LLC (Main Street Lending Program)[8] | | 33,321 |
| Net portfolio holdings of Municipal Liquidity Facility LLC[8] | | 11,536 |
| Net portfolio holdings of TALF II LLC[8] | | 6,405 |
| Items in process of collection | (0) | 103 |
| Bank premises | | 2,210 |
| Central bank liquidity swaps[9] | | 8,463 |
| Foreign currency denominated assets[10] | | 22,043 |
| Other assets[11] | | 41,576 |
| **Total assets** | (0) | 7,442,225 |

Note: Components may not sum to totals because of rounding. Footnotes appear at the end of the table.

**Legend:**

Asset Purchases

Loans to Commercial Banks

Asset Purchases/Loans: Covid-19

**Figure 38:** the Federal Reserve's asset side of the balance sheet (image source The Fed with Eric Yakes additions)[2]

# Implementation of Monetary Policy

The Fed implements discretionary monetary policy by providing banking services and purchasing assets from the market. Through these functions it has, in its own words, "various tools in its toolkit." The goal of this section is to describe how these tools are utilized, flow through the financial system, and directly impact the economy. We'll begin by listing each tool by its technical definition and translating that into language that is easier to understand. (The Fed has a detailed list)[6]

## Monetary Policy Tools:

1. **Reserve Ratio Requirements:** All commercial banks that are members of the Federal Reserve System have an account at the Fed that holds their reserves. There is a legally mandated rate of reserves that banks need to maintain as a percentage of their outstanding liabilities. After the 2008 crisis, the requirement ranged from 3–10%, depending on the nature of the bank. The Fed has the authority to increase or decrease this requirement to contract or expand the money supply. **This rate is important, as it maintains an exponential relationship with credit expansion in the economy, reflected as its reciprocal.** One dollar injected into the economy expands the money supply by $1/reserve-ratio. With a reserve requirement of 10% banks will take a dollar, keep 10 cents in reserves, and lend out the remaining 90 cents. That 90 cents will go to another bank, which keeps nine cents in reserves and lends out the remaining 81 cents. This lending process ripples throughout the economy until there is nothing to lend anymore. Modern economics refers to this as the **money multiplier**. The result is that one dollar of reserves will represent ten dollars in the economy, while only one dollar really exists in the Federal Reserve account. How can a loan from one bank to another represent reserves for the next bank? The answer is in the explanation of the **Discount Window** tool. (Page 109)
    a. **Translation:** Under a gold standard, gold was considered reserves and used to back money. Even with fractional reserve banking, there was some amount of gold

backing demand deposits. Under the modern fiat system, debt backs money, so reserves are just any type of debt that the Fed deems credible (if this is confusing, read the ten-step example below). The Fed decides what percentage of debt obligations back outstanding liabilities and can decrease this mandated rate to allow banks to lend more. As of March 2020, amid the pandemic lockdown, this requirement was lowered to 0%, allowing us all to sleep better at night. Mathematically, credit expansion is currently infinite ($1/0 = \infty$).

2. **Interest on Reserve balances:** The Fed pays interest to banks which have a reserve account with it. Interest is paid on reserves exceeding the required reserve amount. Required are the amounts up to the reserve ratio, and excess reserves are any amounts above that.
   a. **Translation:** The Fed rewards banks for maintaining reserves by paying interest to them. What is important here is that the Fed could incentivize banks to lend out more reserves by reversing this and charging them interest instead. This is how negative interest rates would most likely be implemented. (More on this in the next chapter.)
3. **Discount Window:** The Fed provides loans to commercial banks that are members of the Federal Reserve System. These loans are short-term (no greater than 90 days) with the stated intention to provide liquidity to banks in a time of need and also to influence interest rates.
   a. **Translation:** The Fed creates money by typing on a keyboard and gives it to a commercial bank at whatever interest rate the Fed chooses. There are two impacts that occur from this:
      - These loans increase the amount of reserves the commercial banks have with the Fed because

**once a commercial bank receives a loan in cash, the Fed allows them to reclassify that borrowing as a reserve. This is a key point to understand because at this point what was once considered debt is now considered money, but it is nothing more than an accounting trick.** This in turn allows banks to take that borrowed money and lend the amounts above the legally required reserve ratio to another bank.

- The interest rate the Fed charges on the original loan affects at what rate the commercial bank subsequently lends. If the Fed lowers their lending rate, the commercial bank can then lower its lending rate to attract borrowers. This is one way the Fed lowers interest rates.

b. The lower the interest rate charged by the Fed on these loans, the more likely banks are to borrow and the more money (credit) expands. Given this relationship, **the reserve requirement ratio and the discount window tools work together to expand money in the banking system.**

4. **Open Market Operations (OMO):** The purchase and sale of securities in the open market by a central bank. This policy tool is uniquely separate from the other functions of the central bank and hence governed by a separate body, the FOMC. Historically, the range of securities purchased via OMO was limited to government debt securities of short-term maturity. Recent financial crises have expanded the role of OMO into what the Fed calls **large-scale asset purchases**. In 2008 the **Quantitative Easing (QE)** program expanded the Fed's purchases of securities from only short-term to long-term government debt, including the mortgage debt owned by Fannie Mae and Freddie Mac. This was in response to two

facts: (1) the Fed had pushed short-term interest rates to zero and long-term rates were the next option for expanding credit; and (2) the mortgage market was crumbling and needed buyers.

   a. **Translation:** The Fed creates money by pushing buttons on a keyboard and buys assets that would otherwise not be purchased at their current prices. Every time the government issues debt to fund its expenses, the public buys some small amount of it, and the rest the Fed buys. **This is effectively a way for the government to create money, but this circumvention is necessary to keep these actions constitutional.** This practice manipulates asset prices upward and interest rates downward.

5. **COVID-19 Loans and OMO:** As a pandemic response in March 2020 the Fed created a variety of new tools to provide direct loans to non-bank entities as well as to purchase their debt in the secondary markets. The list of entities includes corporations, municipalities, small businesses, money market mutual funds, commercial paper markets, and foreign governments. The Fed did not have the legal authority to purchase these assets directly, so it established six special purpose vehicles (SPVs) as legal structures to make the loans and purchases indirectly. These are the same type of legal structures that were used by Enron, Bear Stearns, and Lehman Brothers to hide assets. **The US Treasury took an equity stake in these legal entities along-side the Fed, putting taxpayer dollars at risk.**

   a. **Translation:** The Fed expanded its lending and purchase of assets to include everything except stocks, and it had to create a separate corporate structure to do so legally. **Most importantly, this has effectively converted the Fed into a "quasi-fiscal" agency by utilizing US tax dollars and supporting fiscal policy**

**programs.** One cannot say the Fed is independent when it works in conjunction with Federal programs in such a way.

In summary, the Fed conducts monetary policy by creating money on its computer and loaning it out or buying assets in the secondary market. It can also adjust the legal reserve ratio to expand the amount of lending banks can do, made possible by our fractional reserve system. Each method effectively takes debt/trust/IOUs and converts it into money. Stated differently, the Fed can create money and inject it into the economy through loans or asset purchases. Once it is flowing through the fractional reserve system, the Fed can expand how much it flows by adjusting the percentage of required reserves.

An illustrative example is the best way to grasp how this happens in practice. Let us go through the process for a $1,100,000 issuance of US Treasury Bonds.

1. The US government spends too much and needs $1,100,000 to pay a supplier, so it issues $1,100,000 in US treasury bonds to the public.
2. Interest rates are 0.7% (which is less than inflation) so the public does not want to purchase these bonds (there are reasons one would purchase these based on future interest rate expectations, but that is beyond the scope of this example). The only interested parties are institutions whose mandate requires them to purchase treasury bonds, so only $100,000 worth is purchased.
3. The Fed steps in to buy the remaining $1,000,000 of bonds and writes the US government a check with money created on its computer – this is how the new money is created. The government issues debt, and the Fed buys it with money on

its computer. This is how our money is "backed" by debt. This is the policy tool of **Open Market Operations,** also described as the function of **Asset Purchasing.**

4. The US government pays the contractor, and the money enters the economy as a deposit in the bank account of the contractor at First Fractional Bank.
5. First Fractional Bank receives the $1,000,000 deposit and recalls it is legally required to maintain only 10% in reserves. So, it puts 10% of the $1,000,000 aside and loans $900,000 to an energy business.
6. The energy business uses Second Fractional Bank, which receives $900,000 and puts 10% of it aside as reserves while loaning the remaining $810,000 to another business that uses Third Fractional Bank.
7. This process continues from bank to bank until there is nothing left to loan. Since the fractional reserve amount at banks is 10%, $1/10% equals $10. **So, for every dollar the US Government issued in Treasury Bonds, there are ten people running around thinking they are the true owners of that dollar.** If the Fed reduced the required amount to 5%, there would be 20 people running around thinking they own that dollar. This is how fractional reserve banking expands the money supply.
8. Meanwhile, First Fractional Bank just had 11% of its deposits called in by depositors, and it only maintains 10% in reserves.
9. First Fractional bank decides to call up the clerk at the Fed **Discount Window** and ask for a loan to help them cover the difference. The Fed gives them a loan of $11,000,000 that covers 11% of liabilities.
10. First Bank realizes that its reserves are back at 11%, above the required amount, so it loans $1,000,000 to Second Fractional Bank, and the money ripples through the economy ten times over again.

In summary, our money is backed by debt. Money is created when debt is issued. It starts with the government and then multiplies through our fractional banking system. A loan is created and converts to a deposit, which is converted to a reserve, which can be partially converted into new money. Figure 39 is the collateral backing of US dollars at the Fed as of February 2021:

## 7. Collateral Held against Federal Reserve Notes: Federal Reserve Agents' Accounts

Millions of dollars

| Federal Reserve notes and collateral | Wednesday Feb 17, 2021 |
|---|---|
| Federal Reserve notes outstanding | 2,215,334 |
| Less: Notes held by F.R. Banks not subject to collateralization | 161,995 |
| Federal Reserve notes to be collateralized | 2,053,339 |
| Collateral held against Federal Reserve notes | 2,053,339 |
| Gold certificate account | 11,037 |
| Special drawing rights certificate account | 5,200 |
| U.S. Treasury, agency debt, and mortgage-backed securities pledged[1,2] | 2,037,102 |
| Other assets pledged | 0 |
| *Memo:* | |
| Total U.S. Treasury, agency debt, and mortgage-backed securities[1,2] | 6,997,466 |
| Less: Face value of securities under reverse repurchase agreements | 194,269 |
| U.S. Treasury, agency debt, and mortgage-backed securities eligible to be pledged | 6,803,198 |

Note: Components may not sum to totals because of rounding.

1. Includes face value of U.S. Treasury, agency debt, and mortgage-backed securities held outright, compensation to adjust for the effect of inflation on the original face value of inflation-indexed securities, and cash value of repurchase agreements.
2. Includes securities lent to dealers under the overnight securities lending facility; refer to table 1A.

*Federal Reserve Notes are backed by Treasury, Agency, and Mortgage debt*

**Figure 39:** the USD is "backed" by government, agency, and mortgage debt (image source: The Fed with Eric Yakes additions)[2]

This centrally controlled, credit-based, fiat monetary system results in two primary long-term outcomes:

1. **Economic volatility** – driven by a fractional reserve system in which the money used in the economy only partially exists in an exceedingly small percentage of reserves. Since the inception of the Federal Reserve System, the US economy has had a recession, on average, every seven years.
2. **Monetary Inflation** – major contractions always result in the need to create more money to backstop the fractional reserve contraction. This means that **we don't have bank failures anymore because we print money and bail out banks every time.** As a result, each expansion and contraction results in adding a bit more debt to the system. Simultaneously, the money supply continues to expand (one form of inflation). Debt and money are the same thing. In fact, to pay off our debt would mean to eliminate all our money. **Without debt, we have no money.**

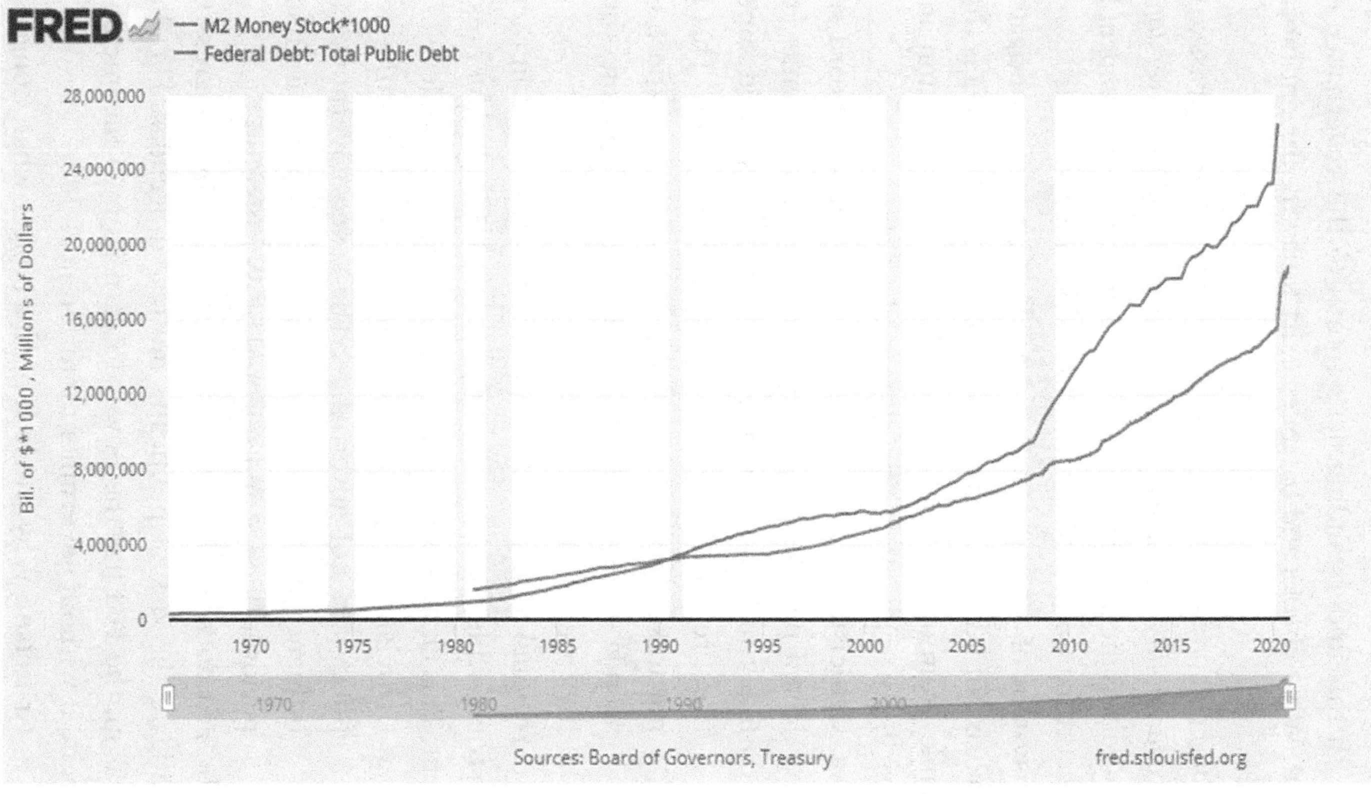


**Figure 40:** the money supply increases with federal debt because of how closely tied the 2 metrics are

## Checks and Balances

With this understanding, let's return to the governance of the Fed. What checks and balances exist today to prevent moral hazard?

The Fed stated in its 2009 annual report: "*The tricky issue is that accountability means being subject to some political oversight, which weakens the perception that the central bank is independent.*"[7]

According to the Fed, it's checks and balances include:

1. A system of 12 banks with a board of governors mitigates the risk of political influence on the system. The idea is that banks from other regions are farther from Washington and less likely to be politically influenced.
   a. **Criticism:** The 12 banks are governed by a board selected purely by Washington. The regional banks are likely influenced by their politically appointed superiors, regardless of distance from Washington. This is not to say they are all acting with a single purpose or agenda – there is observable diversity of opinion – but they are still influenced to a degree.
2. The regional bank presidents are chosen by a board in their district, while the seven governors are chosen by the president. This creates proper accountability at a district level.
   a. **Criticism:** Regional bank presidents can influence policy but not governance. The seven governors can influence both. The governors are in a position of superior influence and selected by Washington.
3. The Fed does not have a budget controlled by Congress to mitigate the risk of politically motivated agendas. For this reason, the Fed has the power to earn its own income and spend it without government interference.
   a. **Criticism:** Why would it need a budget when Congress provides capital by coercing the banking system to hold

accounts at the Fed? The Fed's existence is predicated on the powers of Washington. Further, 99% of its income is given to the US Treasury.

4. Transparent financial reporting is audited by an independent agency.
    a. **Criticism:** The Fed is currently "audited" by the GAO – a government agency – which is prohibited by law from auditing the 4 areas[8] below. The prohibited areas encompass practically everything the Fed does. The statement that the Fed is audited is nominal. In fact, it is so misleading that I would call it deceitful.
        - *Transactions with foreign central banks, governments, and private international financing organizations*
        - *Deliberations, decisions, or action on monetary policy matters, including discount window operations, reserves, open market operations, securities credit, and interest on deposits*
        - *Transactions made under the FOMC*
        - *Specific parts of a discussion or communication among or between members of the board and officers and employees*
5. Fourteen-year staggered office term for governing board members eliminates the ability for a president to stack the board
    a. **Criticism:** None. This is a value add.
6. The Fed is required to report to Congress.
    a. **Criticism:** This reporting to Congress is not actually reporting on salient aspects of Fed policy decisions because those decisions are not even allowed to be audited.

Governance of the Federal Reserve is directly influenced by Washington. Policy decisions are both directly and indirectly influenced by Washington. The audits of the Fed exclude nearly everything that exists on its financial statements. Let us not forget, the primary purpose of the Federal Reserve System is to buy the debt created by Washington that private markets will not buy.

This concludes the discussion of how the Federal Reserve system operates domestically. However, it is important to understand its function on an international level. The next section will describe the international system of the US dollar as a global reserve currency and its cause/effect relationships.

## The Global Reserve Currency

US dollar hegemony was established at the Bretton Woods conference during World War II. At the time, under the gold standard, the dollar was strong and used as a reserve by participating nations. Since the abolition of the US gold standard in 1971, dollar supremacy remains as a product of the former system. The reserve status of the dollar is not maintained by any international agreement. Rather, it is in the interests of the system's most powerful stakeholders for it to remain so.

*Why the dollar?*

1. The US has the deep and developed currency markets – buying and selling the dollar is easy, efficient, and transparent. Europe is not as developed and has a higher degree of political uncertainty.
2. If a new reserve currency emerged, the powers that influence the current system would effectively have to transfer wealth to that currency.

US dollars are used as a common unit of account in the global trade system as contracts and invoices are denominated in them.

As these offshore contracts are outside of the Federal Reserve System, transactions are conducted in what is called the **'Euro-dollar' system** – a credit system which depends on US Treasuries and the like as collateral. Physical settlement is avoided, and **participants are effectively exchanging IOUs.** The offshore dollar is represented by collateral that is actually debt. This is much the same as dollars between US banks representing each other's debt. Because these dollars are simply promises, **the Fed plays a key role in providing liquidity to international markets during financial contractions.**

The monetary fate of foreign countries is closely tied to the monetary decisions of the USA. In 2009 China and Russia called for a new world reserve currency. They wanted a stable currency separated from the credit-based national currencies of today. Since the US dollar underpins the global financial system, it is a systemic point of risk. As of March 2020, China is the 2nd largest foreign owner of US Treasuries and is concerned about its exposure (China has been significantly reducing their exposure in recent years). Were the dollar to rapidly inflate, China stands to lose the most value. The dollar was chosen at Bretton Woods because it was soundly backed by gold reserves. Today, **under a credit-backed fiat system, soundness is determined at the discretion of monetary authorities.**

## The Benefits and Costs of the Dollar as the Reserve Currency

Significant benefits accrue to the USA from this system. Foreign countries are forced to export to the US to attract dollars and conduct trade domestically. Eighty percent[9] of forex trading involves the US dollar, so most countries need dollars to conduct trade. Foreign countries stockpile dollar assets (the dollar is ~60%[10] of all foreign reserves) by running a persistent trade surplus. To entice the US to buy the goods of your country, you must compete against other countries producing the same goods. This can be achieved by lowering the prices of your goods and services, which requires lowering your costs of production, mainly wages. Many people are aware of US companies employing labor from China and India and paying them in dollars. The artificial suppression of foreign wages accrues to the US as cheap labor costs – referred to by France as an "exorbitant privilege."

This privilege is like that which Great Britain possessed in the 19th century: "Australia, Argentina, Canada, New Zealand, and, above all, the United States became prodigious exporters of the food and agricultural raw materials that fed the workers and machines of Europe's industrial revolution."[1]

By way of this system, the Federal Reserve has become the *de facto* **world central bank**. Each international financial crisis calls for Federal Reserve assistance, **increasing the dependence of foreign countries on the Fed**. Non-US banks lend in dollars, amounting to 60% of cross-border lending. In 2008 and 2020, collateral backing loans of foreign banks collapsed as a result of defaults. Those banks needed dollars, but their central banks couldn't create them, so the Fed stepped in.[1] **This dependence is a major point of leverage for the USA.**

Another point of leverage is the global US dollar **payments systems**. As the issuer of the global reserve currency, the USA has created the financial plumbing that comes with it. Participants in dollar markets utilize the Fed-wire, CHIPS (Clearing House Interbank Payments System), and SWIFT (Society for Worldwide Financial Telecommunication) systems. As trade is settled on these systems, this gives the USA another point of leverage to coerce behavior. To quote Schwartz: "*The Fed supplies the carrot of crisis management, while the Treasury wields the stick of exclusion from the payments system.*" [1]

This exorbitant privilege does not come without costs of its own. Generally speaking, this is known as the Triffin dilemma – in which a reserve currency must choose between its short-term domestic and long-term international interests. When applied to the USA, **it contributes to wealth inequality.** The system negatively impacts the working class of the US by facilitating cheaper international competition. Meanwhile, US capitalists employing cheap foreign labor accrue the benefits. US monetary policy has created an unsustainable competitive environment for the American working class.

**Figure 41:** corporate profits rising while employee compensation is falling (image source: Ray Dalio)[3]

Countries have proposed introducing a global currency to solve the problems on both sides. John Maynard Keynes proposed what was called the Bancor, but the closest thing in existence today is the IMF's SDR (Special Drawing Rights). The problem is that in one way or another all these currencies are influenced in some manner. **A global currency would have to be truly decentralized, so that no party could control it to their benefit.**

## Conclusion

The Federal Reserve remains one of the least known and most powerful economic entities in the world. The Federal Reserve System is comprised of 12 banks governed by two separate boards. While the Fed is said to be independent, it is owned by, and its board members are selected by, the federal government. It has a variety of functions but is primarily an asset manager through its OMO monetary policy. It is the largest investor and most profitable company in the world. Money enters the economy when the Fed creates it and purchases securities with it. The Fed can multiply how many people think they possess that money by lowering the reserve requirement for fractional reserve banks. Our money is backed by debt; to increase money is to increase debt and vice versa. Without debt we have no money. This is the volatile, debt-based, inflationary fiat system of modern times.

The US dollar was established as the global reserve at the Bretton Woods conference. It has remained as such during the world's transition to fiat systems. With control of the global reserve currency, the Fed acts as the world's central bank and controls the most dominant foreign payments network. This leverage has afforded it benefits that flow to the rich and costs that flow to the poor. **A global currency would remove the conflicting interests of this system. However, it would have to**

**be fully decentralized.** In the next chapter we will understand where we are today and what possibilities are on the horizon.

## References


1. *The Dollar and Empire*, Herman Mark Schwartz, July 16th 2020
2. https://www.federalreserve.gov/releases/h41/20210211/h41.pdf
3. https://www.linkedin.com/pulse/paradigm-shifts-ray-dalio/
4. https://www.stlouisfed.org/in-plain-english/who-owns-the-federal-reserve-banks
5. https://twitter.com/zerohedge/status/1300092969551364097?lang=en
6. https://www.federalreserve.gov/monetarypolicy/policy-tools.htm
7. https://www.stlouisfed.org/annual-report/2009/a-series-of-checks-and-balances
8. https://www.law.cornell.edu/uscode/text/31/714
9. https://www.tradersmagazine.com/am/88-of-all-2019-forex-transactions-are-in-us-dollars/
10. https://www.brookings.edu/wp-content/uploads/2019/09/DollarInGlobalFinance.final_.9.20.pdf

# 7. THE CYCLE OF CENTRALIZED BANKING

*Another thing that freaks me out is time. Time is like a book. You have a beginning, a middle, and an end. It's just a cycle.*

*– Mike Tyson*

## Modern Monetary Policy

In the wake of the 2008 financial crisis, central banks shifted to a stimulus-at-all-costs mentality. Money printing increased drastically, emergency lending facilities were opened across a majority of markets, and public funding was placed directly into the major banks. These experimental measures were, once again, supposedly temporary.

If you read the transcripts of the Fed meeting minutes during the crisis, they had little concept of what was to come. At the time the central bankers thought inflation was the primary risk stemming from their policy. They were unaware that they were walking off a cliff of systemic bank failure. Following the crisis, they still had little concept of the impacts of their experiments. Muhammed El-Erian summarizes the sentiment of central bankers at a Paris conference years after the crisis:

*Because all this was so far away from the norm, neither central banks nor anyone else, for that matter, had tested playbooks and historical precedents to refer to. It was bold policy experi-*

*mentation in real time, and for an unusually prolonged period of time...Given all that, it soon became obvious to me that I was not the only one feeling anxious in the room in Paris. Many of us felt inherently uncomfortable about where central banks had been forced to operate, and many of us wondered about what might lie ahead.*[1]

The economic recovery that followed fell below expectations, and the exit process was a failure. While the financial media often portray central bankers to have certainty about their decision-making, the reality is that central bankers have a limited understanding of the consequences of their decisions. New York Fed Branch CEO William Dudley in 2014 stated:

*We still don't have well developed macro-models that incorporate a realistic financial sector. We don't understand fully how large-scale asset purchase programs work to ease financial market conditions.*[2]

Despite their uncertainty, the Fed continued to purchase assets for 6 years after the crisis, into 2014. Before the recession, the Fed had roughly $800 billion in assets on its balance sheet. By October 2014 this had become $4.5 trillion. Interest rates remained at 0%.

In 2016, 8 years after the crisis began, the Fed attempted to raise interest rates. This lasted 3 years, only for the Fed to begin lowering them again in the fall of 2019. Not only were interest rates lowered, but asset purchases began again. This was the fourth official asset purchase program since the crisis; it was called QE4 (i.e., QE4eva).

This new stimulus in the fall of 2019 (pre-pandemic) was a response to a **spike of 10% in repo interest rates**. This point is important, **as it shows economic dislocations existed pre-pandemic**. The repo market is basically where companies that own a lot of illiquid securities and need liquid cash, can borrow from banks to obtain cash reserves. Using the securities as collateral, banks will give them short-term cash loans. Interest rates spiked in the fall of 2019 because banks did not want to make these loans and were asking for a rate of 5 times the normal 2% as an enticement to lend. The market was telling the world that the market interest rate was unsustainable because the natural rate of interest is much higher. **The years leading up to the 2020 crash displayed just how dependent the market was on central bank stimulus, as any reduction in stimulus resulted in immediate price volatility.**

## The 2020 Pandemic

In response to national lockdowns, the Federal Reserve:

1. Lowered the reserve ratio to 0%.
2. Lowered interest rates to 0%-.025%.
3. Opened lending facilities to the corporate, municipal, money market, commercial paper, main street markets, and others.
4. Conducted asset purchases in the corporate, municipal, money market, commercial paper markets, and others.
5. Opened dollar new liquidity swap lines with 9 foreign countries.

The 2020 pandemic stock market crash was one of the largest and most rapid in history. The Fed stepped in with historic experimental monetary policy, expanding the money supply by 21% in a matter of months. It further expanded asset purchasing to all categories except stocks and opened lending facilities across the board. Aside from buying stocks directly and implementing negative interest rates, the Fed exhausted all of its policy tools.

In the 6 months following the pandemic, Federal debt increased by 15%, but the Fed still called for more fiscal stimulus. As the Fed is a politically independent institution, this behavior is concerning. Requesting fiscal assistance is counter to their stance that they can still do more. Just as bailouts and a decade of asset purchases pulled us out of the 2008 crisis, it makes sense to expect the same this time. However, a confluence of factors support the proposition that the effectiveness of stimulus is coming to an end.

## Debt Cycles

Ray Dalio (founder of the largest hedge fund in the world) stated in May 2019:"*We are very late in the long-term debt cycle, meaning the capacity of central banks to ease monetary policy is limited.*"

Few people have studied markets for as long and as intensely as Ray. Through his study of economic history, Ray delineated short-term and long-term debt cycles. His distinction is important to understand, as it has major implications for our current economic environment.

**Short-term debt cycles** are familiar to most of us and are often referred to as **business cycles**. These are the fluctuations in credit that occur in periods of, typically, 5 to 10 years. Coming out of a recession, businesses and individuals take on more credit and use it as buying power. Production and consumption increase. Over-consumption and malinvestment eventually occur. Sentiment shifts to an awareness of this state and some negative catalyst causes credit to contract. Bankruptcies ensue and **the Federal Reserve steps in to lower interest rates, buy things people don't want, and lend to people that others won't lend to**. The economy is in a lull for some period and begins to rise again, rinse and repeat. After a few decades of this, a pattern emerges: each time we cycle through this process, the economy is left with a little more debt.

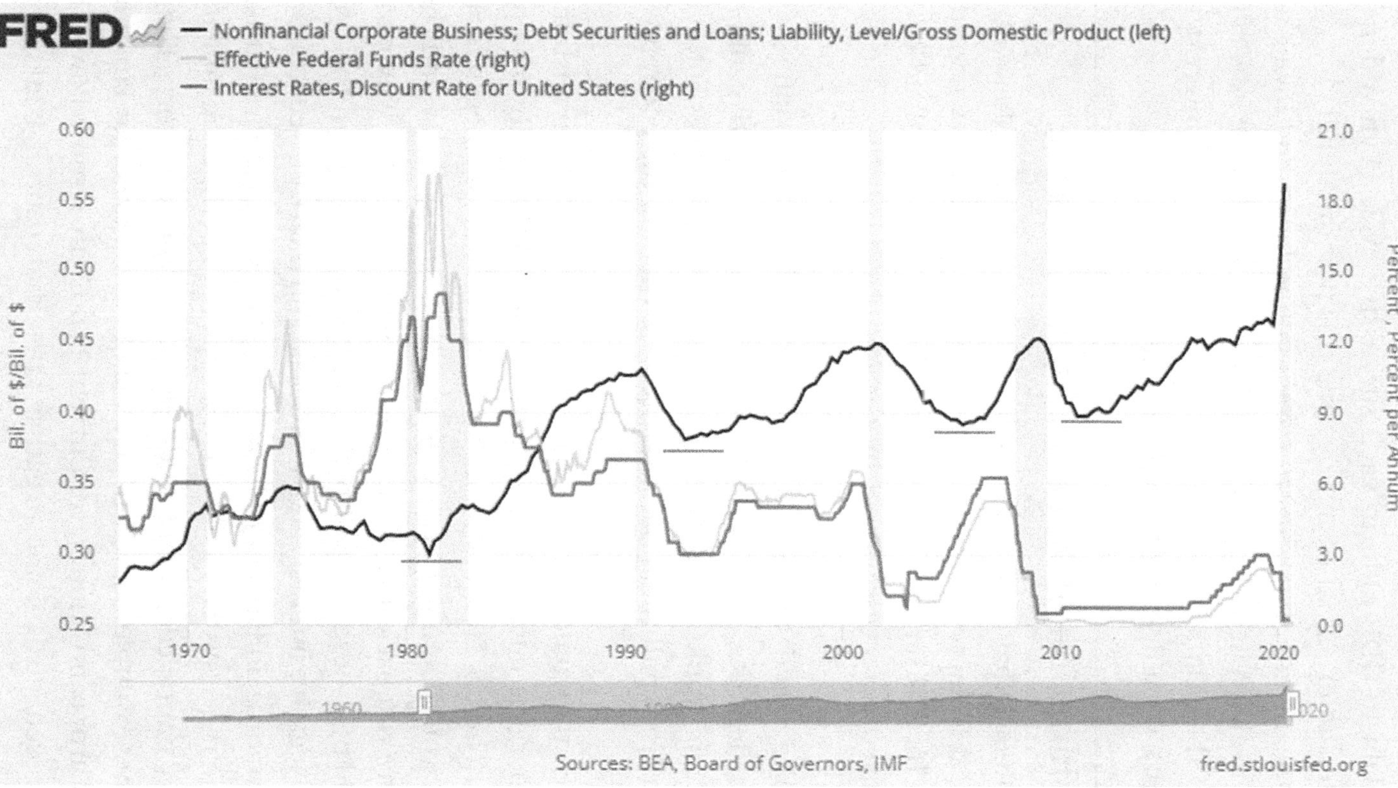


**Figure 42:** debt as a percentage of GDP increases with each cycle

You can see this in the higher highs (Figure 42) achieved in the debt-to-GDP ratio in each successive cycle (Lyn Alden has written an excellent essay covering this point in detail).[4]

Meanwhile, interest rates keep falling lower and lower with each cycle. What is important is that interest rates are now at 0%. Since they cannot fall lower (excluding a negative interest rate policy), what does this mean for debt?

## Explanation of Negative Interest Rates:

Recall that all commercial banks that are members of the Federal Reserve System have an account at the Fed where they keep their reserves. How much they keep is determined by the **required reserve ratio** set by the Fed. Normally, because these reserves are deposits, the Fed pays the banks interest. However, the Fed could theoretically begin to charge them interest on these deposits. This would effectively be a "negative interest rate" and would incentivize any banks holding reserves at the Fed to, instead, pull them out and circulate them in the economy via loans.

Banks would not likely pass along this cost to their customers by charging customers for deposits, but theoretically it is possible. The US Treasury could also issue debt with a negative rate. This would be done by you giving them money today and them paying you back less in the future. The rationale for why people would buy these notes or bonds is beyond the scope of this book.

Negative interest rates are the last and final tool a central bank has to force dollars out of its accounts and get them circulating in the financial system. This is a new type of experimental monetary policy unprecedented in 4,000 years of financial history. The US has never implemented it, but major economies like Japan and the European Union have. Current Fed Chair Jerome Powell has expressed disdain for negative rates, but central bankers are known to occasionally change their minds.

Why do negative rates matter? As of October 2020 $16 trillion in global debt is priced to yield negative. JP Morgan Strategists has stated that the global stock of sovereign debt with negative real yields (yield minus inflation) is $31 trillion. That is 76% of total developed nation sovereign debt, an increase from 57% in 2017. Total global debt was ~$250 trillion in 2019 (source: Grant's Interest Rate Observer). Monetary policy is forcing a lot of debt to yield negative, indicating that **monetary policy options are exhausted in many major global economies**.

**Long-term debt cycles** occur at the intersection of **(1) credit accumulation** through each cycle and the **(2) exhaustion of monetary policy** over time. While short-term debt cycles fluctuate primarily due to consumer behavior, long-term debt cycles fluctuate in accordance with monetary policy. Understand that there are short-term and long-term costs associated with each business cycle. If the Fed did not step in and provide stimulus and bailouts, then both costs would be borne by society with each cycle. Since the Fed stimulates each contraction, there are long-term costs that are avoided each time (kicking the can down the road). **Major signs of a cycle's end are the degrees of**

1. **Malinvestment**
2. **Over-consumption**
3. **Wealth inequality**
4. **Political extremism**

To understand the first two, it is necessary to understand what we can call the **Producer's Trilemma**. People who produce value receive money. Once received, they can do three things with it: (1) save it, (2) spend it, or (3) invest it. Because central banks have pushed interest rates to historical lows, savings make no sense – your money will be inflated away before you can earn anything with your 0.1% deposit interest. This trilemma, created by stimulative monetary policy, forces people to either spend their money or put it at risk by investing it. **This incentivizes people to either spend or invest money that would otherwise be saved.** The results are:

1. **Malinvestment**. Zombie companies, companies that survive by rolling over their debt, are nearly 20% of US firms. Scale and growth are prioritized over sustainable financial practices, resulting in failures like WeWork or bankruptcies like SunEdison created by CEOs who "move fast and break things." The $100 billion Silicon Valley investment fund raised by Softbank is an example of malinvestment. Historical stock market valuation highs are another indicator of malinvestment.

**Figure 43:** stock market valuations are at historic highs
(Data source is Robert Schiller CAPE data)

**2. Over-consumption.** People spend more today than they used to.

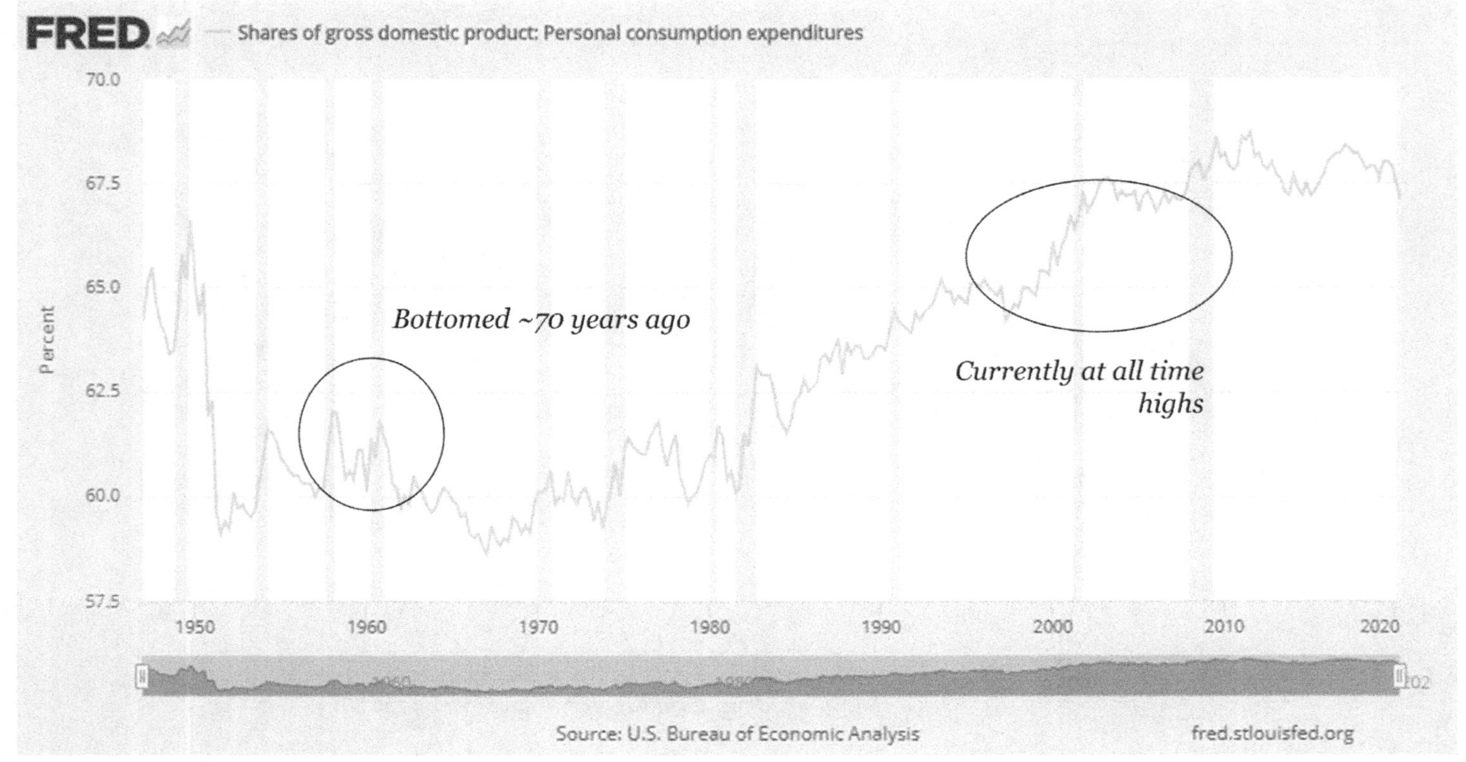


**Figure 44:** personal consumption as a percentage of GDP

We are consuming more than ever but nobody is getting any happier.

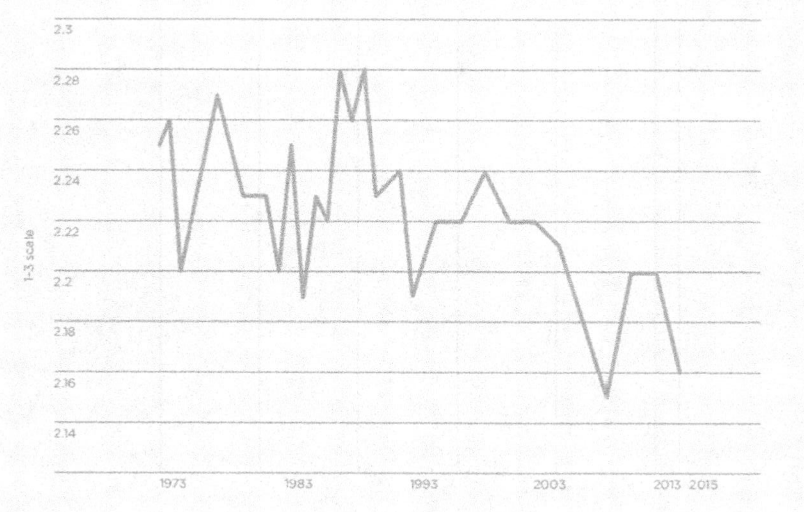


**Figure 45:** US happiness levels survey
(image source worldhappines.report)

Consumer spending is focused on short-term wants rather than long-term needs. A new area of research quantifies the effects of substance and addiction. People are overconsuming short-term wants (social media/internet/leisure) at the cost of spending time on activities that improve long term wellbeing.

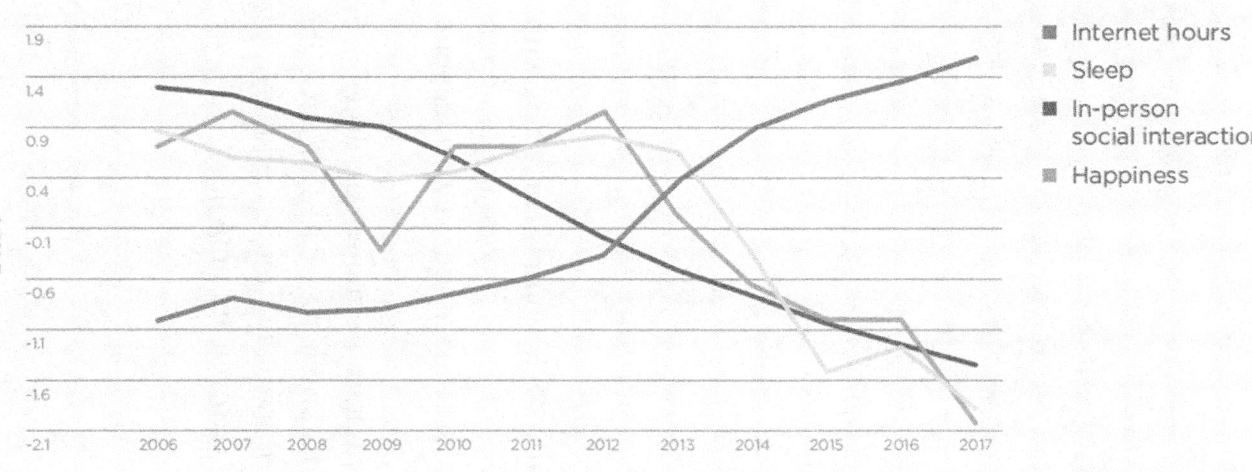


**Figure 46:** people are spending more time on the internet and less on sleep and socialization (image source worldhappines.report)

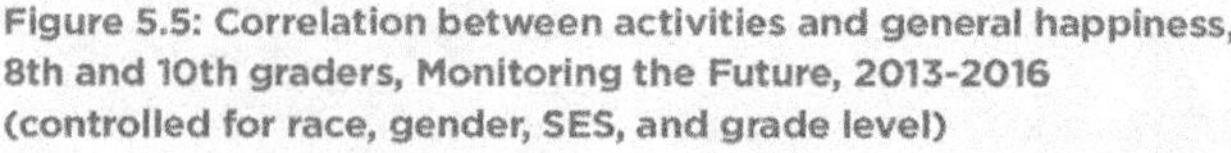


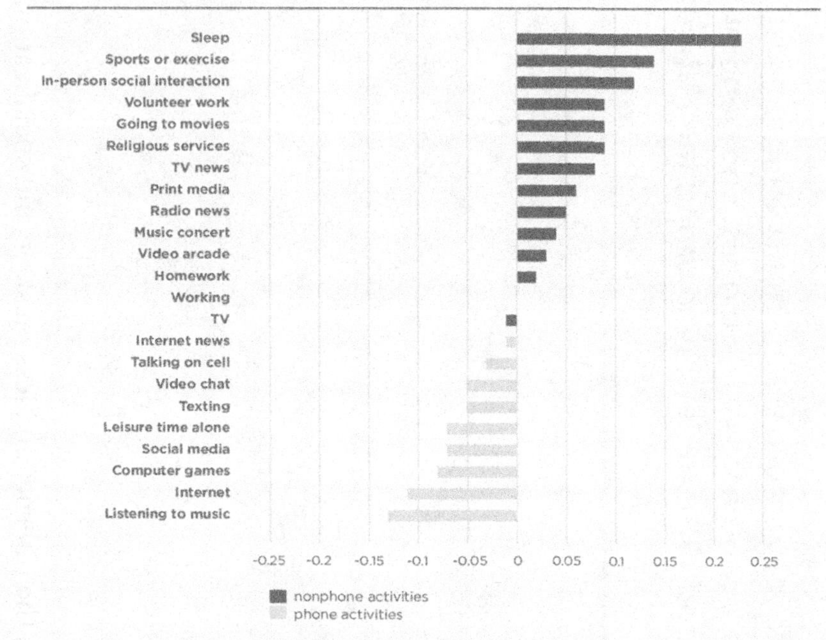


**Figure 47:** happiness correlates with activities that are becoming less common
(image source worldhappines.report)

Spending more money on drugs is becoming the preferred solution to problems related to declining happiness. Drugs are prescribed more and more frequently, often before healthy life practices are even attempted.

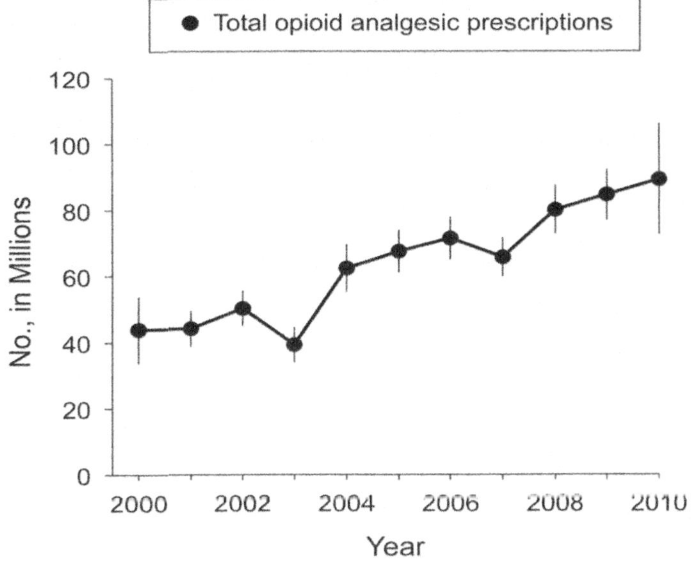


**Figure 48:** opioids are being prescribed more frequently (image source US National Library of Medicine)[5]

Drugs are not free, and this lifestyle is unaffordable. Healthcare expenditure has increased from 4% of income in 1971 to 18% today. (yakes.io analysis)

What's more, our focus on expediency over economic mobility is being financed by debt. Students take on a lifetime of debt to get degrees with hardly any prospects of a job that will help them pay it back. In 1971 the average 4-year college costs were 16% of the median household income but now are 47%. (yakes.io analysis) However, the most debt-ridden aspect of our lives is housing.

Want to buy a house? You will need a loan because everything is unaffordable. How do I get a loan? Well, you need a credit score. How do you get a credit score? By taking on other types of debt like credit cards. How many people actually use credit cards because they need short-term credit? The ones that actually do end up paying 15% rates and are getting poorer. The people who don't fall into credit card debt buy a house 7 years later with more debt. Then a recession occurs, they get laid off, and the bank gets their house.

Meanwhile, credit card companies are doing fine:

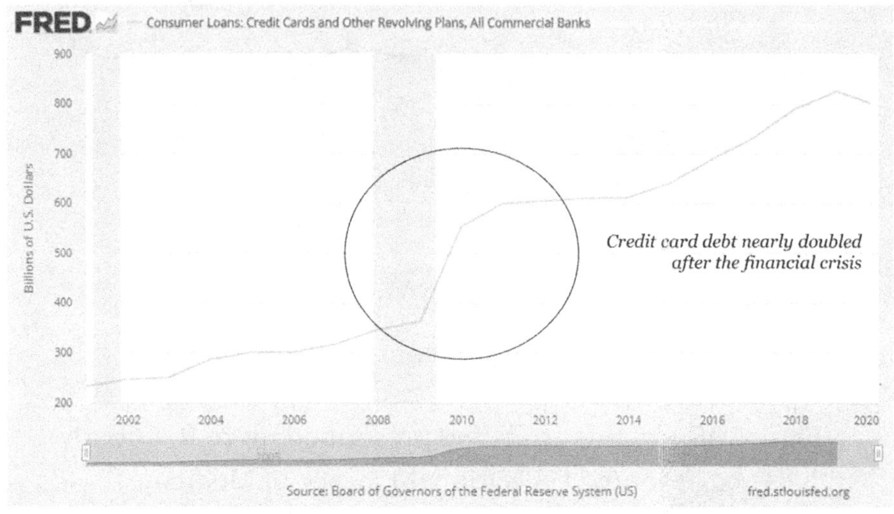


**Figure 49:** credit debt is increasing rapidly

This accumulation of debt results in the two outcomes below:

1. **Wealth inequality peaks towards the end of long-term debt cycles.** Recall the discussion on the **Cantillon Effect.** Extreme amounts of monetary stimulus (i.e., more debt) result in a significant rise in financial asset prices. Wealthy people who are invested in them do very well. Those who do not own financial assets are left out of the party holding cash (if they have any) and not gaining any wealth. Further, their cash is getting devalued by the central bank printing money to keep the economy afloat. **US income inequality is the highest it has been since the Great Depression.** The 2020 lockdown harmed low-income households the most, while according to UBS, billionaire wealth increased from

$8 trillion in April 2020 to $10 trillion by July of that year.[6] Extreme inequality causes tensions between classes and contributes to political extremism.

2. **Political Extremism is fueled by economic malaise**. Today, politics is a sour topic. Many people today form their social groups around politics and have a hard time maintaining relationships across party lines. Political campaigns and debates are increasingly structured around emotion and narrative rather than logic and information. In response, there has been a resurgence in anti-establishment political movements and a rise of populism. In the chart below, you can see that wealth inequality last peaked during the Great Depression, coinciding with a rise in populist sentiment. Economic inequality today contributes in the same way to increasing populist sentiments.

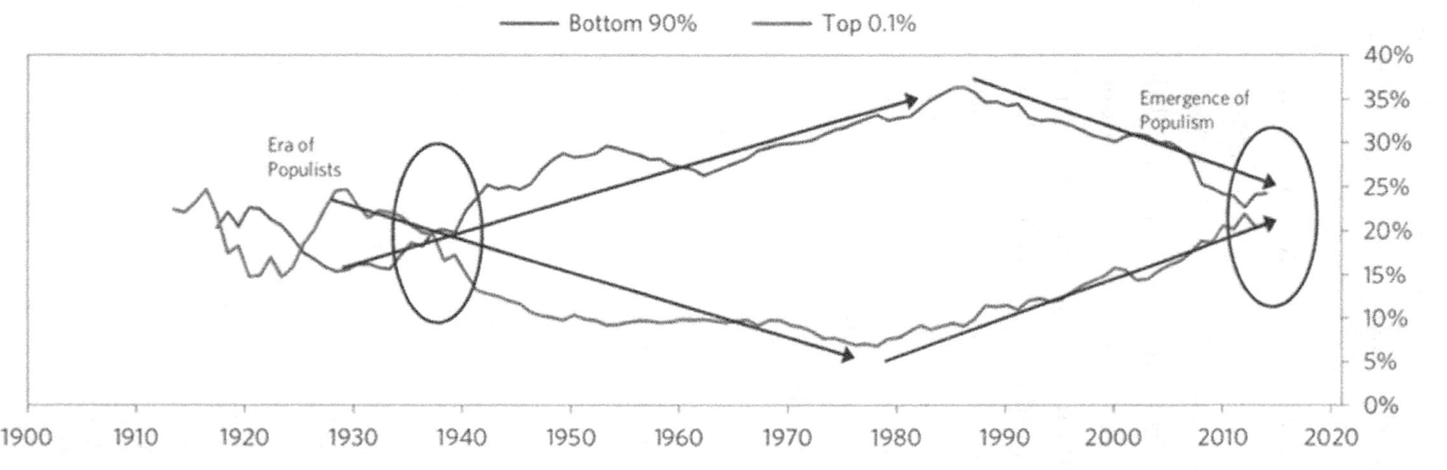


**Figure 50:** the rise of populism is associated with income inequality (Image source Bridgewater Associates)

In summary, the long-term accumulation of debt through the central banking system results in the accumulation of long-term problems. Central bank policy forces people away from saving and into spending and investing. **This results in overconsumption and malinvestment.** The accumulation of debt exacerbates wealth inequality, contributing to a rise in political extremism.

You can take steroids for a long time but each time they will be less effective, and eventually you will grow "boobs." The end of the long-term debt cycle is when the economy starts to grow "boobs."

Like Japan:

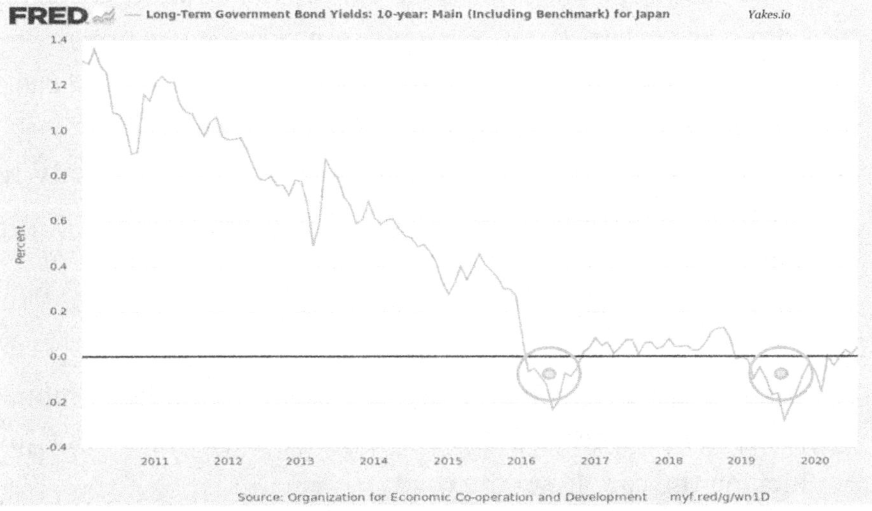


**Figure 51:** Japanese unnatural central bank response to these economic ills – negative interest rates

The point is that waste accumulates over long periods of time, and sooner or later we pay for it. With that understanding, here is the simple logic of each cycle.

Short-term Debt Cycle:

- Our money is *now* completely backed by debt.
- To increase money is to increase debt.
- Debt is a promise to pay someone in the future.
- So, by increasing debt in the economy, we are increasing the amount of promises to do something in the future.
- These promises cause expectations to diverge from our actual productive capability, and once expectations cannot be fulfilled, a crash occurs because people stop trusting one other.
- Productivity then falls below what is achievable because people no longer trust that promises are good.
- Eventually people begin to trust again, and productivity returns to its natural level.
- The cycle repeats.

Long-term Debt Cycle:

- Each time the cycle repeats, monetary stimulus (money printing) soothes the pain by adding more debt, but just kicking the can down the road.
- Each short-term cycle leaves the economy with a little more debt relative to actual productivity.
- The excess accumulates until extreme levels of debt are reached and monetary stimulus options have been exhausted.
- Signs indicative of this include: malinvestment, over-consumption, wealth inequality, and political extremism.
- The economy enters a period of stagnation as we restructure the institutions that created the mess.

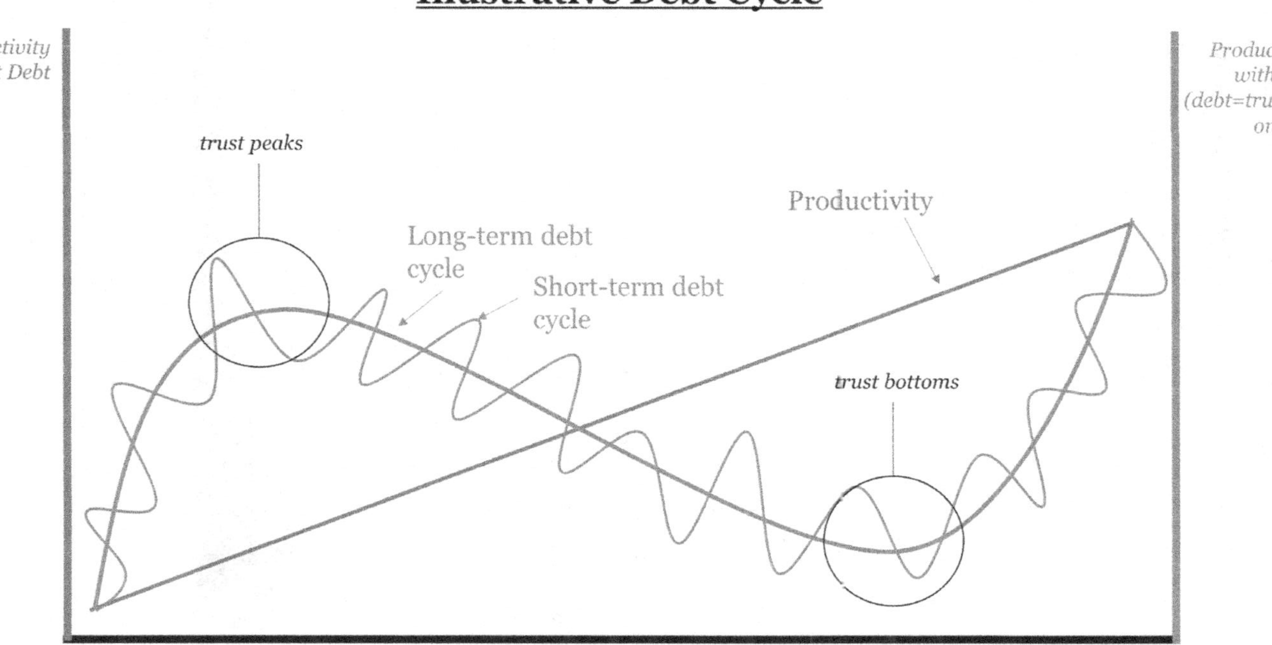


**Figure 52:** short-term and long-term debt cycles occurring under linear growth in productivity

## The End of the Long-Term Debt Cycle

With this understanding of the theory, let's look at the data going back to the Great Depression and compare the cycles.

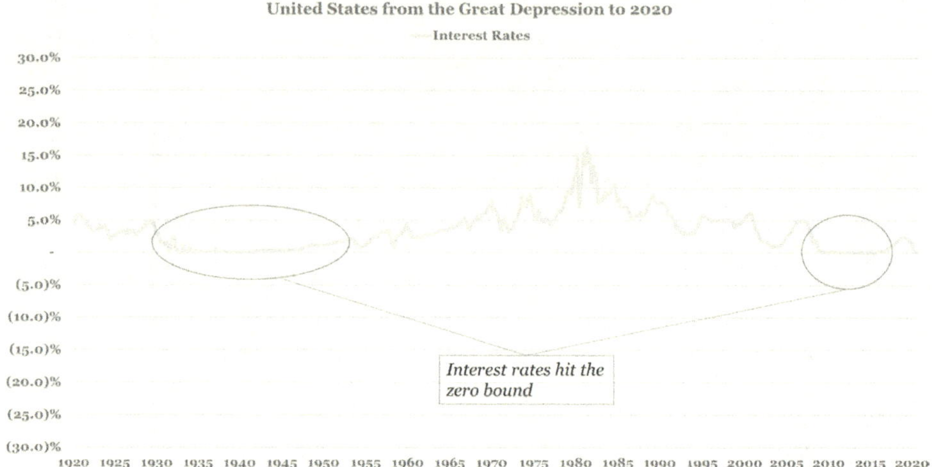


**Figure 53:** interest rates since 1920

1. Interest rates hit the zero boundary. These are the only two times in US history this has occurred.

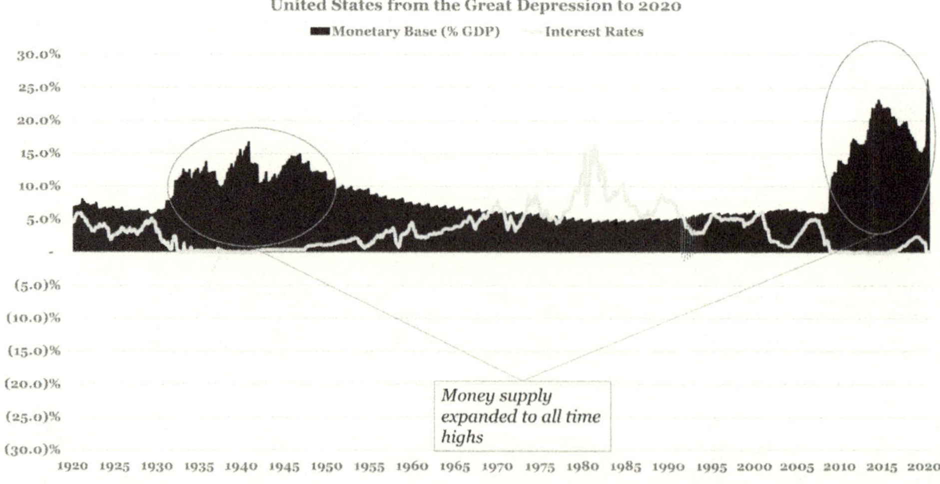


**Figure 54:** money supply and interest rates since 1920

2. Since the Fed could not lower interest rates below zero, they resorted to record amounts of asset purchases to stimulate the economy further, materially expanding the money supply (monetary base).
    a. The monetary base includes bank reserves held at the Fed, plus all currency in circulation. It is the most basic measure of money, including the most liquid forms of it.

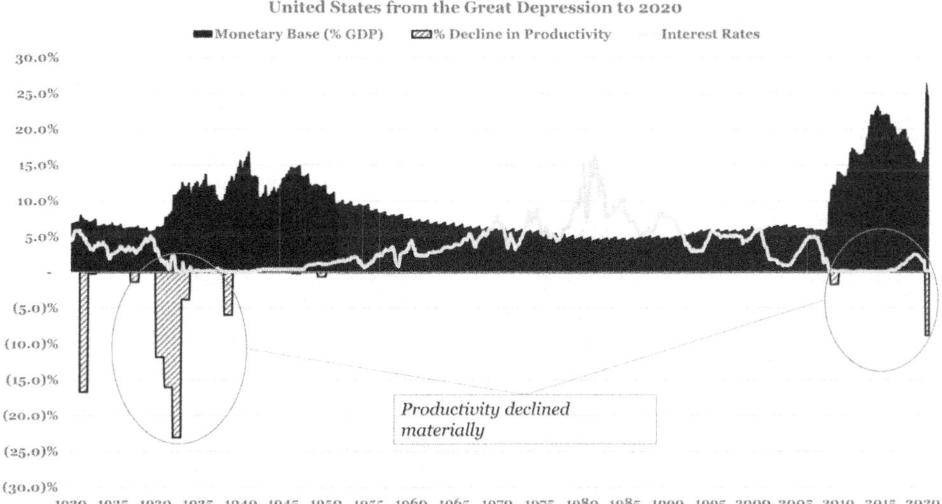


**Figure 55:** money supply, interest rates, and percent decline in productivity since 1920

3. Despite the amount of monetary stimulus, productivity was suffering declines. Note the rarity of productivity declines in the past century. From 1930 to 1950 there were four periods of decline in productivity. Since the financial crisis in 2008, there have been two.

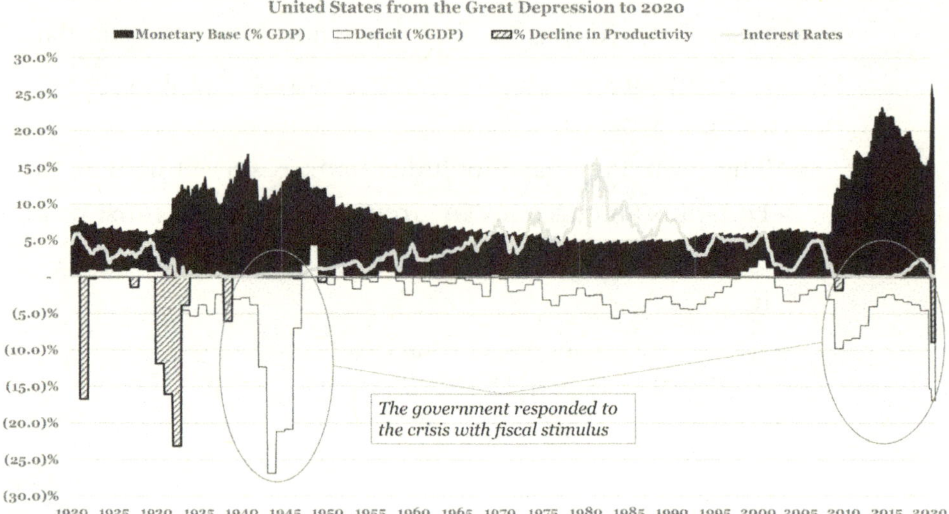


**Figure 56:** money supply, interest rates, percent decline in productivity, and fiscal deficit since 1920

4. Both periods witnessed a major crisis amidst the economic decline. In the 1940s it was WWII; in the 2020s it started with a pandemic. With monetary policy options exhausted, the government responded with fiscal stimulus – the current magnitude of which remains to be seen.

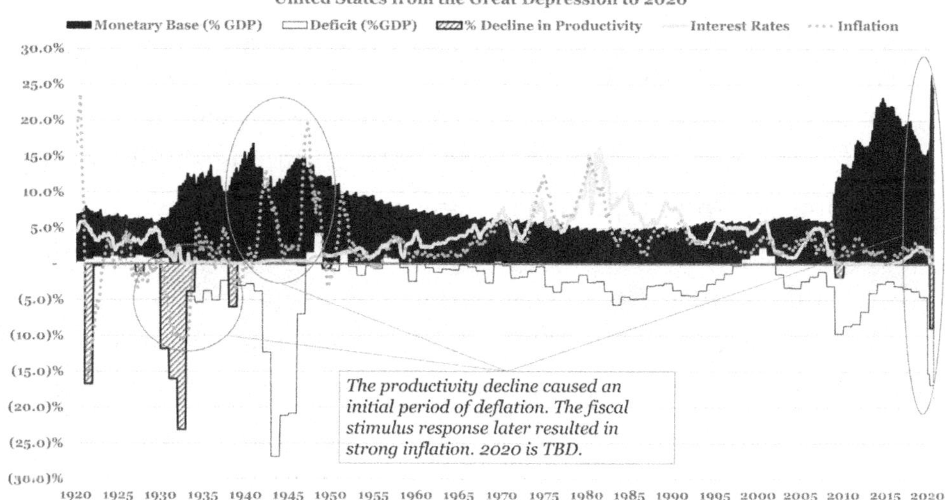


**Figure 57:** money supply, interest rates, percent decline in productivity, fiscal deficit, and inflation since 1920

5. Historically, fiscal stimulus has been generally inflationary. However, what is common between the Great Depression and the 2020 pandemic is that monetary policy measures were exhausted prior to the onset of fiscal stimulus. With a crisis emerging in both instances, fiscal stimulus was the only response left. Here we are in 2021, with the Federal Reserve calling for more fiscal stimulus and stating that there is a low risk of "overdoing it."[7]
   a. Furthermore, in August 2020 the Fed unanimously approved a major shift in its inflation strategy from targeting below 2% inflation to targeting above that rate. The change in strategy was justified with the idea that the "average inflation target" over the long run should be 2%, which it is currently below. So the Fed says we need more inflation because we have not had enough (or perhaps they just need that to be the case).

These periods are not perfectly identical, and will have different outcomes. Differences include the prevailing monetary regimes, the nature of each crisis, and the timing of the fiscal stimulus response. Nobody can say exactly what will happen, or when. However, given the history and the confluence of certain economic factors, I am not holding onto US dollars when their purchasing power is constantly being eroded. **One out of every four dollars currently in circulation was printed in 2020.**

To recap, after the 2008 crisis, interest rates went to zero. The Fed's attempt to raise rates did not work, and after the pandemic hit in 2020 they went back to zero. Many indicators are pointing to the end of a long-term debt cycle. Our current economic environment has material similarities to the Depression era, and many indicators point to inflation. When and if the inflation will come remains to be seen, and whether we will see deflation first is uncertain.

## Conclusion

Here is what is much more certain.

In Antiquity, money was primarily decentralized and 6 defined properties drove the adoption of money over time. The evolutionary pattern was an increase in efficiency at the cost of increased centralization. Money and the emergence of modern banking systems eventually became inseparable. The efficiencies of this evolutionary step required trust in centralized authorities.

This trust was abused by the agents of money (i.e., governments and banks) and it is apparent that immutability has become a desirable 7$^{th}$ property. However, for most of recent history there has not been a viable decentralized solution to the consequential moral hazard of our monetary agents. As a result, history is replete with examples of abuse and fraud caused by fractional reserve systems, leading in turn to repeated boom and bust cycles. Each time this occurred the politically convenient solution was to further centralize the system, which culminated in the creation of the central bank.

As monetary systems have been increasingly centralized, we lack information transparency and are subject to moral hazard by the agents who control our money. Societies subject to a fiat monetary system are transacting in a monetary medium which benefits the agents of the system at the cost of the participants, who assume the agents are acting in good faith. There is a conflict of interest between government agents and market participants.

Today we have the most centralized global banking system in the 4,000 years of financial history. It has a track record of failure and is on the brink of failing yet again. Fiat money means value by decree as opposed to merit.

What can you do? Well, there are various securities and assets you could purchase. Stocks, bonds, real estate, and gold are all near or at all-time highs. The winners of that game have emerged over the past decade. Although a defensive portfolio allocation could protect you from a market crash, in all major financial crises, asset values have deflated, and today there are few places to hide your money. In a crisis it will be hard to make money as an average investor; all you can do is protect what you have.

For the first time in history, the world has been given an alternative to this oppressive system. **Bitcoin** is an emerging digital form of money that is purely decentralized. For years it has been mocked by government figures, powerful banking interests, and everyone else who has listened to them and not done their own research. However, being a joke was one of its strengths. That allowed it to fly under the radar without being attacked by regulators.

Now the same bankers that mocked Bitcoin are investing in it, and as a result, changing their narrative. JP Morgan and Goldman Sachs are creating divisions devoted to Bitcoin. Citigroup thinks Bitcoin will be worth $318,000 by the end of 2021.[3] It is used by Paypal, Square, Cashapp, and Robinhood. Public corporations like Tesla are putting their treasury dollars in it to protect themselves from inflation.[8] Major insurance companies like Mass Mutual are investing in it. Prominent investors such as Paul Tudor Jones, Stanley Druckenmiller, and Tim Draper are investing significant amounts of wealth in Bitcoin.

Why are they all doing this? The remainder of this book will explain why.

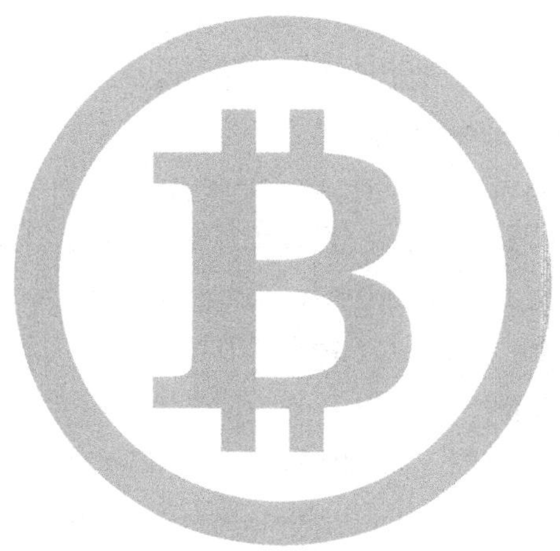

## References

1. *The Only Game in Town: Central Banks, Instability, and Avoiding the Next Collapse*, Mohamed A. El-Erian, 13
2. Remarks by Mr William C Dudley, President and Chief Executive Officer of the Federal Reserve Bank of New York, at the American Economic Association 2014 Annual Meeting, Philadelphia, Pennsylvania, 4 January 2014
3. https://twitter.com/classicmacro/status/1327381449000034307?s=20
4. https://www.lynalden.com/fiscal-and-monetary-policy/

5. https://www.ncbi.nlm.nih.gov/pmc/articles/PMC3955827/
6. https://www.ubs.com/global/en/global-family-office/reports/billionaires-insights-2020.html
7. https://www.cnbc.com/2020/10/06/fed-chair-powell-calls-for-more-help-from-congress-says-theres-a-low-risk-of-overdoing-it.html
8. https://www.cnbc.com/2021/02/08/tesla-buys-1point5-billion-in-bitcoin.html

# 8. THE HISTORY OF BITCOIN

*I feel like I'm too busy writing history to read it. – Kanye West*

In October of 2008, amidst a global recession resulting in government bailouts of the banking system, a white paper was released under the pseudonym Satoshi Nakamoto titled *Bitcoin: A Peer-to-Peer Electronic Cash System*. The paper summarized a confluence of technologies that, when combined, created digital money. These technologies were the product of 4 decades of attempts and failures to create digital money – Figure 58 is a list of about 100 failed attempts:

| | | | | |
|---|---|---|---|---|
| ACC | CyberCents | iBill | Mondex | Polling |
| Agora | CyberCoin | iKP | MPTP | Proton |
| AIMP | CyberGold | IMB-MP | Net900 | Redi-Charge |
| Allopass | **DigiCash** | InterCoin | NetBill | S/PAY |
| **B-money** | DigiGold | Ipin | NetCard | Sandia Lab E-Cash |
| BankNet | Digital Silk Road | Javien | NetCash | Secure Courier |
| Bitbit | e-Comm | Karma | NetCheque | Semopo |
| **Bitgold** | E-Gold | LotteryTickets | NetFare | SET |
| Bitpass | Ecash | Lucre | No3rd | SET2Go |
| C-SET | eCharge | MagicMoney | One Click Charge | SubScrip |
| CAFÉ | eCoin | Mandate | PayMe | Trivnet |
| CheckFree | Edd | MicroMint | PayNet | TUB |
| ClickandBuy | eVend | Micromoney | **PayPal** | Twitpay |
| ClickShare | First Virtual | MilliCent | PaySafeCard | VeriFone |
| CommerceNet | FSTC Electronic Check | Mini-Pay | PayTrust | VisaCash |
| CommercePOINT | Geldkarte | Minitix | PayWord | Wallie |
| CommerceSTAGE | Globe Left | MobileMoney | Peppercoin | Way2Pay |
| Cybank | **Hashcash** | Mojo | PhoneTicks | WorldPay |
| CyberCash | HINDE | Mollie | Playspan | X-Pay |

**Figure 58:** notable attempts to create digital money; those in bold will be discussed later in the chapter (Data sourced from Princeton)[3]

PayPal is on that list – their original idea was cryptographic payments on hand-held devices. They were not able to create this and survived by pivoting away from it. It's no surprise that the major founders of PayPal are all public supporters of bitcoin (e.g., Peter Thiel and Elon Musk). This group of people was a primary catalyst of Silicon Valley's growth.

Many of the projects in the above table have a similar story of attempting to make something like Bitcoin. In hindsight we realize that their fundamental problem was they tried to be a company in the first place. However, with each failure knowledge was gained, and the world came one step closer to digital money.

## The Cypherpunks

Many attempts to create digital money were spawned by **the Cypherpunk movement,** which originated in the 1990s along with the growth of the internet. Cypherpunks believed the internet would become a government surveillance apparatus unless defensive technologies were created.

**Figure 59:** May/June 1993 cover of *Wired*.
(Image source *Wired*)

Below is a summary of the Cypherpunk manifesto[5]:

- Privacy is a fundamental right and necessary for an open society in the electronic age.
- Privacy in an open society requires anonymous transactions systems which can be achieved via cryptography.
- We cannot expect powerful institutions to grant us privacy, as it is not to their advantage to do so.
- We must defend our privacy if we expect to have any.
- Today electronic technologies enable us to defend our privacy because software cannot be destroyed and widely dispersed systems cannot be shut down.
- Electronic technologies can enable private systems via:
    - Cryptography
    - Anonymous mail forwarding systems
    - Digital signatures
    - Electronic money
- For privacy to be widespread it must be part of a social contract whereby people deploy these systems for the common good.

Before governments implemented national firewalls, before social media websites were selling our personal data, before the NSA's PRISM program, and before big tech was systematically censoring political movements, the Cypherpunks were at work anticipating this new world. They were able to anticipate it because of their uncommon intersection of various kinds of knowledge – including cryptography, computer science, Austrian economics, and libertarianism.

Cryptography enables digital encryption, which removes the power of sovereign influence over the internet. However, an autonomous form of digital money is also required to have an economy free from government control. **Digital money enables**

**an encrypted online economy to freely transfer value and thus the ability to freely organize in the digital world.**

Let's walk through the 30-year history of digital money to illustrate the incremental problems that led to where we are today. The story begins with the invention of long-distance communications and the subsequent cryptography used to secure them.

***The Cypherpunks possessed an uncommon confluence of knowledge, which they used to make the internet an enabler of freedom instead of a tool for control.***

## Cryptography

Cryptography is the practice of securing communications in the presence of **3rd party adversaries**. It emerged as a response to communications over long distances (the telephone), which could be easily intercepted.

In the simplest sense, communications are just energy being sent over a line. Consider a flashlight – it has a battery, a bulb, a switch, and a wire that connects them. Imagine you made this wire 4 miles long and gave the bulb to your friend 4 miles away from you. You can now turn the switch on and off and your friend will see that happening. If he knows in advance what on and off means, you can successfully communicate with each other. All forms of telecommunications and computing can be boiled down to this idea – **using a switch to send binary (on/off) signals via electricity**.

Morse Code (named after telegraph inventor Samuel Morse) was used to send and interpret binary signals as alphanumeric characters. This allowed people to use a single switch to communicate anything in the English language. However, with new technologies come new problems.

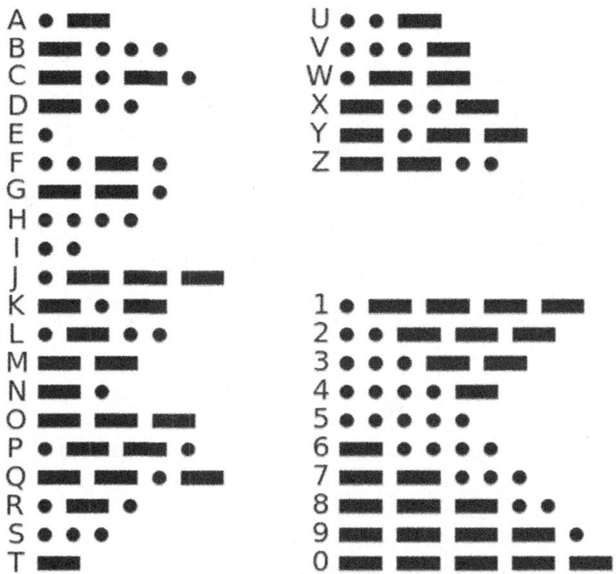


**Figure 60:** Morse Code

More and more frequently, long distance communications were at risk of interception by a 3rd party. This was of particular importance during the World Wars, and cryptography was the solution. In its most basic form, cryptography was the use of a **cipher** to encrypt text. A cipher is a document used to encode letters into an alternative system (e.g., A = O, T = H, C = Q, K = Y). If both parties use the same cipher, they can read each other's encoded messages. For example, if 2 parties are communicating and they both know that ATTACK = OHHOQY, then OHHOQY can be sent over the communication channel and, if it is intercepted by a 3rd party, it will be unintelligible to that 3rd party. As more ciphers were used, more ciphers were decoded, and cryptography continued to increase in complexity.

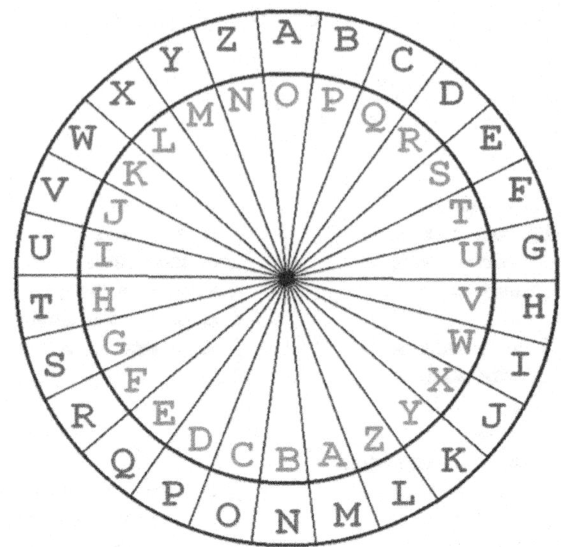


**Figure 61:** a cipher disk
(Image source Michigan Tech)[4]

The use of **ciphers (also referred to as keys)** came with security issues and increased complexity. In order for 2 parties to decode each other's messages, they both need to know the key. Thus, **keys had to be exchanged between the communicating parties beforehand, often over insecure channels.** If somebody intercepted the key, then they could decode all of your encrypted messages. For this reason, everyone on a network had to use different keys. The more people that used a particular key, the greater the security risk of interception. Things got complex as the number of keys required increased exponentially with the number of network members. If there are 10 members of a network, $10^2$ keys are required.

These problems resulted in the invention of **public-key cryptography** in the 1970s – "publickey" meaning a public key can be sent over channels freely without revealing a private key.

## Government Response to Cryptography

As expected, the government attempted to control this new technology. Steven Schlesinger of Fordham University summarizes the scenario:

> *Instead of embracing encryption and adapting to its adoption, the U.S. government sought to fight its citizens' encryption use. Ultimately this resulted in unnecessary and prolonged litigation. This culminated in the government's push to compel technology companies into implementing "backdoor access" within encryption platforms that would enable government access should they deem it necessary.* [1]

The battle emerged when PGP (Pretty Good Privacy), the standard encryption system used for email, was created by Phil Zimmerman. When Zimmermann exported PGP to countries with oppressive governments, the US Justice Department launched a 3-year criminal investigation of him. The NSA publicly argued that his software would be used by child molesters and criminals. In reality PGP was going to make the NSA's job of surveilling the world much harder, and it gave many people privacy on the internet. Just like any enabling technology, it can be used by good and bad people. The Cypherpunk Timothy May best described this phenomenon:

> *Child pornographers, terrorists, money launderers, take your pick. These are the people who will be invoked as the bringers of death and destruction...But all technologies have had bad effects, the telephone [caused], extortion, death threats, bomb threats, kidnapping cases.* [2]

This narrative that bad people can use technologies is continuously invoked by the government to garner public support to extend its power. In this case it was used to argue for backdoor access to encryption protocols. The Cypherpunks argued that PGP code is published speech, and controlling it is a violation of the First Amendment. To prove a point, Phil Zimmerman convinced MIT to publish the PGP source code in books and ship these to European bookstores. The government knew they could not go to court and attempt to suppress the publication of a book from a university. Subsequently, 2 federal judges found that encryption is protected by the First Amendment.[2] The battle for private encryption was won, but the war still continues today.

***Public-key cryptography enabled privacy for the digital world. To this day the US government attempts to control it.***

Aside from the legal battle, public-key cryptography enabled a wealth of inventions. I will cover the relevant details of this in the next chapter, but for now understand it made possible the invention of **digital signatures**.

## Digital Signatures

Satoshi Nakamoto (the pseudonymous Bitcoin creator) stated in a post:

*Talking about the old Chaumian central mint stuff, but maybe only because that was the only thing available. Maybe they would be interested in a new direction. A lot of people automatically dismiss e-currency as a lost cause because of all the companies that failed since the 1990's. I hope it's obvious it was only the centrally controlled nature of those systems that doomed them. I think this is the first time we're trying a decentralized, non-trust-based system.*

Satoshi is here referring to the cryptographer David Chaum, who is considered a father of the Cypherpunk movement. In 1983 he created the concept of a **blind signature** and in 1989 he founded **Digicash**.

Recall the goldsmith-bankers who developed our modern checking system. Bankers were handing out receipts, which provided a guarantee of redemption for gold. People began trading these receipts as if they were money. People trusted that the bankers would keep their promise and that these receipts were **unforgeable**. This meant that the banker's signature on the receipt was, in fact, his and the note was therefore not counterfeit.

Digital money is different. Because it is digital, it is infinitely replicable as the money is just bits on a computer, indistinguishable from any other set of bits. Digital money created the **double spending problem** – if you send me digital money, what is stopping me from multiplying it and sending the same money to multiple people?

Until Bitcoin, this problem was solved in digital systems via some sort of centralized authority. For example, when you give someone a check, your bank works with their bank to update both of their electronic ledgers – subtracting the money from yours and adding it to theirs. Both banks verify that you are who you say you are. This centralized system works but is highly cumbersome, and the process cannot be performed anonymously.

Chaum's blind signature solved the double spending problem and could be done anonymously (mostly), but still required centralized servers to do the verification. People needed to trust these servers, and if they ever went down, the network would as well. He implemented his idea with the company Digicash in 1990, although Digicash ultimately failed. However, his **digital signatures** allowed people to encode their identity so that no other party in the network could decode it. When you spent a coin, the recipient would require you to decode a random subset of the encoding, and they kept a record of this. If you ever tried to double spend the same coin, both recipients could go to the bank to redeem their notes, and when they did, the bank could put the 2 pieces of information together to decode your identity completely.[3]

This was the first major advance in digital money. Digicash ultimately failed because it was hard to persuade merchants and banks to adopt it. It also was not peer-to-peer, which made it hard to bootstrap a network if merchants were not going to use it (i.e., peer-to-peer systems can at least be used between individuals until institutions decide they are useful).

***Digital signatures solved the double spending problem without revealing one's identity, but the verification process was done through centralized servers.***

## Digital Scarcity

Other attempts came and went, but what was common among them was their **pegged value systems**. What made your digital cash worth $100? Nobody had tried to implement a currency that maintained fundamental monetary properties. Instead, they were all tied to some other currency. In Digicash, you had to trade $100 to get 100 Digicash. Others did the same. NetCash attempted to get governments to authorize services to mint digital money out of thin air. E-Gold tried to 100% back their money in gold, and Digigold attempted to partially back it.[3] **Every idea was an attempt to peg the digital currency to the dollar or a commodity because attempting to bootstrap monetary value was a monumental task.**

To create a free-floating digital money with monetary value, that digital money needs to maintain monetary properties. Recall the process of convergence in a market – step 1 for a good to become a monetary medium is to function as a valid store/cache of value. The most important property needed to achieve this is scarcity. Digital money is infinitely replicable, so making it scarce was a problem.

Achieving digital scarcity was ultimately done by using **computational puzzles.** The idea traces back to 1992 from cryptographers Dwork and Naor as a solution to email spam. If your computer must solve a puzzle that takes a few seconds every time you send an email, it would not really bother you but would significantly hinder a spammer's ability to send thousands of spam emails per second. Adam Back implemented computational puzzles in his proposal for HashCash in 1997. Hal Finney, the first bitcoin recipient in history, has also been mentioned to have used computational puzzles in the first **proof of work system.**[3] The proof of work system was ultimately used in bitcoin, requiring computers known as miners to solve a computationally intensive puzzle to create new bitcoins. This makes bitcoins costly to create and thus scarce. This will be discussed in detail in a later chapter.

***Digital scarcity was solved by requiring computers to solve computationally expensive puzzles to create new digital money.***

## The Blockchain

The last key development was the **blockchain,** the origin of which can be traced back to a paper by Haber and Stornetta in 1991. A blockchain is a database structure. It was not created to be used in digital money but rather as a method to preserve a database with timestamps.[3] The idea was for people to send different versions of a document to a server over time. The server would add a hash pointer to the prior document, a time stamp, and a digital signature of the server to verify that it was, in fact, the server that signed off on this (i.e., verified it). This meant that the most recent version in the list had a link to its prior version, thus creating a chain between them all.

A **hash pointer** is a **hash function** that hashes the prior document in a temporal list of documents. We will discuss hash functions in my next chapter, but you should understand that it is an algorithm that enabled this data structure by being able to take any amount of data and compress it into a 256-bit string of text (these are also known as compression functions). This allowed large databases to be compressed into a string of text for storage, and a single change in any part of the database would be reflected in the string of text.

If each document created has a hash pointer to its prior version included, then any changes to its lineage would be apparent through a change in the hash pointer of the current document. Add a time stamp to each document so that you have a temporal list, and then use a digital signature to prove it was the server that signed off on the document update. **All of these measures combined produced a verified chain of information where any tampering with its history would be immediately apparent.**

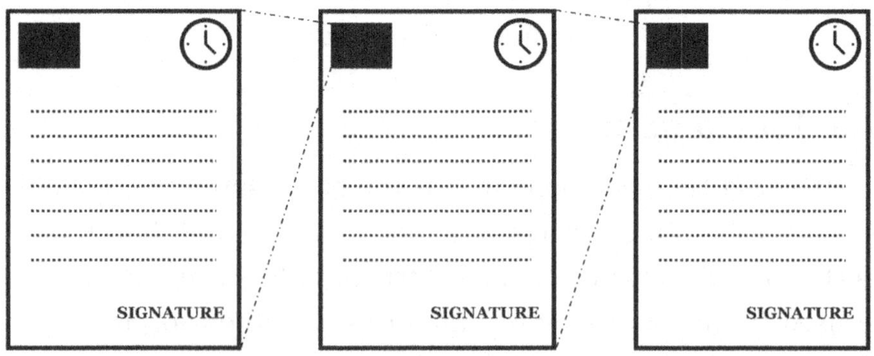


**Figure 62:** documents include a digital signature, time stamp, and hash of the previous version

This process was made more efficient by incorporating each pointer into blocks using what is known as a **merkle tree** (named after cryptographer Ralph Merkle, who invented hash functions). It is the same concept, except instead of having one string of documents, you have a string of blocks. Within each block is a tree structure of the hash of each document. This structure organized the data more elegantly and significantly compressed the amount of memory required to store it. However, this system had **one problem – to trust the blockchain data you also must trust the centralized server you are sending the documents to** (the same problem Digicash had). Bitcoin uses this system to create an immutable record of all of its transactions but leverages a decentralized network to do so, thus removing the need to trust centralized servers. (More on this in a later chapter.)

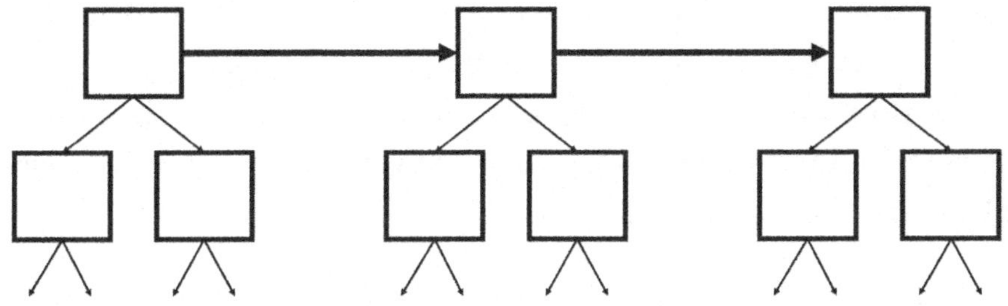

**Figure 63:** blocks contain tree structures of documents, and each block contains a hash pointer to its prior version

***A blockchain is a temporal method of data storage in a list where each document is linked (and thus dependent) on its prior version.***

To recap, digital signatures created a verifiable method of confirming an identity digitally without disclosing it. This digital signature, when incorporated in a blockchain data structure, creates a temporally-linked, immutable record of data. These technologies could be used to counteract the double-spend problem inherent to digital money. However, the supply of that digital money needed to be scarce, and this problem was solved using computationally intensive puzzles (via hash functions) to regulate supply.

Prior to bitcoin, proposed digital monies utilized a blockchain to time stamp a ledger to prevent **double-spending**, as well as a computational puzzle to regulate scarcity of the currency. **Wei Dai** proposed **b-money** in 1998 and **Nick Szabo** proposed **Bitgold** in 2005. (There's a theory that Szabo is Satoshi, but he denies it.) These proposals utilized a decentralized network of nodes (nodes are computers connected to a network) to run the verification process and eliminate the need for trust. However, **their proposals did not communicate a clear way to resolve disagreement between nodes on the recorded ledger**. They also did not propose a mechanism to adjust the difficulty of the puzzles being solved.[3] Ultimately, it was Bitcoin that solved these problems by utilizing a network with clever incentives. This should not make complete sense yet, so if you are confused, please just keep reading.

***Bitcoin utilized digital signatures, the blockchain data structure, and computational puzzles to successfully create, for the first time in history, decentralized digital money.***

## Bitcoin

Satoshi says he started coding Bitcoin around May 2007 and registered bitcoin.org in May 2008. In October 2008 he released the Bitcoin whitepaper and code. The Bitcoin network was up and running by the start of 2009. The first transaction was sent to Hal Finney, and a community of Cypherpunks began encouraging the use of bitcoin for peer-to-peer transactions. Satoshi stated in a forum post:

*It might make sense just to get some in case it catches on. If enough people think the same way that becomes a self-fulfilling prophecy.*

In hindsight this quote seems laughable, but back then Bitcoin was a longshot. Satoshi's resolve was admirable. Here is an anonymous programmer throwing his life into a project in the face of 30 years of failed attempts. The possibility that it would work probably seemed remote. It is now a $1 trillion network and is challenging a monetary system controlled by the world's most powerful institutions.

The foresight of the Cypherpunks is astonishing, and what they did took courage. They existed at an interesting intersection of knowledge across cryptography, computer science, Austrian economics, and libertarianism. In fact, much of their quest to invent internet money was inspired by economists rooted in the Austrian school.

In 1984 Nobel laureate economist Friedrich Hayek was quoted stating:

*I don't believe we shall ever have a good money again before we take the thing out of the hands of government, that is, we can't take it violently out of the hands of government, all we can do is by some sly roundabout way introduce something that they can't stop.*

In 1999 Nobel laureate economist Milton Friedman stated:

*I think that the Internet is going to be one of the major forces for reducing the role of government. The one thing that's missing, but that will soon be developed, is a reliable e-cash, a method whereby on the Internet you can transfer funds from A to B, without A knowing B or B knowing A.*

In 2008 this vision started its journey toward reality. Satoshi had created decentralized digital money while standing on the shoulders of giants.

## Conclusion

The Cypherpunk movement enlisted libertarian cryptographers to develop technologies that would enable freedom in the digital world. Digital money was at the center of these technologies. Bitcoin was created after 4 decades of failed attempts to create digital money. With each attempt building off prior ones, progress was made. The major discoveries of digital signatures, digital scarcity, and the blockchain database structure were combined to create digital money. Bitcoin solved the final problem that was necessary to combine these major discoveries: disagreement among participants on the history of the blockchain database. The resulting decentralized digital money emerged in a sly, roundabout way that can no longer be stopped. Read on to understand how.

## References

1. *DEFEND YOURSELVES: THE RIGHT TO DATA ENCRYPTION*, Steven W. Schlesinger, Fordham University, 4
2. *When Encryption Was a Crime: The 1990s Battle for Free Speech in Software*, ReasonTV
3. *Bitcoin and Cryptocurrency Technologies,* Arvind Narayanan, Joseph Bonneau, Edward Felten, Andrew Miller, Steven Goldfeder, 10 – 17
4. https://pages.mtu.edu/~shene/NSF-4/Tutorial/VIG/Vig-Devices.html
5. https://www.activism.net/cypherpunk/manifesto.html

# 9. WHAT BITCOIN DOES

*I'm really bad with answering questions. Usually, I don't even answer them. I try to find inspiration inside of the question. I think, and I jump from one beam of inspiration or energy to the next, as opposed to explaining the energy.* – *Kanye West*

Bitcoin is at the intersection of multiple technologies. This chapter will cover what Bitcoin does, how digital signatures work, how transactions are sent, and how they are compiled into a blockchain.

What Bitcoin does is a separate question from why it is valuable. What makes Bitcoin valuable is the network of people who have decided to use it. To understand why these people have decided to use it, you need to understand how it works. This can be challenging, as Bitcoin's technology is a confluence of technical concepts unfamiliar to most people.

Bitcoin is software. It was created by Satoshi Nakamoto and is currently maintained by a group of developers. The software allows people to:

1. Store bitcoins in a wallet.
2. Send/receive bitcoins between other people using the software.
3. Create new bitcoins by using a computer to solve a mathematical puzzle.

That's it. That's the chapter.

**Figure 64:** Mike Tyson meme

## Bitcoin vs. Legacy Finance

The Bitcoin software allows you to send money to anyone in the world who also has the Bitcoin software. This ability sounds simple, but it is powerful. Call your bank right now and ask them to wire a significant amount of money to somebody in another country for you. Enjoy spending the next week trying to make that happen and subsequently getting tracked by the government. The ability to move large amounts of value within minutes over a digital network does not exist anywhere else.

You might ask, what about Paypal or Venmo or CashApp?

These are all **trusted 3rd parties**. Trusting 3rd parties has consequences.

- You have to play by their rules
- You have to tell them who you are

- You have to trust they will keep your information safe
- You have to give them control over your money

Let's append "trustless" to my last statement: the ability to move large amounts of value within minutes over a **trustless** digital network is incredibly powerful. It is trustless because you don't have to trust a 3rd party. This is possible because it is a **decentralized network** which has no **3rd party intermediaries** and thus nobody can control it; more on this later.

In April 2020 $1.1 billion in bitcoin was moved in a transaction for a cost of **68 cents, and it was done** in a matter of minutes.[2] This was done cheaply and efficiently without the transactors having to play by anybody's rules, tell the third party who they were, trust anyone with their information, or give anyone control over it. **No other payment system in the world can move that amount of value, for that price, in that amount of time, without oversight from a 3rd party.**

To understand how this works we need to eat our vegetables first. The remainder of this chapter will focus on the functionality of Bitcoin. We will start with some math that is fundamental to **public-key cryptography**. This will allow us to explain **hash functions** and **digital signatures**, which are the foundation of Bitcoin. Lastly, we will cover how transactions are aggregated and stored in the blockchain. This will be the most conceptually challenging aspect of Bitcoin. Read through this slowly, and if you can wrap your mind around it, understanding the rest of Bitcoin will be like eating cake.

## The Discrete Log Problem

The **discrete log problem** is a mathematical problem that has yet to be solved. It is the foundation of public-key cryptography which allows people to send information over insecure channels without worry that it could be decrypted. In the simplest sense it allows us to produce **one-way calculations** – a calculation where if A*B=C you can only find A or B if you know them (e.g., if you have A and C you CANNOT divide them to find B). This problem arises when you apply **finite field math** to **elliptic curves.**

**Finite field math** uses operations such as addition, subtraction, multiplication, and division in a way different from normal math. It is different in that it works like a clock with the maximum being 12 hours, and if you exceed this amount, you start again at 1 (e.g., if it is 10am and you add 15 hours, you cycle around the clock until you end up at 1am). This is why it is called finite field math – a clock operates in a finite (limited) field of 12 hours. What this means is that addition, subtraction, multiplication, and division produce different answers than in normal math. Continuing with the example of a clock, 12 is the maximum value in the field. 4*4 = 16 but the maximum of the field is 12. 16-12 = 4. The remainder of 4 is your answer. Thus, in finite field math with a maximum of 12, 4*4 = 4.

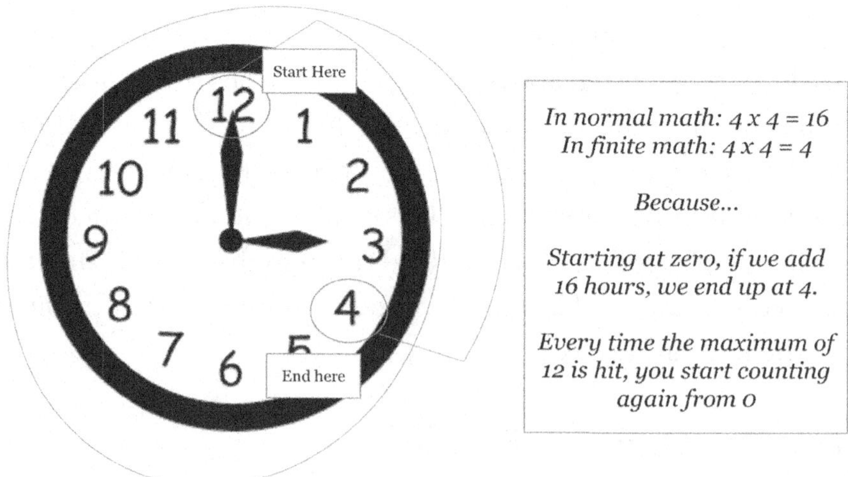


**Figure 65:** finite field mathematical operation example

**Elliptic curves** are a type of graph that allows you to do point addition. This means that every time you add 2 points on the elliptic curve you will always get a 3rd point (barring a few exceptions but these can be controlled for). Further, it is a completely symmetrical graph, which means you can take your 3rd point and find its reflection on the other side of the graph.

Below you can see that the addition of point A+B = C:

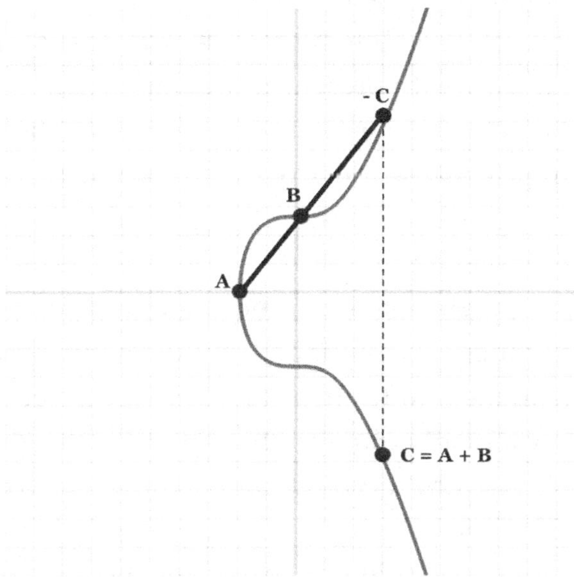


**Figure 66:** the secp256k1 elliptic curve with point addition

This also applies to multiplication using an integer and a point. **What** cryptographers realized is that **if you multiply a point and integer using finite field math, you can produce random outputs with a standardized method**. Meaning, if we know the integer and point, we can multiply them and produce the solution. But what if we only have the point and the solution? Well, we could simply use algebra and divide the solution by the point we have to get the integer, right?

The answer is yes and no. If the order (order meaning the maximum number like 12 for a clock) is a prime number, then certain theorems can be used to divide efficiently. However, theorems become increasingly less able to divide numbers as the order gets larger because computers solve division of these numbers through trial and error. If you can find a large enough prime number, the only option is to let a computer randomly try inputs until it finds the desired answer. Modern computers have enough computing power to make a lot of iterative guesses. To defend against a computer's rapid iterative guesses, an exceptionally large prime number needs to be used so that it is computationally impossible (at least with present-day computers).

So, if you choose a large enough prime number, division is practically impossible to do when attempting to reverse point multiplication. This is the **discrete log problem** and is the basis of modern cryptography. Mathematicians currently have no way of dividing these numbers, they can only use computers to guess what number was multiplied by the known point to get the answer. **This makes multiplication problems over large prime finite fields practically impossible to reverse through division.**

Much of modern cryptography rests on this unsolvable problem. If it is solved, most of our cryptographic systems will crumble. Computers could theoretically become fast enough to guess solutions through iteration (e.g., through quantum computing). However, this is very unlikely. To give you a perspective on this, the prime number used by bitcoin is $2^{256}$ ~ or $10^{77}$. The estimated number of atoms in the universe is $10^{80}$. A trillion computers doing a trillion computations every trillionth of a second for a trillion years is still less than $10^{56}$ computations.[1] If computers are ever able to use brute force to arrive at the solution, then we will likely be able to find much larger prime numbers as a result. If we reach this stage, bitcoin's failure would be the least of our problems.

What does this all mean? Public-key cryptography is

extremely secure as it will take the most advanced computers trillions of years to break. Further, it allows encrypted communications to be verifiable. This advancement led to the creation of the **digital signature,** which is the foundation of digital money. Fundamental to digital signatures (as well as many other applications in bitcoin) are **hash functions**.

## Hash Functions

A **hash function (algorithm)** is a one-way algorithm that takes a variable length of inputs and outputs a fixed length.

1. One way means it cannot be reversed without knowing the inputs (discrete log problem).
2. These are more commonly known as compression algorithms. They can be used to encode a **variable** length set of data into a **fixed** length set. Meaning that you can input an encyclopedia, or a single letter, and it will return the same length string of text every time. Bitcoin uses the **SHA256 hash algorithm** (Secure Hashing Algorithm 256 bits) throughout its software. You can run any length of data through this algorithm, and it will always produce a 256-bit code of the data with no discernable pattern. SHA256 was created by the NSA, is well known, and is sometimes legally required as an encryption security measure. Go to freeformatter.com and try it out.[3]
    a. For example, if I input "yakes" it returns:
        - 2534c8d79c95cbe9d1b742d9c82d-8780f6a071c442536993d3af7eea06d5ff47
    b. If I input "yakes1" it returns:
        - 2181013eb9f5c896710914a9bed34fa7f23e32315e7850c4f7199879c6745919
    c. Notice there is not a discernable pattern it produces, no matter how minor the differences. If a 3rd party inter-

cepted either of these hashes and knew I used SHA256, they would not be able to backsolve (reverse the calculation to find the inputs) because of the **discrete log problem**.

## Digital Signatures

To send transactions on the Bitcoin network you need an address and a private key. Think of your address as your account number and your private key as a password to that account. A private key is the cipher that can be used to decrypt an address. To send bitcoins you need to prove you have this private key without showing it; that is what a digital signature allows you to do. **Digital signatures** are algorithms which allow individuals to **(1) generate keys, (2) generate signatures,** and **(3) verify signatures.** The specific digital signature algorithm used by bitcoin is the **ECDSA** (Elliptic Curve Digital Signature Algorithm). Let's walk through the Figure 67 graphic step by step to understand how bitcoin uses ECDSA:

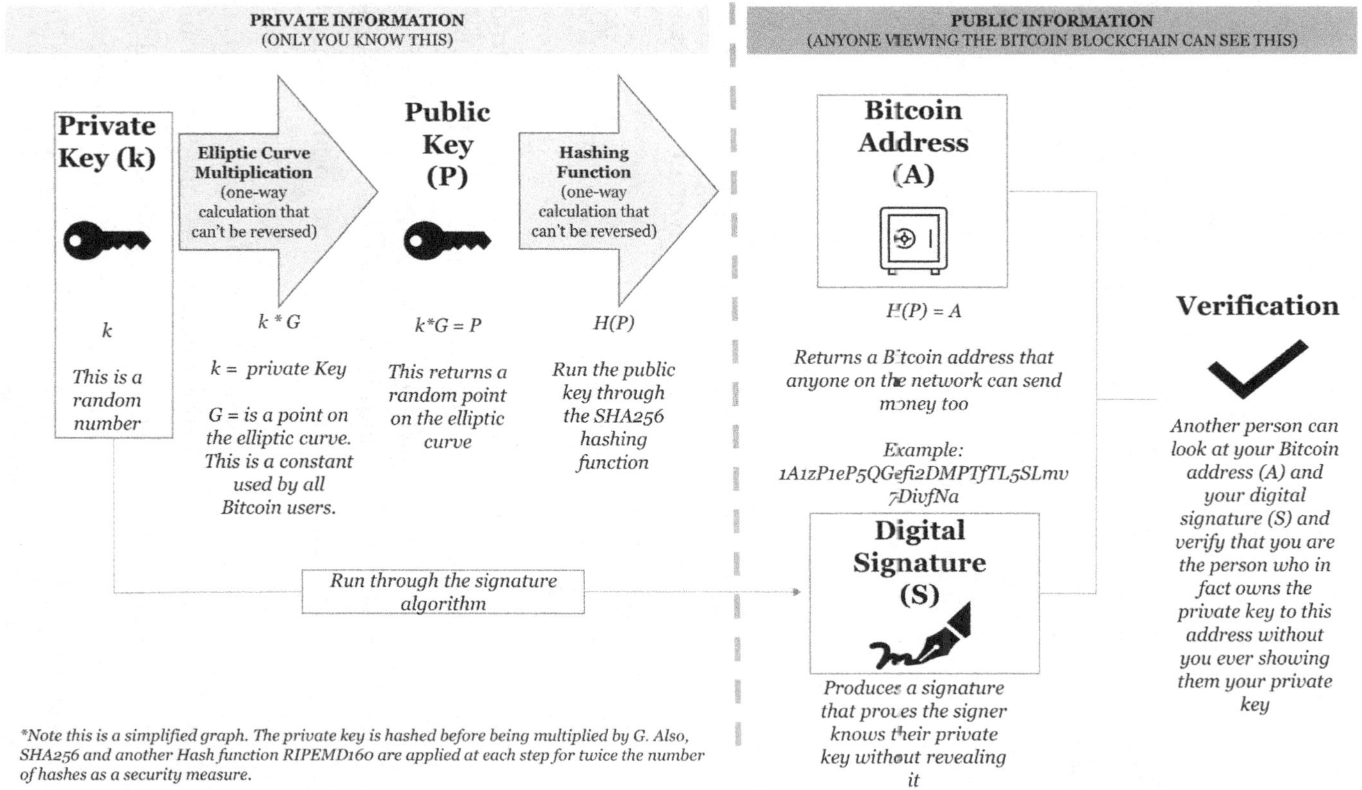

PRIVATE INFORMATION
(ONLY YOU KNOW THIS)

PUBLIC INFORMATION
(ANYONE VIEWING THE BITCOIN BLOCKCHAIN CAN SEE THIS)

**Private Key (k)**

$k$

This is a random number

**Elliptic Curve Multiplication**
(one-way calculation that can't be reversed)

$k * G$

$k$ = private Key

$G$ = is a point on the elliptic curve. This is a constant used by all Bitcoin users.

**Public Key (P)**

$k*G = P$

This returns a random point on the elliptic curve

**Hashing Function**
(one-way calculation that can't be reversed)

$H(P)$

Run the public key through the SHA256 hashing function

**Bitcoin Address (A)**

$H(P) = A$

Returns a Bitcoin address that anyone on the network can send money too

Example:
1A1zP1eP5QGefi2DMPTfTL5SLmv7DivfNa

Run through the signature algorithm

**Digital Signature (S)**

Produces a signature that proves the signer knows their private key without revealing it

**Verification**

Another person can look at your Bitcoin address (A) and your digital signature (S) and verify that you are the person who in fact owns the private key to this address without you ever showing them your private key

**Note this is a simplified graph. The private key is hashed before being multiplied by G. Also, SHA256 and another Hash function RIPEMD160 are applied at each step for twice the number of hashes as a security measure.*

**Figure 67:** the process of generating a bitcoin address, producing a transaction signature, and verification using the ECDSA algorithm

1. The first step is to generate a private key:

**Figure 68:** private key generation

   a. Theoretically this could be anything, but strong random number generators are a minimum layer of security in any digital signature system.
   b. A good source of randomness means something that will be hard to predict.
   c. Randomness is typically derived from a source, so finding things that occur in the world that are truly random are how strong **random number generators** (RNGs) work. What these are and how they work is beyond the scope of this chapter, but you can read about them on wikipedia.[4]
   d. If 2 people were to produce the same random number as their private key on the bitcoin network, this would compromise the security of the funds controlled by whoever produced it first. This is called a **collision.**
   e. Just how this works will make sense once we get to the discussion of Bitcoin addresses.

***A private key is generated as a random number, a good source of randomness is critical for security purposes.***

2. Your random number is then multiplied by the **Generator Point (G):**

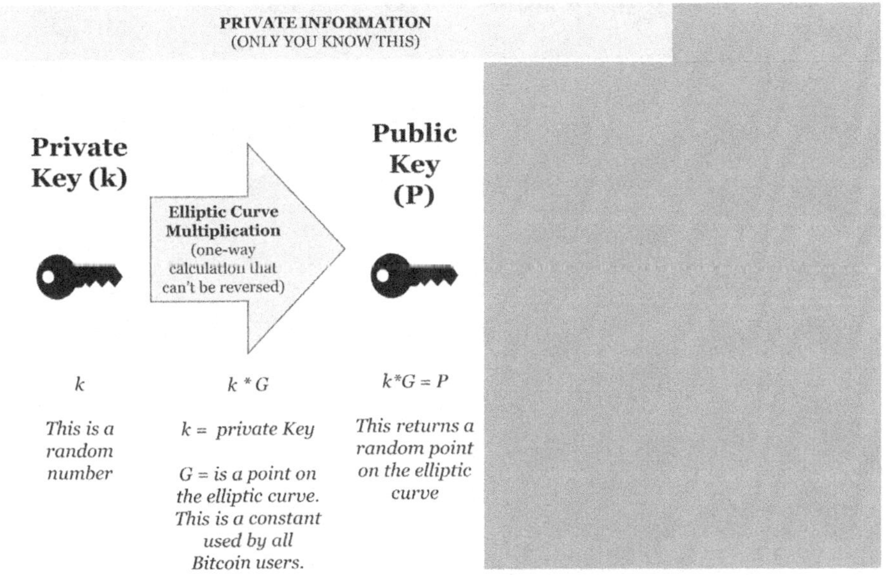


**Figure 69:** public key generation

a. G is a standard point used by everyone in the Bitcoin network and is on the **secp256k1 elliptic curve**.
b. All this means is that we have now used a finite math multiplication process on an elliptic curve to create a public key.
c. This is a one-way calculation that is impossible to reverse because of the discrete log problem.
d. Now, this needs to be converted into a standardized format that everyone can use as their own unique public address, just like your home address.

***The private key is multiplied by a standard point on the Bitcoin elliptic curve to create a public key that can be shared without revealing the private key.***

3. The **Public-key (P)** is run through a hash function to produce your **Bitcoin Address (A)**:

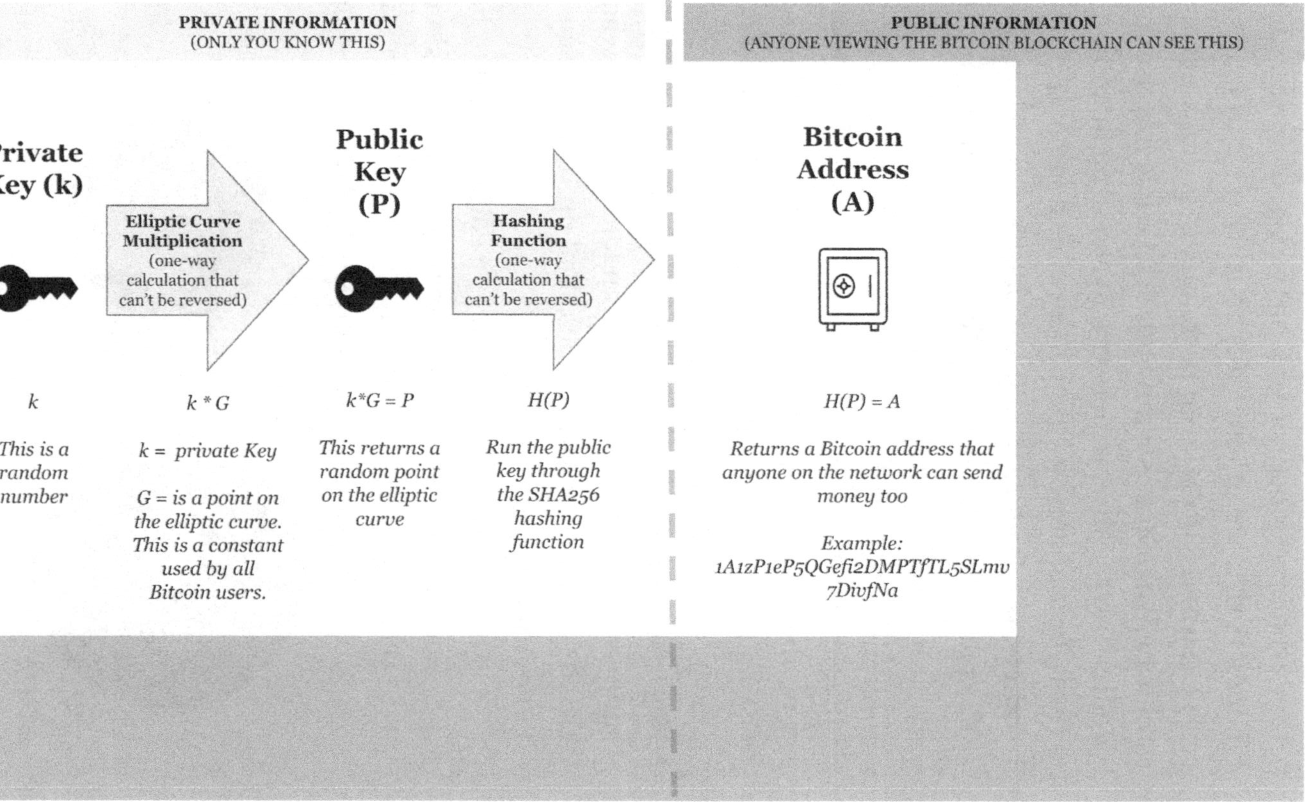


**Figure 70:** bitcoin address creation

a. The public key is run through the SHA-256 hash function which produces a 256-bit string of letters and numbers that are unique (it is actually run through the SHA256 and RIPEMD160 hash functions, but we'll just refer to SHA256 to keep it simple). People can use this address on the Bitcoin network to send you bitcoins.
b. These first 3 steps in the process are done by **Bitcoin wallets,** which store the Bitcoin addresses of a user and of which there are many different types that vary in terms of quality (e.g., security).
c. If you download wallet software, it will use a random number generator to create a private-key (k), multiply it by the generator point (G) to produce a public-key (P), and run that through a hash function to create your new bitcoin address (A).
d. **Key question:** Since everybody is generating Bitcoin addresses independently with random numbers, what are the chances that they would end up with the same Bitcoin address?
    - This would be referred to as a **collision** and to be secure, your wallet software needs to be **collision-resistant**. Meaning, it is infeasible (not impossible) for two different inputs to produce the same

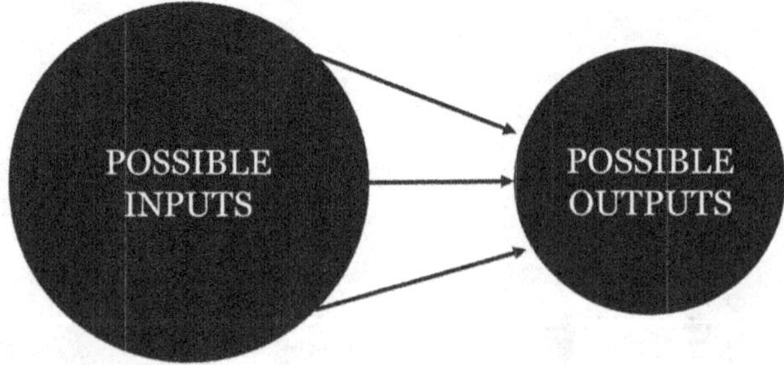


**Figure 71:** the number of possible inputs is greater than the number of possible outputs, and it is therefore certain at least 1 output maps to more than 1 input

- For ECDSA to be secure, both your **(1) source of randomness** and your **(2) hashing function** need to be **collision-resistant.**
  - o Your source of randomness needs to be strong (mentioned in the private key discussion above). A weak example would be one that produces a number between 1 and 100. It would only take 100 addresses to produce a collision with 100% probability.
  - o The same applies to the hashing function. Bitcoin uses SHA-256, which has a $1/2^{256}$ possibility of a collision, which is infinitesimally small.

e. The SHA-256 collision resistance does not matter if your original source of randomness is poor. Thus, for a wallet to be optimal, its source of randomness needs to produce outputs in a range equal to $2^{256}$. Anything greater is unnecessary as the hashing function will bottleneck the probability to $2^{256}$, and anything less is unnecessarily increasing the chance of a collision.

f. **Key point:** The source of randomness and the hash function used are critical to the security of a wallet. Wallets are made by many different people who may or may not use a good source of randomness.

***The public key is then hashed to create a bitcoin address. If your private key used a poor source of randomness, your address could have a security issue.***

4. Now that we have an address, we can send and receive bitcoins. To do so we need to produce a **digital signature:**

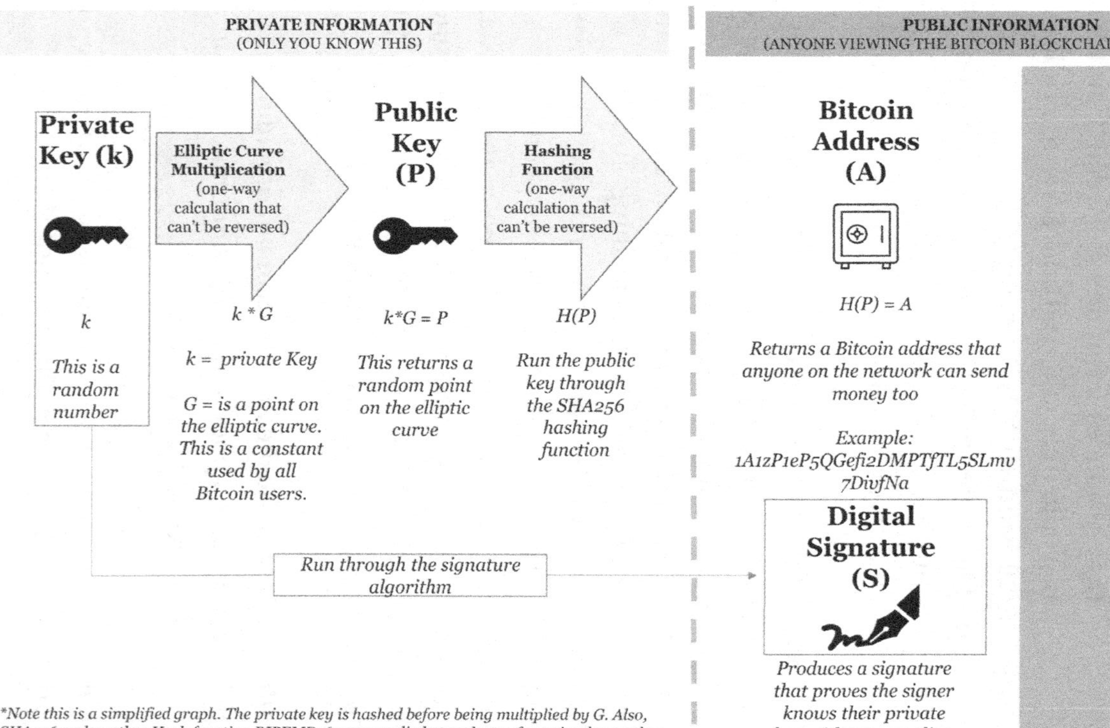


**Figure 72:** the digital signature is produced to prove ownership of the private key without revealing it

a. Why do you need to produce a digital signature? In Bitcoin, the software allows you to send something with your private key, but other people will only accept it as a valid transaction if you can confirm that you possess the private key.
b. A **digital signature** allows you to do this without revealing your private key.
c. How does it do this? This step is mathematically more complex. It isn't necessary to understand the details here, but what is important to grasp is that your private key gets mixed in with other variables (not shown in the above graphic) that hide your key while proving it is still there. Think of it like mixing paint. You can take red paint (your private key) and white paint (other variables) and mix them together in a ratio of exactly 50/50 to create pink paint. If someone else were to find your pink paint, they would be able to deduce that you mixed red paint with white but would not be able to deduce exactly how much of each paint color you used.

***The ECDSA algorithm creates a digital signature from your private key. Using this signature and your bitcoin address, you can now send bitcoins to other people on the network.***

5. Finally, with a Bitcoin address and a digital signature, another participant in the Bitcoin Network will be able to verify that you are in fact the owner of the address and will accept your transaction as valid:

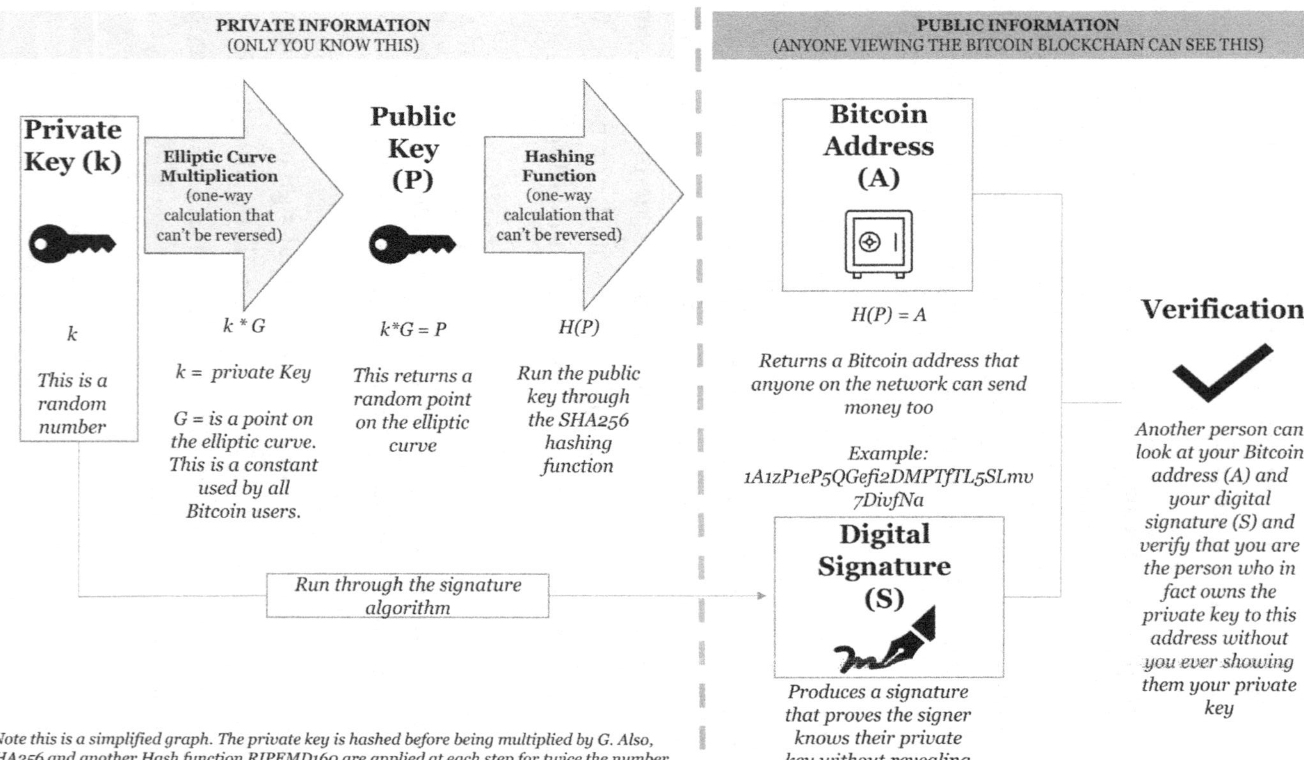


**Figure 73:** participants in the network can verify that the digital signature matches the bitcoin address

a. In Bitcoin, verification by other network participants is necessary for a transaction to be accepted.
b. This is analogous to cashing a check at a bank. To do so the bank must verify the check and signature of the person, as well as that they have the available funds in their account.
c. Traditionally, banks provided this function. Digital money attempts before bitcoin used a centralized server.
d. In Bitcoin everyone on the network verifies the transaction in a decentralized manner. For every transaction you send, there are thousands of computers that hear about it and all run the same check to (1) verify your signature with your address and (2) verify you are not spending more bitcoins than you have (this is protection against the **double spending problem**).
e. Lastly, the only thing you ever need is your private key. Your address can be recreated from your private key. But you can never go backwards and recreate a private key from an address. **Proper security and storage of private keys is your primary responsibility as a Bitcoin owner.**

***When you send bitcoins, every node on the network that hears about your transaction verifies your signature with your address and checks that you have at least as many bitcoins as you are attempting to send. If verification of your signature fails, or if the number of bitcoins you own is insufficient, your transaction is dropped from the network.***

## Transaction Mechanics

We're used to thinking of transactions from the perspective

of a double-entry ledger, but Bitcoin is different. Transactions are structured as a chain. For every Bitcoin transaction there is an input and an output (barring one exception).

Assume Kanye West sends 1 bitcoin to Mike Tyson:

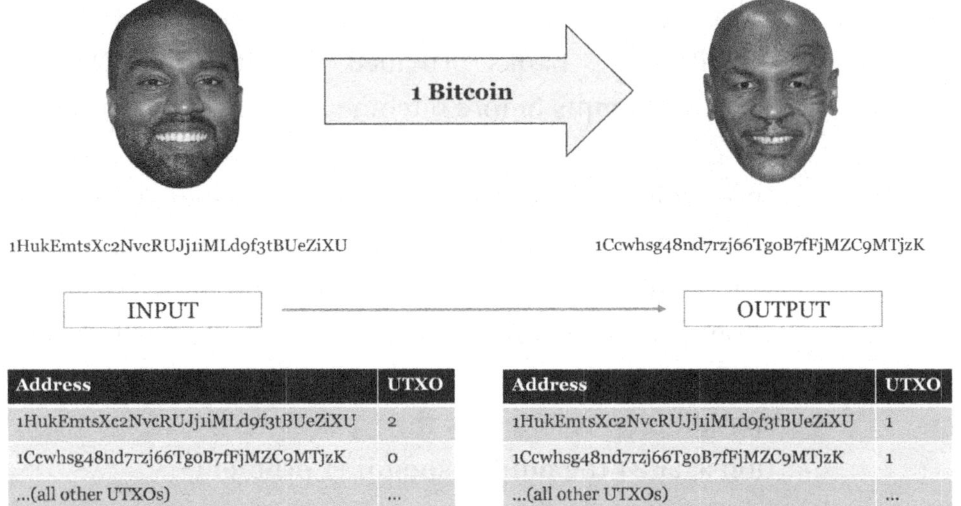


| Address | UTXO |
|---|---|
| 1HukEmtsXc2NvcRUJj1iMLd9f3tBUeZiXU | 2 |
| 1Ccwhsg48nd7rzj66TgoB7fFjMZC9MTjzK | 0 |
| ...(all other UTXOs) | ... |

| Address | UTXO |
|---|---|
| 1HukEmtsXc2NvcRUJj1iMLd9f3tBUeZiXU | 1 |
| 1Ccwhsg48nd7rzj66TgoB7fFjMZC9MTjzK | 1 |
| ...(all other UTXOs) | ... |

**Figure 74:** Kanye West sends 1 bitcoin to Mike Tyson

The input is the number of bitcoins at Kanye's address. The output is the amount he wants to send to Mike's address. If we look at Kanye's address, he has 2 bitcoins. If he sends 1 bitcoin to Mike's address, that is his output. Participants on the Bitcoin network all verify that his address of 2 bitcoins is greater than or equal to the transaction he is sending to Mike's address. Since it is, this transaction is accepted, and Mike now has 1 bitcoin.

Mike's new bitcoin will now sit at his address until he chooses to spend it. Until he does, it will be on the list of **unspent transaction outputs (UTXOs)**. At any given point in time there is a running list of all bitcoins that exist at each address. These are all effectively outputs from prior transactions which have yet to be spent (hence the name). This list is what network participants referenced to confirm that Kanye had the 1 bitcoin he sent to Mike. After the transaction, Kanye's address decreased by 1 bitcoin and Mike's address increased by 1 bitcoin. Mike now has 1 bitcoin to spend, which can be verified from the updated list of UTXOs.

The only exception to this transaction structure is the **coinbase transaction** – when a miner solves a computational puzzle to find a new block, new bitcoins are created and sent to the miner's address. These coins do not have an input. This will be discussed in more depth in the next chapter. Now that we understand the basics of a transaction, let's see how they are aggregated and stored on the blockchain.

***Transaction inputs must be greater than outputs. Network participants verify this using the UTXO list. Coinbase transactions are the only exception to this rule.***

## The Blockchain Data Structure

A blockchain is a chain of blocks. **Blocks are batches of transactions.** We covered the basics of the blockchain in the last chapter, but here we will discuss specifically how it works with Bitcoin.

Bitcoin allows people to create transactions. These transactions are aggregated into blocks. These blocks are linked together to form a blockchain. The blockchain is used as a ledger that cannot be changed. Let's start by walking through the structure of a block.

Kanye sends 1 bitcoin to Mike:

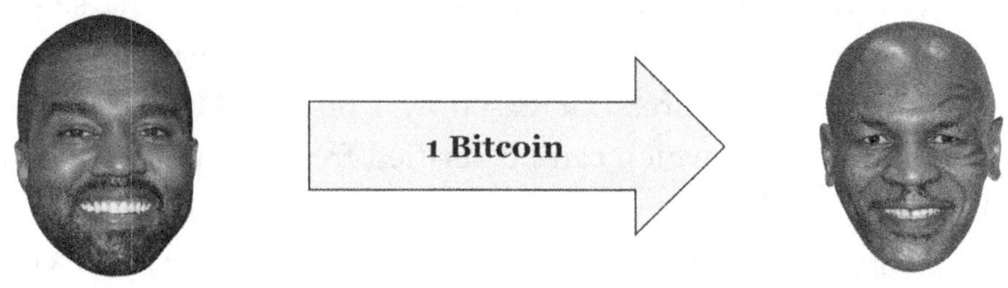


**Figure 75:** Kanye sends 1 bitcoin to Mike

The transaction is then verified via the ECDSA and hashed (run through the SHA256 hash function) and the 256-bit string of text is the output, called the **transaction hash**:

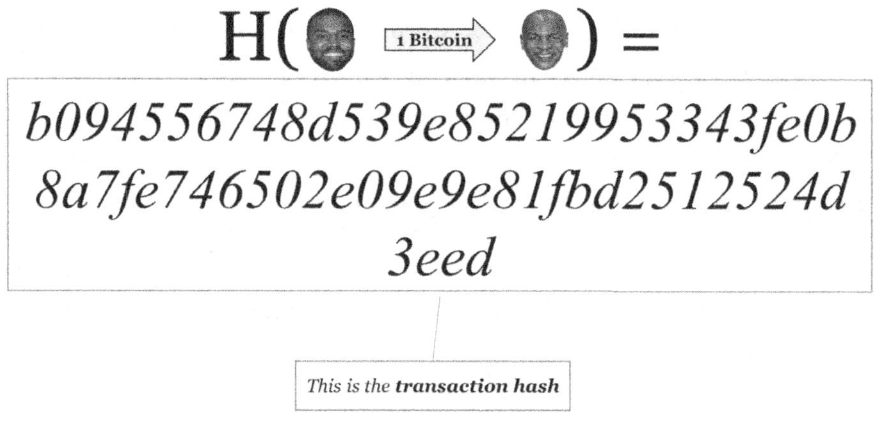


**Figure 76:** hash of the Kanye to Mike transaction

The **transaction hash** is then added into the most recent block. It is intuitive to think these are just lists of transactions, however they are organized as a binary tree of hashes, known as a **merkle tree**. This structure is shown in the image below, where each transaction is hashed, concatenated with its sibling transaction, and then hashed again. This process repeats until we are left with one hash of all the data.

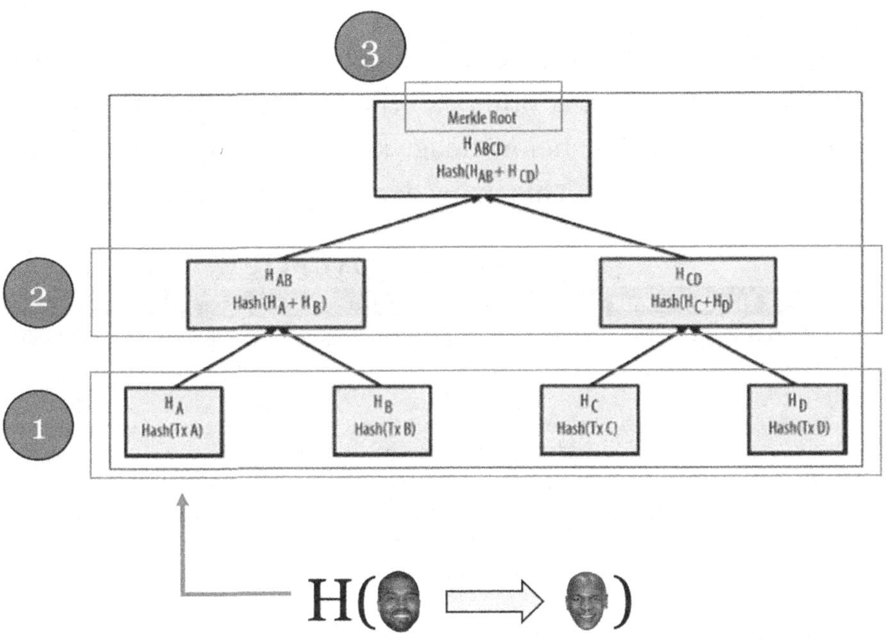


**Figure 77:** the hash of the transaction is included in a merkle tree with all the other transactions
(Image source Mastering bitcoin with Eric Yakes additions)[1]

1. Here you can see that transactions A through D are each hashed.
2. These hashes are then combined in pairs, and each pair is then hashed.
3. We are left with 1 hash at the top of the tree, called the **merkle root**. This is the root of all the transactions – if one of these transactions were subsequently changed, this would be immediately noticeable in the merkle root.

***Transactions are hashed and then added to a merkle tree. Each pair of branches is hashed continuously until there is a single hash left, the merkle root.***

The merkle root is then added into the **block header**. The block header is the title of each block in the block chain. It includes information that others on the Bitcoin network can use to verify the block. The below image shows how the merkle root is one of the items in the block header along with 5 others:

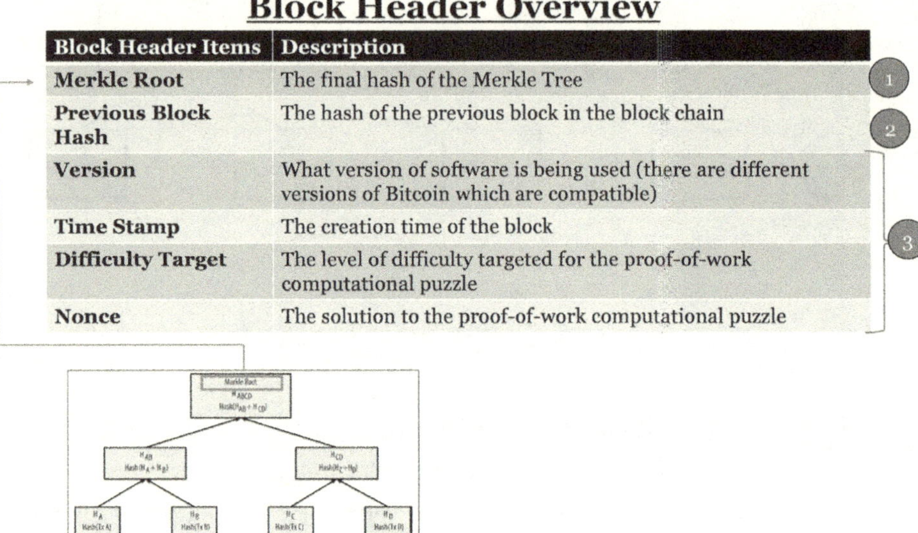

**Block Header Overview**

| Block Header Items | Description |
|---|---|
| Merkle Root | The final hash of the Merkle Tree |
| Previous Block Hash | The hash of the previous block in the block chain |
| Version | What version of software is being used (there are different versions of Bitcoin which are compatible) |
| Time Stamp | The creation time of the block |
| Difficulty Target | The level of difficulty targeted for the proof-of-work computational puzzle |
| Nonce | The solution to the proof-of-work computational puzzle |



**Figure 78:** block header items, the hash of the merkle tree is the merkle root item

1. The **merkle root** is used by network participants to quickly verify that all of the transactions incorporated into a new block are the same across different copies of the blockchain. To be discussed later; each network participant carries their own personal copy of the blockchain, which can vary from person to person.
2. **Previous block hash** is the hash of the prior block, generically known as a **hash pointer** because it points to the prior block. This item is what links all the blocks into a chain. If a single thing were to change in the data of any prior block since the beginning of Bitcoin, the previous block hash

would not match whatever it was before the change. This allows other Bitcoin network participants to look at this field and quickly verify all of them are working off the exact same historical blockchain.

3. **Version, time stamp, difficulty target, and nonce** all refer to items related to the mining process, which will be discussed in the next chapter.

So, blocks are just batches of transactions. The block header is metadata about the transactions in the block as well as a hash of the previous block. At the highest level, a block includes the below information:

| Block Items | Description |
|---|---|
| **Block Header** | Includes all the block header items |
| **Block Size** | The size of the block in bytes |
| **Transaction Counter** | How many transactions are included |
| **Transactions** | The data of all the transactions included in the block |

| Block Header Items |
|---|
| **Merkle Root** |
| **Previous Block Hash** |
| **Version** |
| **Time Stamp** |
| **Difficulty Target** |
| **Nonce** |

**Figure 79:** the block header items are included in the block header field next to the other block items

At the highest a level, a block includes

- the batch of transactions
- how many transactions there are
- the byte size of the transactions all combined
- The block header data.

***Blocks include the batch of transactions, a hash pointer to the previous block, and metadata of the block.***

Within the block header data, the previous block hash item is used to chain the current block to the previous block. Below is a full graphic of the block chain:

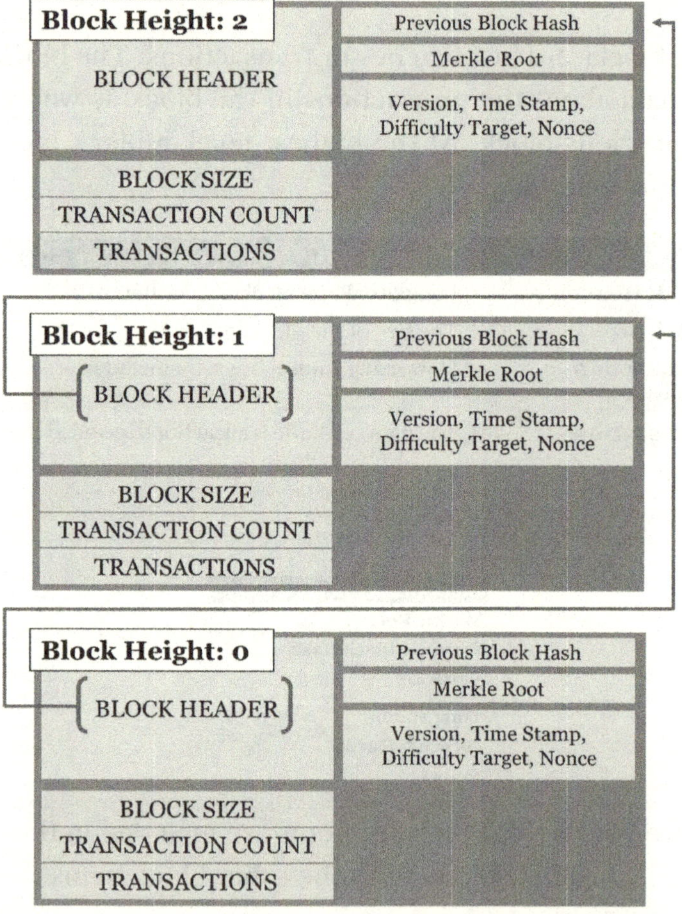


**Figure 80:** the blockchain showing both the block items and the block header items

The blockchain is conceptualized as a vertical stack of blocks so the term **block height** is used to identify blocks. The first block, also known as the **genesis block**, was block height 0. The current height of the blockchain as of this writing is 672,000. New blocks are created on average every 10 minutes. Why and how this works requires an understanding of the mining process, the topic of the next chapter.

You can see that the block header of each block is subsequently hashed and included in the next block. As a reminder, this is called the **previous block hash** (which is a **hash pointer**) and is how the blocks are chained together. **Any change in a previous block will be instantaneously reflected in the current block because the previous block hash would change.** This structure was implemented to quickly allow participants to understand they are both working off the same history of bitcoin transactions. This is basically a method of version control that protects against bad actors. A full explanation of this requires an understanding of the Bitcoin network, the topic of the next chapter.

Lastly, it is important to understand the **memory pool** – a period between the creation of a transaction and its ultimate recording in the blockchain. During this period, a transaction is held by every participant who has heard of it in their respective memory pool. This is like a waiting room where it sits until a miner has solved the computational puzzle that publishes the transactions to the blockchain. The memory pool can vary for each network participant. The memory pool of the miner who ultimately found the next block is the one that will be inserted in the block chain; any transactions that were sent but not included by this particular miner will simply have to wait to be included in the next block.

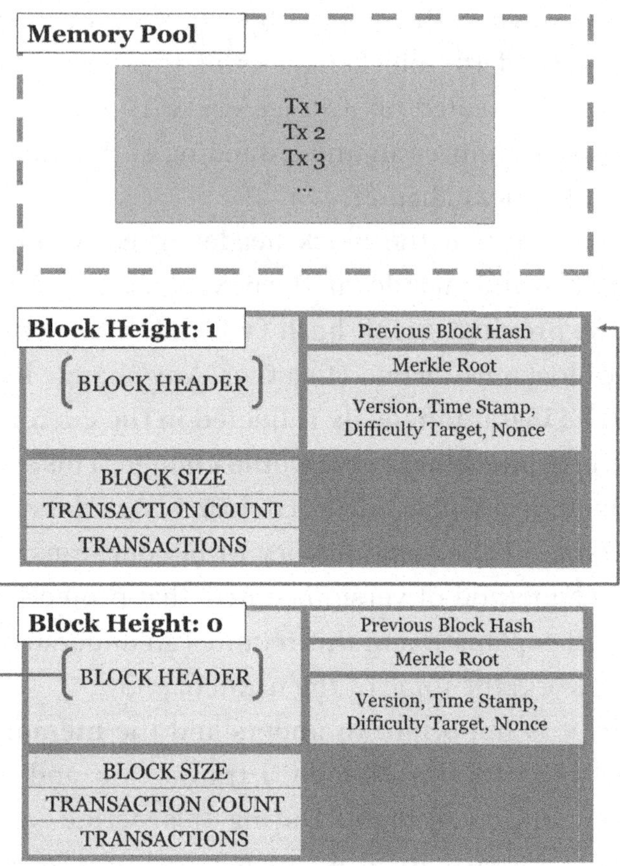


**Figure 81:** the memory pool of transactions are soon to be included in the blockchain

***While network participants are mostly all working off the same history of the blockchain, the memory pool can vary. The miner who mines the new block adds their memory pool of transactions to the block chain.***

## Conclusion

Bitcoin allows people to send digital money peer-to-peer. Transactions can be done anonymously without requiring permission from a 3rd party. No other payment system can transact large amounts of value as cheaply and efficiently as Bitcoin.

The discrete log problem allows for one-way calculations, which underlie all of modern cryptography. One-way calculations are used to create Bitcoin addresses and the ECDSA allows an address to prove knowledge of a private key to other nodes without showing it. The Bitcoin network uses ECDSA to send transactions and subsequently verify them. Verification requires checking the signature with the addresses and that the address is not spending more bitcoins than it has. Once verified, these transactions are structured in blocks. Blocks are chained together by incorporating a hash of the previous block into every new block – allowing participants to immediately verify if the history of blocks has chained. New blocks are added once miners solve a computationally intensive puzzle and transactions sit within the miners' multiple memory pools until a solution is found.

We now understand the structure of the blockchain. This summary of the blockchain is incomplete without understanding the Bitcoin network. How does everyone hear about transactions? Does everyone agree on the same transactions? If not, how is consensus achieved among thousands of different participants when multiple versions of the blockchain are being referenced? The next chapter will explain.

## References

1. *Mastering Bitcoin*, Andreas Antonopolous, https://github.com/bitcoinbook/bitcoinbook
2. https://www.cryptovantage.com/news/here-are-the-5-biggest-bitcoin-transactions-in-history/
3. https://www.freeformatter.com/sha256-generator.html#ad-output
4. https://en.wikipedia.org/wiki/List_of_random_number_generators

# 10. HOW BITCOIN WORKS

*I gotta new strategy it's called no strategy. And I gotta way to sell more music it's called make better music.* – *Kanye West*

Bitcoin can send transactions and incorporate them into a public blockchain, which serves as a ledger. Bitcoin is valuable because we can be certain the transactions included in the ledger are legitimate and not fraudulent. We can be certain they are not fraudulent because of the size of the Bitcoin network. This chapter will explain how the decentralized network incentivizes independent participants to organize and create legitimate transactions on the blockchain.

## Decentralized Software

A computer is made up of memory and processing power. Memory is stored information that some computers have more of than others. Processing power is the ability to convert inputs into outputs and some computers can process faster than others. Software comprises rules that a computer is told to follow. A computer takes in inputs, applies the rules it is given, and produces outputs.

Bitcoin is software, but its nature is different from what we are used to because it is decentralized. Most software we are familiar with uses a centralized network to function. Consider Facebook and how it works. When you log in to create an account, your information is uploaded to one of the many computers Facebook uses for storing the information of its users. Every time you make a post or comment that information is added to the computer. If the CEO wanted to delete or change your information, then he would call the guy who manages the computers, give him your name, and tell him what to do with it. This is all possible because Facebook is a centralized company.

Indeed, most companies we are familiar with operate in a centralized manner and for good reason. The fact that the CEO is a phone call away from making these changes allows the company to function efficiently. In return for this efficiency, the stakeholders of the company (employees, shareholders, and customers) must trust the CEO is doing what is best for all of them simultaneously. Roughly speaking, the CEO of a company does not require consensus of agreement from the stakeholders to enact change, and this allows a company to be agile in a competitive market.

At the other end of the spectrum is a decentralized company – where decisions are made by achieving consensus among a group of participants. In its purest form, this system does not require trust in a central authority because the will of the stakeholders will always be achieved. **This process is inefficient but necessary for enacting operations that are highly subject to moral hazard.**

The founding fathers knew this when constructing the balance of powers and our democratic process for electing officials. It allowed society to maintain a high degree of control over those they elect to be in charge. Put simply, **purely decentralized systems are slow and inefficient, but necessary to eliminate the agency problem** where a conflict of interest exists.

The age of computing enabled decentralized systems because the ability to transfer information at the speed of light made the requirements of decentralization much less onerous. Software became the ideal medium for decentralization. With computing advances came a new universe of ideas that could now be decentralized but remain operationally feasible.

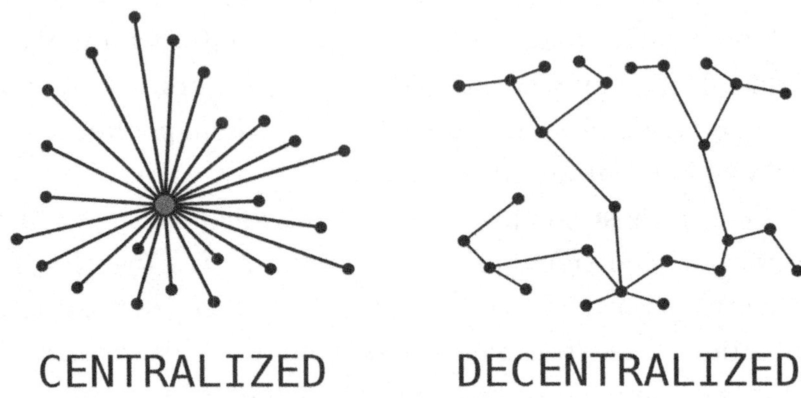


**Figure 82:** centralized vs. decentralized network (Image source Wikipedia)[3]

***Decentralized systems trade efficiency to eliminate moral hazard. Applying decentralized systems to digital environments significantly reduces their inefficiencies.***

Decentralized software is code that is automated enough that there does not need to be a centralized owner (like a CEO). Instead, it is a set of rules that everyone who interacts with the software is required to follow. Once the rules are set, they cannot be changed, UNLESS most network participants agree to make a change.

This agreement is achieved through action because the software is **open source – everyone has their own copy of the code, which they can change in whatever way they wish**. However, if you change your code too much, you might not be able to interact with other people's code anymore. Everyone can change their own code however much they would like, but the rules that are followed are those that most of the network chooses to follow. Anybody that does not want to follow the rules can change their code, but this means they can only interact with others who have made this change as well. Simply put, if somebody wants to change the Bitcoin software, then they need to convince the majority of participants to do the same. If they cannot, Bitcoin will not change.

For this reason, there are a bunch of different offshoots of Bitcoin: Bitcoin Cash, Bitcoin Gold, Bitcoin Diamond, etc. They were created by groups of people that wanted to change the rules, could not get the majority to agree, and decided to change their own rules anyway, which created a new software and network they all began to use. These are called **forks**, which are a category of **altcoins (alternative coins)**. Minor changes to Bitcoin have been agreed upon in the past, but there have been no changes to the fundamental rules – which is a testament to the truly decentralized nature of Bitcoin and why it is so valuable. More on this later.

***Decentralized systems follow a set of rules. The rules change when the majority of participants download software with the rule change. If they do not, the rules remain, and the minority must decide to stay or leave.***

## The Bitcoin Network

The Bitcoin Network exists as the sum of all network participants. Participants are called **nodes** – a computer with compatible Bitcoin software connected to a network. Each node in the network can participate in multiple ways, depending on the software it uses, and **is constrained by its memory and processing power**. Below is a map of the ~10,000+ current Bitcoin nodes:

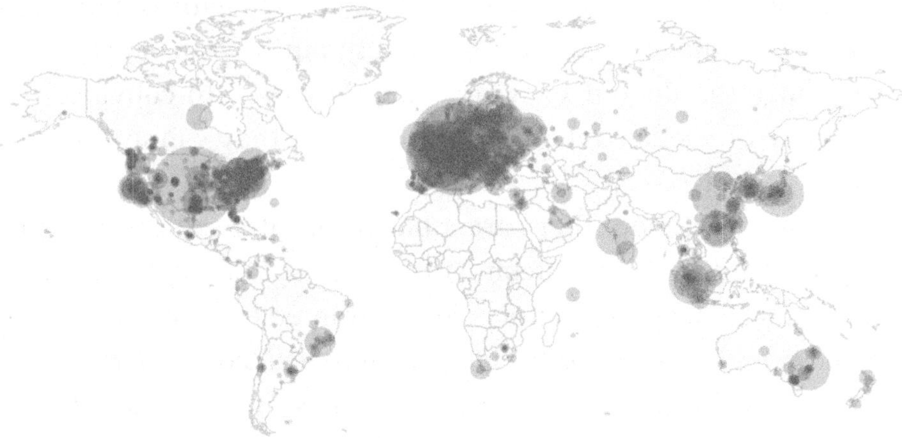

**Figure 83:** a map of the active nodes on the bitcoin network as of January 2021
*(Image source bitnodes.io)*[4]

Nodes participate in the network via 3 primary functions: **routing**, **verification,** and **mining**.

1. **Routing** – All nodes are continuously discovering and connecting to their peers (other nodes). No node is connected to every node. Every node has a few peers it connects to (typically 8) so that it can broadcast new transactions or new blocks to them. Information spreads throughout the network through a **gossip protocol** – one node tells other nodes what it is hearing, and those nodes then tell more nodes. This process rapidly propagates information throughout the network.
2. **Verification** – when a node hears about a transaction, it runs checks to ensure the transaction is valid. It checks that:
    a. The inputs of the transaction are previously unspent. Nodes verify that the bitcoins are spendable by checking the transaction against a list of **UTXOs (unspent transaction outputs)**. UTXOs are a running list of all the bitcoins that exist at each address. This list can

be used to quickly check the number of bitcoins at an address to ensure that address has enough bitcoins to spend. This prevents **double-spending**.

b. The sum of the inputs is greater than or equal to the sum of the outputs. This ensures no new bitcoins are created.

c. The signature successfully unlocks the public key. This ensures that the person sending the transaction is the owner of the private key.

d. If this all checks out, the node adds it to their pool of potential transactions that are not yet included on the block chain – **the memory pool**. If a node hears about a transaction that is already in its pool, it does not relay that transaction to other nodes.

3. **Mining** – to convert the memory pool of transactions into an official block on the blockchain, mining nodes need to solve a computational puzzle. If a miner solves the puzzle, it communicates the solution to its surrounding nodes and creates a new block with all the transactions in its memory pool. The surrounding nodes check that the solution is correct, add the new block to their blockchains, communicate it to more nodes, and begin mining for a new block.

A node's ability to partially or completely fulfill these three functions is based on the constraints of its memory and processing power. Because of these constraints, there are different types of nodes.

All nodes can route and verify transactions. However, their ability to **independently verify** them against the blockchain is **constrained by their memory**. As I write these words, the Bitcoin blockchain requires 350 GBs of storage, which exceeds the memory of many consumer laptops. If a node does not have the ability to download the full blockchain, it must depend on a peer that does. Then once it hears about a transaction, it runs its checks against the peer's copy of the blockchain. These nodes are called **lightweight nodes** and are the most basic type of node. Nodes that have downloaded the full blockchain are called **full nodes.**

**The ability for a node to mine is constrained by its processing power.** Mining is an intensive computational process that only highly specialized computers can do economically. More on this later.

Many nodes are wallets. All nodes can be a **wallet** if they want, but do not have to have this functionality. When you download a Bitcoin wallet software, your wallet is also functioning as a node in the background by relaying and verifying transactions. When you send or receive a transaction with your wallet, you are interacting with other nodes to relay the transaction to the network.

You can see these relationships in the below chart:

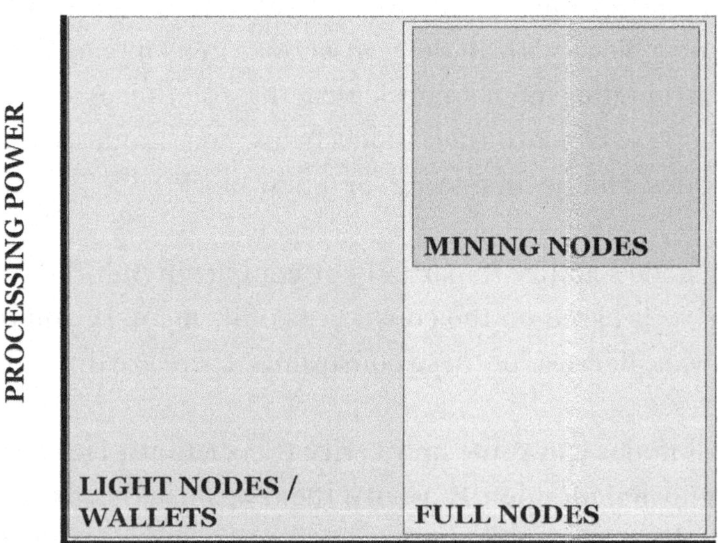


**Figure 84:** node types are constrained by memory and processing power

Below is a general description of each nodes type:

1. **Wallet Node** – allows you to create Bitcoin addresses and send/receive transactions.
2. **Lightweight Nodes** – allow you to route and verify transactions with minimal memory usage. However, this comes at the cost of dependency on a full node's blockchain. A full nodes' ability to take advantage of lightweight nodes will be discussed in the next chapter.
3. **Full Nodes** – the ability to independently verify all transactions. An individual running a full node can be certain that their blockchain is the true blockchain.
4. **Mining Nodes** – can earn you valuable bitcoins. But this is computationally expensive to do, as it requires a significant amount of energy to compete with other miners to find solutions.

***Different types of nodes participate in the network via different functions. A node's ability to perform 3 primary functions (i.e., routing, verification, and mining) is constrained by its memory and processing power.***

## The Mining Process

Mining nodes provide the most important function to the network. At this point we understand how transactions are formed, aggregated into blocks, and eventually published to the blockchain. This process is enabled by nodes verifying transactions and relaying them to other nodes. **The final step of publishing a new block to the blockchain is when miners come in, and this is the primary innovation of Bitcoin as opposed to prior forms of digital money**. This system created an elegant way to protect the network from bad actors, not just through technology but through game theory incentives as well. This step is what all digital money creators prior to Satoshi could not figure out. First, we'll cover how this process works, and then we'll discuss why it is important.

For a new block to be mined and included in the blockchain, a mining node must solve the **proof-of-work (PoW)** computational puzzle. The **proof-of-work algorithm is solved by generating a hash of the block header items that fall below the difficulty target**. Because a hash function's output is random, the only way to produce a low enough number is by guessing. The **difficulty target** is used to increase or decrease the chance that a miner solves the proof-of-work algorithm. The lower the difficulty target is, the harder it becomes to solve because the range of possible answers is smaller.

Recall the block header items from the prior chapter:

| Block Header Items | Description |
|---|---|
| **Merkle Root** | The final hash of the Merkle Tree |
| **Previous Block Hash** | The hash of the previous block in the block chain |
| **Version** | What version of software is being used (there are different versions of Bitcoin which are compatible) |
| **Time Stamp** | The creation time of the block |
| **Difficulty Target** | The level of difficulty targeted for the proof-of-work computational puzzle |
| **Nonce** | The solution to the proof-of-work computational puzzle |

**Figure 85:** block header items with time stamp, difficulty target, and nonce highlighted

The below formula combines all of these items and hashes them to calculate the **block header hash:**

***block header hash*** =

*SHA256(merkle root + previous block hash + version + time stamp + difficulty target +* ***nonce)***

Miners can change what the block header hash is by changing what they put into the **nonce field** - a blank field where miners insert guesses to change the block header hash. They cannot change any of the other fields.

To show you this, let's look at block 661,803.[11] Its block header hash is

*0000000000000000008acdc94cf82ee2d6a2caebe83d359ae39be-7f075016c6*

**That string of text is actually a number, but it is in hexadecimal format**, which is how hashes are shown on the blockchain. Notice the number of zeros that are leading it, 19 to be exact. That is quite a coincidence for a random algorithm. There are a total of 64 spots in that string of text. For the first spot, the probability that it is a 0 is .0625. In this case we have 19 spots being zero, which equates to a probability $.0625^{19}$. This is an incredibly small probability of about a 1 in $10^{22}$ chance (10 trillion trillions of a chance). In hexadecimal format, the greater the number of leading zeros, the lower the number is. So, it was a 1 in $10^{22}$ chance the block header hash was that low of a number.

This occurred because thousands of miners all around the world are iterating over the **nonce field** to produce a hash that is less than the target. None of the fields other than the nonce field can be changed by a miner (there is another field they can use inside the merkle root, but let's just assume the nonce for the sake of simplicity). The nonce field is an empty field where miners input random digits with the goal of producing a hash that is less than the target. Looking at block 661,803 we can see that the nonce which produced the hash that satisfies this requirement was 1,638,968,946.[11] When you input that number into the nonce field, it returns the following block header hash (in hexadecimal format):

*0000000000000000000 8acdc94cf82ee2d6a2caebe83d359ae39be-7f075016c6*

While the target is

*0000000000000000000f1372000000000000000000000000000000000000000000000*

Notice the number of leading zeros is equal for both (19 for each). If the block header hash had more zeros in front of it, we would know that it is lower. Because they have an equal amount of leading zeros, we have to convert to numeric format to see which is lower (it is currently in hexadecimal format). Below is an output of the code to show the comparison:

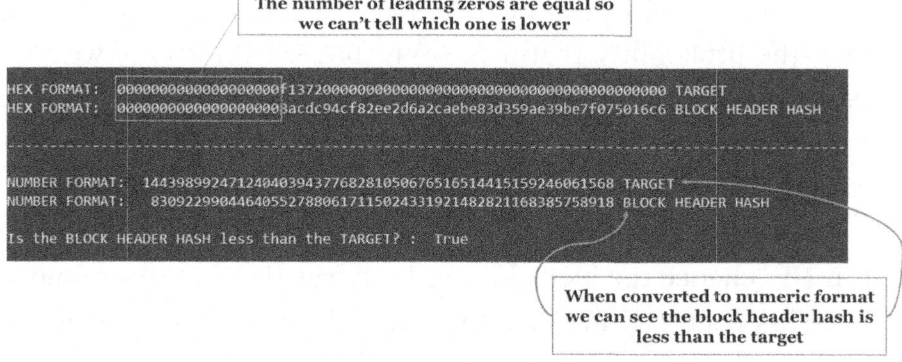


**Figure 86:** comparing the calculations of the block header vs. the target for block height 661,803

So, because the block header hash is less than the target difficulty, the block was successfully mined. The reason you cannot just pick a low number is because the hash functions output is random (there is no way to just make it produce a low number).

***Miners compete to solve the proof-of-work computational puzzle by iterating the nonce field until it produces a block header hash less than the difficulty target.***

## The Longest Chain Rule – Resolving Disagreements

Once a miner finds a solution, they immediately broadcast it to their peers (i.e., nodes they are connected to). Those nodes then verify that the solution is correct and, if so, broadcast it to their peers. Within a matter of seconds the majority of the network is aware that the most recent block has now been mined. The chart below shows that 95% of the blockchain will be aware of it in about 40 seconds on average.

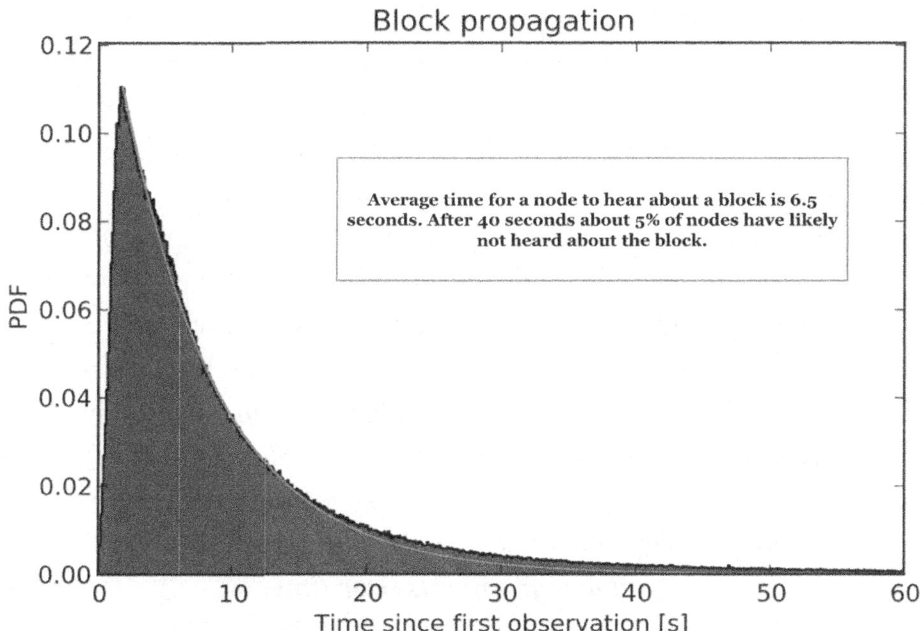


**Figure 87:** probability density function of block propagation time
(Image source Christian Decker and Robert Wattenhofer with Eric Yakes additions)[2,5]

Nodes accept this new block by incorporating it into their copy of the blockchain. Miners accept it and begin mining the next block, with the newest block added to their blockchains, thus restarting the process. This cycle occurs on average every 10 minutes – the difficulty target automatically adjusts to make it so.

What if different copies of the blockchain from different nodes are solved simultaneously? If there are disagreements between nodes, they follow the **longest chain rule**. This mechanism resolves disagreements between block chain copies. Satoshi summarized it best:

> *Nodes always consider the longest chain to be the correct one and will keep working on extending it. If two nodes broadcast different versions of the next block simultaneously, some nodes may receive one or the other first. In that case, they work on the first one they received, but save the other branch in case it becomes longer. The tie will be broken when the next proof-of-work is found, and one branch becomes longer; the nodes that were working on the other branch will then switch to the longer one.*
>
> *New transaction broadcasts do not necessarily need to reach all nodes. As long as they reach many nodes, they will get into a block before long. Block broadcasts are also tolerant of dropped messages. If a node does not receive a block, it will request it when it receives the next block and realizes it missed one.*

***Nodes follow the longest chain rule, which resolves all disagreements over time.***

## The Bitcoin Supply Schedule

Blockchain copy differences are resolved in time, and mining nodes are continuously finding a nonce that produces a hash less than the difficulty target. In recent years, the network difficulty has increased exponentially. (Note, this means the difficulty target is getting smaller, which makes it more difficult to mine.) This phenomenon is due to more mining computers joining the network to earn bitcoins.

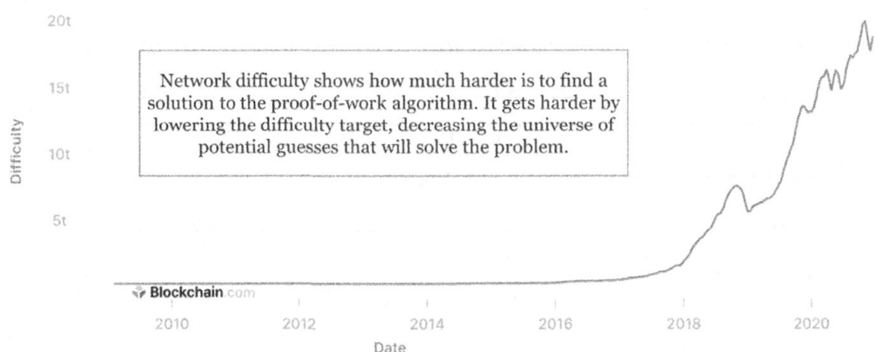


**Figure 88:** network difficulty
(Image source blockchain.com with Eric Yakes additions)[6]

Satoshi designed the difficulty target to self-adjust every 2 weeks on average, using the **time stamp** item in the block header, which records the creation time of new blocks. Using the time stamp, **every 2,016 blocks the bitcoin software checks to see how long it took to find a block on average.** If the average is below 2 weeks, the difficulty target adjusts to make it harder to find blocks (i.e., harder to find a solution to PoW). If it is above 2 weeks, the difficulty target makes it easier to find blocks. For 2,016 blocks to occur in 2 weeks means a block is being found on average every 10 minutes. **Thus, this self-adjusting mechanism ensures that a new Bitcoin block is found every 10 minutes on average over the long run.**

Why do miners go through the trouble of doing this when it only gets harder as they get better? Because they are rewarded in bitcoin to do so through the **block reward.**

***block reward** = coinbase transaction + block fees*

When a miner successfully mines a new block, there is a

special transaction in Bitcoin called a **coinbase transaction** (the company Coinbase is named after this) which sends a defined number of bitcoins to the successful miner. This is the only way that new bitcoins can be created. At the start of Bitcoin in 2008, the block reward was 50 BTC (bitcoin) but now it is 6.25. This is because the block reward is cut in half (called a **halving**) every 210,000 blocks (or 4 years) by design (50, 25, 12.5, 6.25, etc.). Bitcoin has a hard coded supply schedule for new bitcoins produced embedded in its software:

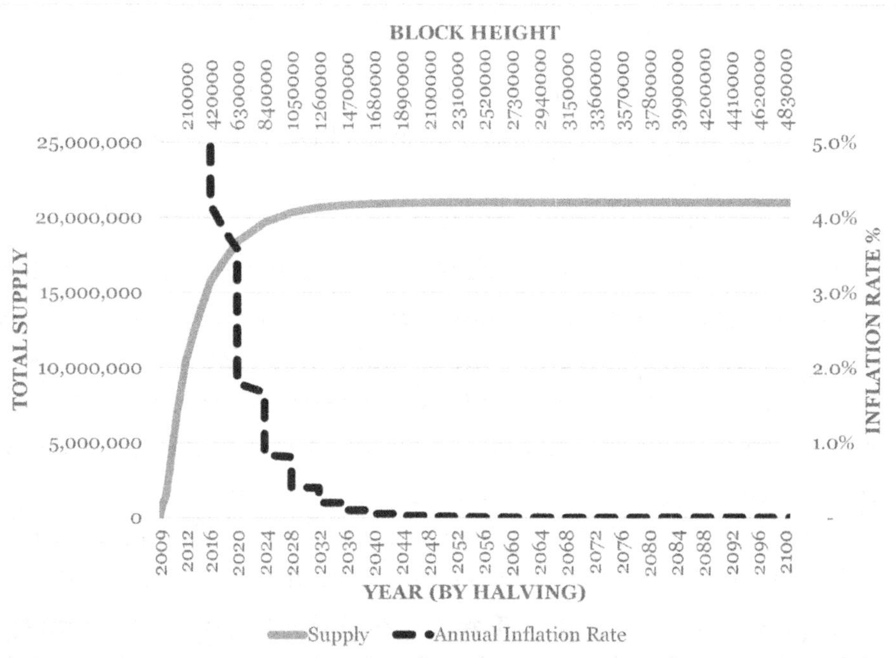


**Figure 89:** bitcoin total supply and annual inflation rate by each halving year and block height (Data sourced from bitcoin.it)

**This is a disinflationary supply schedule that will end near the year 2140 with a maximum total supply of 21 million bitcoins.** After this there will be no more coinbase transactions of new bitcoin created, and miners will only be **compensated in**

**fees for transactions.** Today, most mining is done for the coinbase transaction and small fees are paid to miners.

Fees are voluntary in Bitcoin, and miners prioritize transactions that include higher fees. If your transaction is urgent, then including a large fee will ensure it is quickly added to a new block. If you do not include any fees, it will likely still be included, but it might take a few blocks before it is. You can see below that fees have historically been a small but increasing percentage of the block reward. The highest point was 30% of the reward at the end of 2017, and today they are closer to 10%.

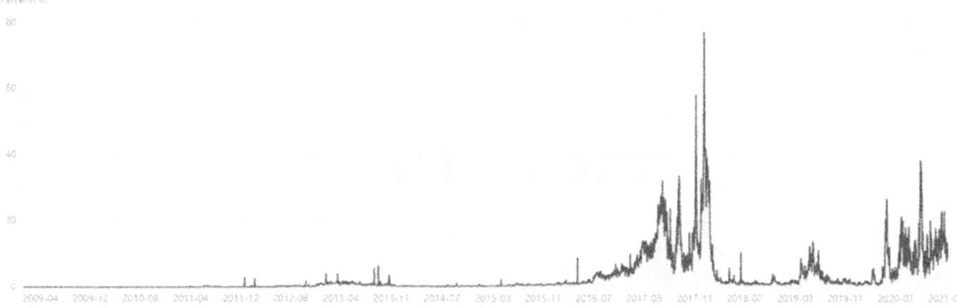


**Figure 90:** transaction fees as a percentage of the block reward since 2009 (Image source btc.com)[8]

To summarize, miners are incentivized to mine by earning block rewards, which include new bitcoins and transaction fees. As more miners attempt to mine bitcoins, it becomes increasingly likely that someone will find a nonce that produces a hash lower than the difficulty target. Said differently, blocks get found more quickly when there are more miners. This increases the rate at which new blocks are included in the blockchain, and thus the supply of bitcoins. Any increased/decreased supply rate can only sustain for a maximum of 2 weeks, as the difficulty target will adjust to adhere to a supply schedule that averages a block reward every 10 minutes.

***There will only ever be 21 million bitcoins.***

As more miners enter the Bitcoin network, the more competitive the mining process becomes. The number of miners on the network is expressed by the total amount of computing power contributed to finding a low block header hash, known as the **network hash rate**. This has increased exponentially in recent years along with the price of bitcoin:

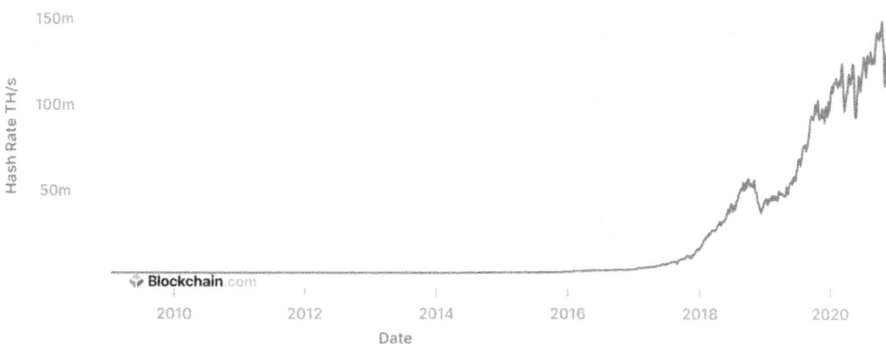


**Figure 91:** total network hash rate since 2009 (Image source blockchain.com)[9]

You might think 6.25 bitcoins (currently $150k USD) every 10 minutes is enticing, but I can convince you otherwise. Mining for blocks has become so competitive that the odds of doing it yourself are strikingly low. To understand this, take the total network hash rate (150 million TH/s in the above chart) and divide it by the number of hashes per second you could contribute. This will tell us how many blocks it will take to find a solution. One of the fastest miners on market currently can achieve 110 TH/s which means it will take this miner on average 26 years to find a solution.

To counteract this uncertainty of cash flows, miners have formed **mining pools** – miners combine their computing power as a group. When the group finds a solution, the rewards are distributed equitably, according to the amount of computing power contributed to the pool. This provides more certainty of cash flows, but the managers of the pool take a small fee from your earnings. This also causes concentration of the mining network into a handful of pools, increasing centralization. This is a key criticism of Bitcoin to be discussed in a later chapter.

At the beginning of Bitcoin, mining machines were general CPUs. All you needed to mine was to download the Bitcoin reference client (reference client is the most basic Bitcoin software called Bitcoin Core) and your computer would start searching for nonces on each block. This quickly became uneconomic, as the typical CPU is not specialized enough to find nonces quickly, and consumes more energy than you would ultimately earn in bitcoin. As mining became more competitive, people started using GPUs that could iterate nonces more quickly. This evolution concluded with manufacturing of ASIC (application specific integrated circuits) computers. Your laptop is a general-purpose computer, and its brain is designed to do a lot of different functions. ASIC mining computers have a brain designed for the single purpose of finding nonces. The use of ASICs effectively pushed out the mom-and-pop miners, as they mostly require industrial-size electricity and infrastructure to run. This increased centralization and is a key criticism of Bitcoin to be discussed later.

***Mining has become exponentially more competitive over the years. As this industry scales, there are concerns that centralization will become a risk to the network.***

Further, mining computers use large amounts of energy. Many critics note this type of energy consumption is not environmentally friendly, which is discussed further in the final chapter of this book. The argument is that the energy is being unnecessarily expended to solve a purposeless puzzle. To understand why this energy use is necessary, we need to discuss the fundamental purpose of mining.

## Incentives – the Proof-of-Work Algorithm

An important question to answer: why isn't some miner's blockchain just randomly picked every 10 minutes to be published? Why do we have to waste all this energy? To answer this, we need to understand a 51% attack, summarized well by Decker and Wattenhofer:

> *Bitcoin never commits a transaction definitively. Every transaction can be invalidated if a longer chain that started below the block including the transaction is created. If a single entity could control a majority of the computational power on the network, and thus be able to find blocks faster than the rest of the network combined, it could revert any transaction. If an attacker attempts to revert a transaction that was included in block bh it would create a new transaction that conflicts with the original transaction and include it into a block bh0 with h 0 < h. The attacker would then proceed to create blocks on top of bh0 until this new chain overtakes the original blockchain and thus becomes the new blockchain.* [2]

The primary purpose of the proof-of-work algorithm is this: **it makes mining a block awfully expensive, which makes the blockchain secure**. The larger the bitcoin network grows, and the more miners that contribute their computing power, the more competitive it gets and thus the more expensive it becomes to mine a block.

Since bitcoins are valuable, people will attempt to steal them. Let's think through how this might take place. Someone attempting to steal bitcoins would likely do so by modifying information in the blockchain. For example, they would want to include a type of transaction that would not be verified and accepted by other nodes – such as a double-spend. The attacker could send 2 bitcoins to someone to buy a car and then attempt to reverse this transaction in a later block, receiving both the car and getting back the 2 bitcoins. They could accomplish this by retroactively changing the transaction so that the 2 bitcoins go to an address they control, instead of to the other person. **To include this fraudulent transaction in a block (that honest nodes would reject quickly through the verification process) the attacker would have to mine that block into existence himself.**

**Mining a fraudulent transaction into existence would require computing power greater than 50% of the entire network in order to make the fraudulent chain longer than the predominant one.** Given that the current hash rate of Bitcoin is so large, it would likely take cooperation among the largest governments to attempt such an attack. Gobitcoin.io[10] estimates it would require a hardware cost of $30 billion and an energy consumption of $20 million per day to build this kind of processing power. With its defense budget of ~$700 billion, the USA could theoretically attack Bitcoin. This will be discussed further in later chapters.

Even if an attacker was able to assemble more computing power than all honest nodes, he will likely find it more profitable to play by the rules. His choice is between defrauding people by stealing back payments or using his control to generate new coins for himself. In Satoshi's words:

> *He ought to find it more profitable to play by the rules, such rules that favor him with more new coins than everyone else combined, than to undermine the system and the validity of his own wealth.* [1]

In other words, if someone successfully attacked Bitcoin, it would simultaneously destroy the value of bitcoins (because the network is no longer secure, so nobody would want bitcoins) and the attack would be worthless. **This game-theoretic incentive is a major defense of Bitcoin against bad actors.**

Thus, **the only reasonable expectation of an attacker would consist of a group with a significant amount of wealth in a competing monetary system who would benefit from the destruction of Bitcoin.** An alternative cryptocurrency group would not attempt this if they were rational, because destroying Bitcoin would signal to the cryptocurrency market that none of the currencies are secure, given that Bitcoin is the hardest to attack. An attacker would most likely be a government with a fiat system. It would be easy to see why the US government would want to end Bitcoin as people continue to sell their dollars for it.

To round it all out, the proof-of-work algorithm is like a school test. Tests are an unproductive expense of energy as they do not produce anything of value. However, a test provides proof that you have done the work to understand the material. This protects the validity of the school by not simply graduating students who say they've read the curriculum but rather students who've spent the time and energy to prove it. Much time and energy has been spent by students to take tests that produce nothing of tangible value other than proof of their knowledge. By doing so, schools gain credibility from the performance of their graduates and feel comfortable graduating them because they have proven their knowledge.

Similarly, Bitcoin gains credibility by the security of its network. Its security is in the fact that people know with certainty there will only ever be 21 million bitcoins. The cost of mining is what makes this certain. Securing the Bitcoin network means securing a trustless, decentralized monetary medium that is not subject to moral hazard. A monetary system is the foundation of an economy, and in turn its security is of the utmost importance. In Bitcoin, the necessity of verification is made evident by the millions of mining nodes expending resources every day for it to function. Fiat money is more like a school without tests.

## Conclusion

Bitcoin is a decentralized network where nodes willingly follow the rules of the software by participating. Nodes can participate in a variety of functions and are constrained by their memory and processing power. Mining nodes provide all functions to the network and mine blocks into the blockchain. To do so they randomly guess inputs to the nonce field in order to produce a block header hash that is lower than the difficulty target. Once an answer is found, they add it to their blockchain and broadcast it to the network. Other nodes verify that it is correct, add it to their blockchains, and begin mining the next block. Miners do this because they are rewarded with newly created bitcoins and fees to do so. New bitcoins are created with each successfully mined block, increasing the total supply. The supply increases at a decreasing rate, as the rate is cut in half every 4 years. There will only ever be 21 million bitcoins by the year 2140 (under the current set of rules). Mining is an expensive process and is necessary to secure the blockchain.

The mutually agreed upon rules that dictate the processes discussed in this chapter can theoretically change. Just how they could change is the topic of the next chapter.

## References


1. *Bitcoin: A Peer-to-Peer Electronic Cash System*, Satoshi Nakamoto
2. *Information Propagation in the Bitcoin Network*, Christian Decker and Roger Wattenhofer
3. https://en.wikipedia.org/wiki/Decentralised_system#/media/File:Decentralization_diagram.svg
4. https://bitnodes.io/
5. https://tik-old.ee.ethz.ch/file/49318d3f56c1d525aabf7fda78b23fc0/P2P2013_041.pdf
6. https://www.blockchain.com/charts/difficulty
7. https://en.bitcoin.it/w/images/en/4/42/Controlled_supply-supply_over_block_height.png
8. https://explorer.btc.com/btc/insights-fees?chart=daily-fees-reward-percent
9. https://www.blockchain.com/charts/hash-rate
10. https://gobitcoin.io/tools/cost-51-attack/
11. https://www.blockchain.com/btc/block/00000000000000000008acdc94cf82ee2d6a2caebe83d359ae39be7f075016c6

# 11. THE RULES OF BITCOIN

*I completely lost everything, but I gained everything because I lost the fear* – *Kanye West*

With an understanding of what Bitcoin does and how it works we can now summarize the most salient rules that nodes of the Bitcoin network follow. Bitcoin is software, so if you want to know the rules, the best way to do that is to review the code. If you don't know how to do that, below is a summary. These rules are necessary to grasp how Bitcoin's software forms transactions, compiles them into blocks, secures the blocks into a chain, and secures a fixed supply schedule of new bitcoins. Below the rules are delineated between the transaction level and block level for ease of understanding, although some rules are not mutually exclusive and could be included in either category. Study this table briefly and move forward to understand how these rules could change.

TRANSACTION LEVEL RULES

- A Bitcoin address is derived from a private key
  - **Private keys** are generated **randomly**, and the source of randomness is critical to its security
  - The **secp256k1 elliptic** curve is used to transform **private keys to public keys**
  - **Addresses are the hash of the public-key** via both the **SHA256 and RIPEMD160** hash functions
- There are **2 types of transactions**:
  - **Peer-to-peer transactions (P2P)** – a transaction sent from one address to another. Each transactions input is the address and private key signature of the owner and the output is the address of the recipient.
  - **Coinbase transactions** – sends new bitcoins to the miner who solved the proof-of-work algorithm
    - This transaction requires no inputs and is only an output to the address of the miner
    - **Coinbase transaction** reward automatically **halves every 4 years until the year 2140** approximately
    - In 2008 it rewarded **50 Bitcoins**, as of 2021 it is **6.25 Bitcoins (~1.8% inflation)**. This is a fixed supply schedule that will likely never change (more on this later).
- P2P transactions require that **outputs are equal to or less than inputs**.
  - The difference between the input and output is an implied fee that goes to the miner who mined the block
- **ECDSA algorithm:** for an address to send bitcoins to another address, the input address must present an ECDSA signature that can be used to verify knowledge of the private key
- Transactions propagate across the network through a **gossip protocol** – nodes only relay transactions that they haven't already heard of and pass the verification process

Figure 92 (1): salient transaction level rules present in the bitcoin code (block and transaction level categories are not necessarily mutually exclusive)

BLOCK LEVEL RULES

- When a node hears a transaction that is valid, it adds it to its **memory pool** – its temporary copy of transactions to soon be added to the block chain
- Differences between nodes over memory pool and blockchain copies are resolved by following the **longest chain rule**
- There is a **block size limit of 4 megabytes** as of 2017.
    - This determines the number of transactions that can be included in each block and thus how many transactions per second the network can process
    - It was originally 1 megabyte, but the Bitcoin community decided to change this (more on this later)
- Transactions are hashed and structured into a **Merkle Tree**
- The **Merkle Root** is a hash that includes all transactions of the **Merkle Tree** and is included in the **Block Header**
- The **Block Header** includes a **link to the previous block** which chains all blocks together, forming a blockchain
- For a block of transactions to be published to the block chain, a **mining node needs to solve the proof-of-work (PoW) algorithm**
    - The PoW algorithm requires producing a hash (random number) that is less than the difficulty target
- **Bitcoin's are created every 10 minutes on average** via the **difficulty target**.
    - The difficulty target **increases/decreases every 2 weeks** so that miners average solving the PoW algorithm every 10 minutes
- Miner's are rewarded for solving the PoW algorithm via the **Block Reward** which includes the **coinbase transaction** and **transaction fees**
- **There will be a maximum of 21 million bitcoins by the year 2140**

Figure 92 (2): salient block level rules present in the bitcoin code (block and transaction level categories are not necessarily mutually exclusive)

These rules exist from **consensus as network participants willingly accept them**. Participants accept them by downloading the Bitcoin software and utilizing it. However, Bitcoin exists not just by achieving consensus about the rules (code) but also by achieving consensus about its **history** and the **value** of the coins.

## Consensus

The writers of Bitcoin and Cryptocurrency Technologies[1] summarize this concept well:

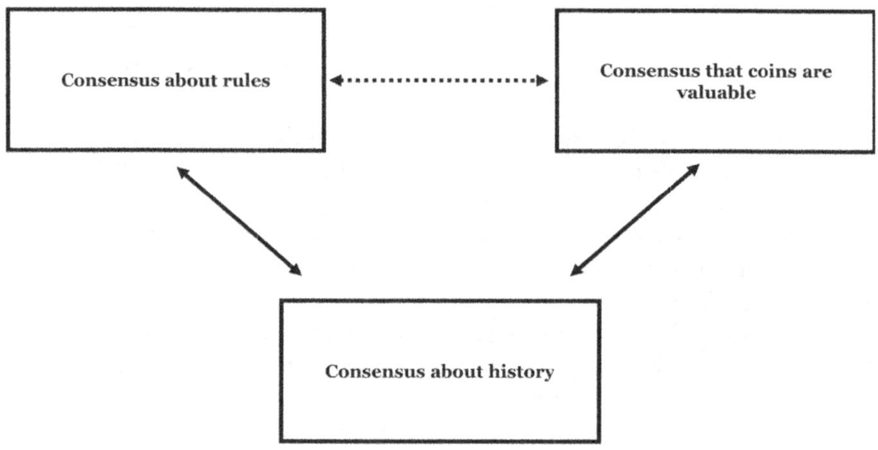


**Figure 93:** the relationship of consensus among rules, history, and value of bitcoin

1. **Consensus about the rules** – the rules listed above are agreed upon by the network participants willingly accepting them. They accept them by using the Bitcoin software, which they can change if they wish. However, if they do change it, they may not be able to interact with the network. Consensus about these things allows different participants in the systems to communicate and agree on what is happening.
2. **Consensus about history** – history, meaning what is and is

not included in the blockchain or, more specifically, which transactions have occurred. The result being consensus about the UTXO list (what bitcoins exist at what addresses).

3. **Consensus about value** – people need to agree that bitcoins are valuable. This was a challenge when the Bitcoin network was originally bootstrapped, but as it has grown, the network effect has created a self-fulfilling prophecy of its value.

Let us compare this to fiat currency. A fiat currency only requires consensus on value but only partially because it was coerced upon us as legal tender for taxes. The history and rules are determined by agents who control the fiat currency. **Rules do not emerge by consensus but by decree** (the definition of the word fiat). We do not vote on our monetary policy. Rather, monetary policy is influenced by politicians and controlled by these people:

**Figure 94:** the Federal Reserve Board of Governors April meeting 2019

Their decisions affect the livelihood of each citizen more so than decisions made by anybody within government, and yet their decision-making is centralized and outside of our democracy.

***Bitcoin forces its participants to achieve consensus about its rules, its history, and its value while fiat currency partially requires consensus on its value – all else is by decree.***

Bitcoin's different forms of consensus have a circular interplay, which is illustrated as follows:

- Some people believe bitcoins have value because they have fundamental monetary properties that make it the world's best savings technology (or at least it will be once its acceptability is wide enough).
- That drives them to speculate on its price by buying it and holding it through ups and downs. They hold it through the downs because they understand its monetary properties.
- This brings in more speculators who want it to go up, further driving up the price. As the price increases, mining bitcoin becomes more profitable, attracting more miners.
- These miners add more computing power, increasing the number of hashes per second that can be calculated to solve the proof-of-work algorithm, causing solutions to be found more quickly (i.e., in less than 10 minutes).
- Bitcoin's rules then require the difficulty level to increase so that miners find a solution every 10 minutes.
- Through this process, more and more miners keep coming to the network to earn bitcoins, and it continues to get harder and harder to do so. Some less profitable miners drop out, but the net effect is an increase in overall hashing power.
- This continuously expands the size of the network, increasing its computing power and security so that it cannot be 51% attacked.

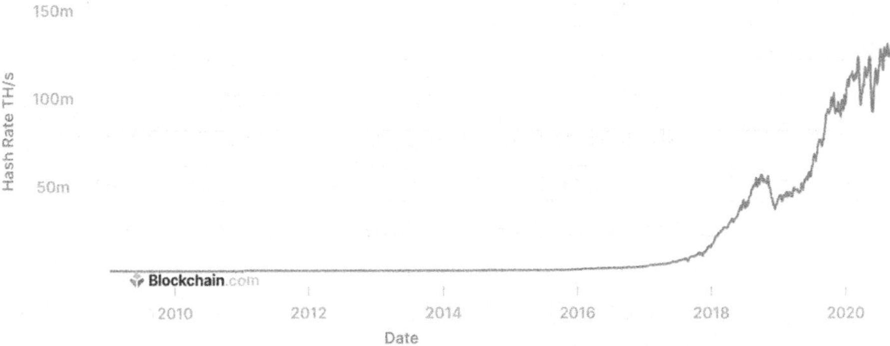


**Figure 95:** total network hash rate since 2009 (Image source blockchain.com)[2]

- This increase in security ensures that consensus about the rules and history is more secure than before.
- In turn, the value of bitcoin increases and the cycle repeats.

To summarize, speculative price increases attract more miners, expanding the computing power of the network, and making the network more secure and more valuable. This further increases the price over time. **As the bitcoin price rises, it creates a positive feedback loop** in which participants believe it will continue to rise. That is the power of a network effect when applied to a standard of value. Aside from the network effect, there are fundamental monetary properties that drive bitcoin's adoption by those who understand them. Without these properties, people would not have speculated on bitcoin in the first place. The monetary properties of bitcoin will be covered in the next chapter.

This structure of incentives did not happen by chance, but was the result of clever design by Bitcoin's creators. They had to initially bootstrap the network for this dynamic to begin playing out at scale. This process formed a community of people who evangelized bitcoin and used it where they could. Once it took hold, all the pieces were in place for the community to drive it forward.

***The achievement of consensus across each dimension creates a positive feedback loop, generating a strong network effect, increasing the value of bitcoin.***

The Bitcoin of today is different from what it once was. Along the way, there have been updates and changes to the software. The changes emerged by achieving consensus among the community.

## How the Rules Can Change

The Bitcoin software is called **Bitcoin Core**, which can be downloaded bitcoin.org. This is the most widely used Bitcoin software, but there are other versions of Bitcoin software. The other versions must maintain a minimum level of similarity with Bitcoin Core to participate in the Bitcoin network. **This minimum level is that a node needs to check for the validity of transactions and blocks in the same way as other nodes**. If it does not, the transactions/blocks it creates and relays will likely not be accepted by other nodes and vice versa. Bitcoin Core is the standard of these rules and thus the de facto rulebook of Bitcoin.

Bitcoin Core can change by **Bitcoin Improvement Proposals (BIPs)**. A BIP is a formal proposal to change something, how to do it, and the rationale for doing so. Each BIP is ordered and submitted by number – you can see the full list of BIPS at github.com.[3] Each one of those has an author who creates it and, whether through himself or a group, evangelizes in favor of it. The community then discusses it, and if consensus is achieved, Bitcoin

Core will be changed. This does not mean the nodes (users) will choose to download Bitcoin Core, but it is the default software most use.

Agreed upon changes are implemented by Bitcoin Core developers. Bitcoin Core developers have "commit" access to the Bitcoin Core software. Anyone can propose any change, but whether it is implemented into the software is determined by those with commit access. This access can only be given by someone that already has rights to it. Satoshi Nakamoto was the initial creator of Bitcoin, and once he left the project, Gavin Andresen, who had access, took over.

How powerful are the developers? Any change they make can be implemented in Bitcoin Core and followed by default. However, if the community does not like what they are doing, it can always go in another direction – this is called a **fork**. There are **hard forks** and **soft forks** – soft forks are backwards compatible, while hard forks are not. Since hard forks are not backwards compatible, they require a split in the blockchain. This means that some miners accept the rules, while other miners leave to start a new blockchain.

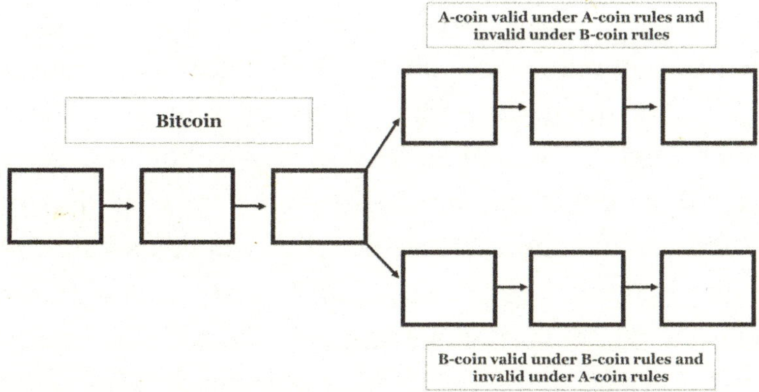


**Figure 96:** illustrative example of a hard fork splitting into 2 separate blockchains that follow new rules

When a fork occurs, all owners of the bitcoin would also own an equivalent amount of the new forked coin. They can either hold both currencies, sell their bitcoin for the new currency, or sell their new currency for more bitcoin. Both coins will have separate networks and rules. The goal for the new forked coin is to eclipse the network of Bitcoin. Bitcoin has yet to be eclipsed by a forked network.

***To change the rules requires consensus. If consensus is not achieved within the community, the network will fork creating a new network with different rules.***

The most prominent example of a Bitcoin hard fork resulted in the creation of Bitcoin Cash. It started in late 2015 with a BIP (Bitcoin Improvement Proposal) by Peter Wuille known as **SegWit** (segregated witness), which effectively increased the block size limit from 1mb to 2mb. The goal of SegWit was to reduce the size of each bitcoin transaction, allowing more transactions to take place at once, increasing the throughput of the network. This BIP was a soft fork as it was backwards compatible (nodes did not have to adopt the update to continue functioning on the network). However, in response to SegWit, a hard fork was implemented by community members which created the coin Bitcoin Cash. SegWit stored more transactions by reducing their sizes in the block, effectively allowing 2mb of transaction storage, so as to not cause a hard fork. Bitcoin Cash supporters wanted to increase the block size beyond this amount and believed a hard fork was necessary to do so. SegWit was a soft fork solution to transaction throughput, while increasing the block size was the hard fork solution that other community members wanted.

When the hard fork occurred, each bitcoin holder received an equivalent amount of Bitcoin Cash. At this point, everyone was a holder of both coins and could either hold both or sell 1 for the other. This is how network participants can democratically and economically vote. If a majority sold their bitcoin for Bitcoin Cash, this would have made mining Bitcoin Cash much more profitable, attracting more miners, and growing the network.

However, since then the price of bitcoin has grown significantly, and Bitcoin Cash has remained relatively flat. Technologically, Bitcoin Cash is superior to Bitcoin, but Bitcoin has a much larger network, and competing with its network effect has yet to be successful. **In fact, a primary value proposition of Bitcoin is that it is so hard to get the community to agree on any changes.** This provides more certainty that Bitcoin will not change. Since Bitcoin Cash forked, it has forked thrice more creating BSV (Bitcoin Satoshi's Vision), BCHN (Bitcoin Cash Node), and BCHABC (Bitcoin Cash ABC).

In Bitcoin's 12-year history, the nodes that chose to own and operate in bitcoin have received materially more value than any competing network. Many altcoins you see today were created through forks. This is a natural process of disagreement between network participants. How this phenomenon is likely to end, I cover in my final chapter.

***In its 12 years of existence, Bitcoin has continued to expand its network at a faster pace than any forked alternative currency.***

## Stakeholders

There is a strong interplay that exists between the stakeholder groups of Bitcoin. Each depends on the other to serve a function.

| Stakeholder | Function | Consensus Control | Influence |
| --- | --- | --- | --- |
| **Developers / Community** | Gatekeepers of the rulebook (code) that most nodes use | Control consensus about the rules | They can stop updating Bitcoin:<br><br>Proposed changes cannot be implemented without the developers, which could prevent necessary changes from occurring |
| **Miners** | Determine control what transactions are included in the history of Bitcoin | Control consensus about history | They can stop mining:<br><br>What the miners choose to mine determines which network is secure and thus valuable |
| **Investors** | Buy and hold bitcoin through ups and downs | Control consensus about value | They can sell Bitcoin:<br><br>Influences community decisions on the developers<br><br>Makes mining bitcoin unprofitable |

**Figure 97:** the stakeholders of the bitcoin network

You can see that each group has a form of power, but none have full control. Think of this like an **intransitive structure,** which is analogous to the game of rock/paper/scissors.

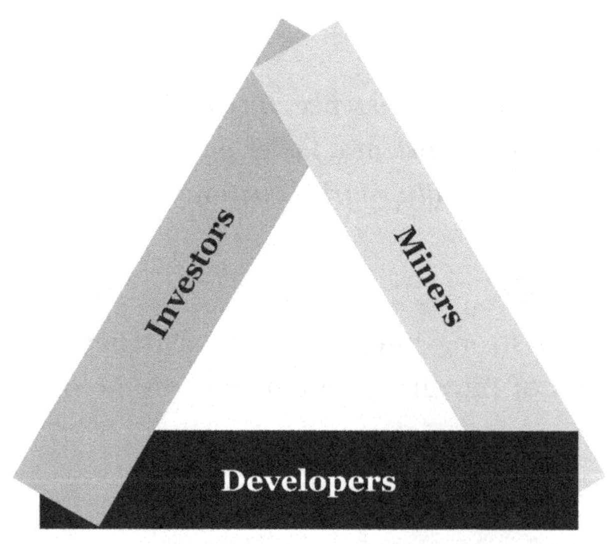


**Figure 98:** the intransitive structure of Bitcoin's stakeholder groups

The developers control the code that the miners use. The miners control network computing power that the investors desire. The investors influence the community that the developers need to download their software.

However, it is not quite this simple. Investors also have power over the miners, developers have power over the investors, and miners have power over the developers. Further, **these groups are not mutually exclusive**. The point is that these primary stakeholder groups all need each other in some form and there is a balance of power that exists as a result. **If something is to change in Bitcoin, then consensus needs to be achieved across these 3 groups for it to occur.**

An important point to reiterate is that the developer group is materially smaller than the others. There are many investors and many miners but only a handful of developers. However, the developer group is enabled by a development community. Bitcoin is open-source software so anyone can submit a proposal to change Bitcoin and evangelize it to the community. There are many developers out there without commit access working to support Bitcoin for a variety of reasons. Think of the developers as the community, with the smaller group that has commit access as the gatekeepers.

***The Bitcoin rules are created by the community and implemented by developers with commit access. Both must agree for a rule to change.***

What if somebody attempted to control this small group of developers with commit access? Well, they have the power to make new software for the community to willingly download but cannot make them download it. Further, all changes to the software are reviewed by community members because it is open source – any changes are quickly identified. Thus, if the government interrogated this group and forced them to tamper with the software, it would be quickly known in the community that something was wrong.

Could the government take over those with commit access and control any new updates to Bitcoin? No. If something like this happened, thousands of nodes could use their own copy of the software and select a new group of developers to control it for the community. The community would simply start taking software updates from this new group. The community is really in control here.

***The developer group could be replaced in a crisis.***

What about the merchants that accept bitcoin? Don't they have influence? Well, at the start of Bitcoin the answer was yes, but today not so much. Bitcoin can exist without their adoption. Bitcoin does not need to be used for payments if it is effectively storing value. The reasoning behind this will be covered in the next chapter. Bitcoin is peer-to-peer and does not require merchants to function as a value transfer system.

## Conclusion

The rules of Bitcoin are its software. Bitcoin Core is the most commonly used software and the de facto rulebook of Bitcoin. Changing this rulebook requires consensus across all 3 stakeholder groups. Each stakeholder group has some form of power and lacks other forms, creating an interdependence that demands consensus. If consensus is not achieved, the dissenters have to fork a new network to play by their new rules. The necessity of consensus to enact change is a primary value of Bitcoin, as it creates certainty that Bitcoin will not easily change.

Our current financial system is controlled by a highly centralized group. You have a choice of whether you want to abide by the democracy of the Bitcoin system or the continuously changing rules of the present fiat system. As more people adopt the Bitcoin system, this decision will become much easier. However, this adoption will require significant development of the current ecosystem that supports it, the topic of the next chapter.

## References

1. *Bitcoin and Cryptocurrency Technologies,* Arvind Narayanan, Joseph Bonneau, Edward Felten, Andrew Miller, Steven Goldfeder, 195
2. https://www.blockchain.com/charts/hash-rate
3. https://github.com/bitcoin/bips/blob/master/README.mediawiki

# 12. THE BITCOIN ECOSYSTEM

*I am not a fan of books.* – *Kanye West*

Bitcoin's software leverages a decentralized network to make peer-to-peer transactions. This functionality allows it to act as **a base monetary layer for a new financial system**. Bitcoin can exist on its own but requires an ecosystem of enabling products and services to replace our current financial system. This ecosystem is necessary for further mainstream adoption because it impacts the ease with which Bitcoin can be used. Bitcoin cannot yet function as an alternative financial base layer to the USD. Bitcoin still needs to develop the variety of financial services that support our current banking system.

To understand the key aspects of this ecosystem, let's walk through the graphic below step by step. After that we will discuss how the regulatory environment can impact this ecosystem.

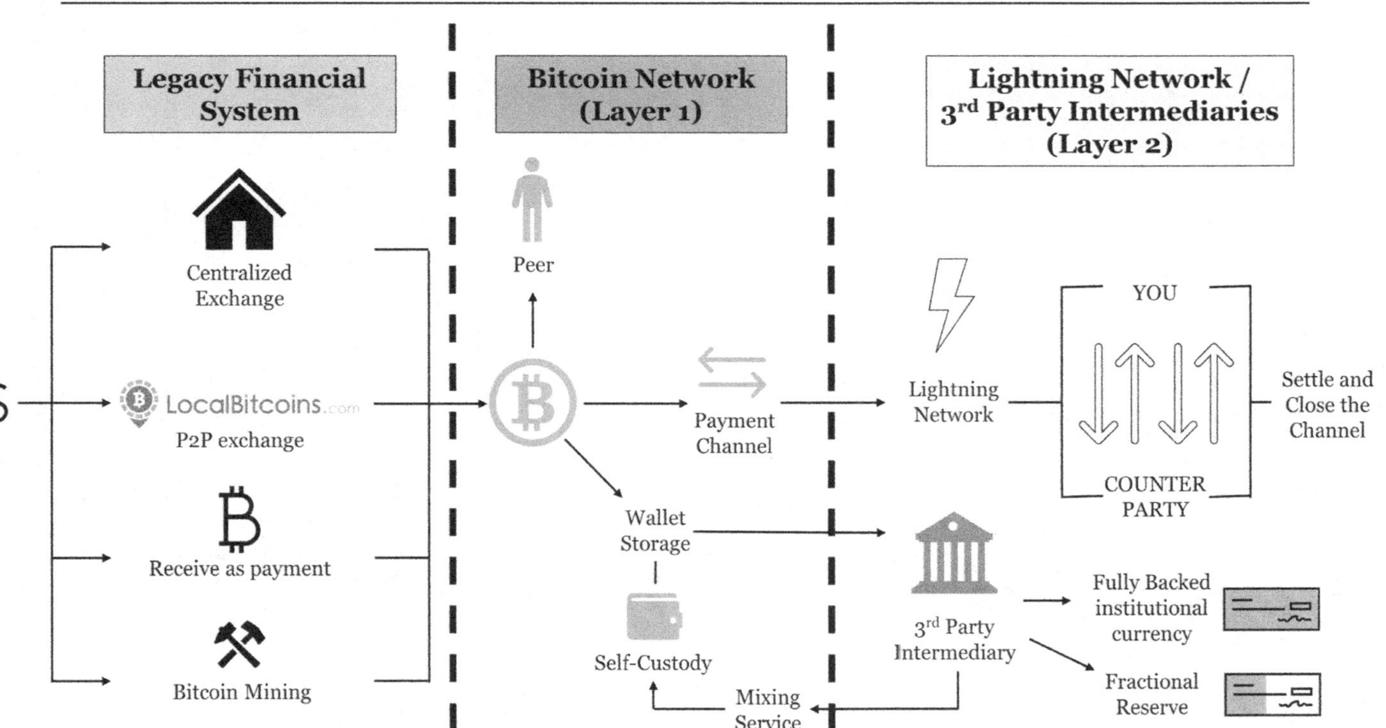


Figure 99: the ecosystem of Bitcoin

## Legacy Financial System

The first element is the link between the legacy financial system and Bitcoin. This link allows people to trade fiat currency for bitcoin through 4 primary avenues:

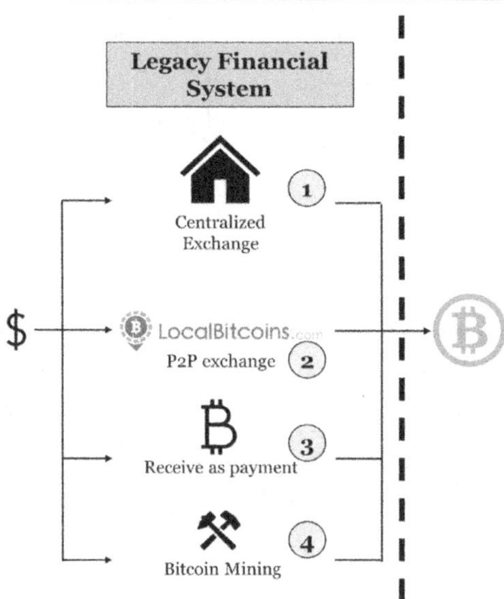


**Figure 100:** onramps from the legacy financial system into bitcoin

1. **Centralized exchanges** – online exchange of fiat currency for cryptocurrency. It is centralized because it is a company with a CEO that is regulated by its local government. Good examples are the companies Binance and Coinbase.
2. **P2P exchanges** – localbitcoins.com is an online exchange where you can convert your fiat to bitcoin directly with your peers, like Craigslist.
3. **Receive as payment** – as bitcoin adoption has grown, more people are willing to pay for goods and services in bitcoin. If you can find someone willing to pay you in bitcoin, this is

another way to accumulate it. If a government attempted to shut down centralized and P2P exchanges, then bitcoin could still be earned this way.

4. **Bitcoin Mining** – exchanging your fiat currency for a specialized mining computer and paying for the energy it consumes is another way to obtain bitcoin. Mining has become very specialized, with expensive computers and equipment in order to do it economically. There are large-scale mining companies that are making mining highly competitive. While an individual can do it economically, it is a time-consuming process. Your investment in time, energy, and equipment is likely better spent by just buying bitcoin directly. However, if exchanges are attacked, then computers can still earn you bitcoin.

These are the primary **on-ramps** to Bitcoin, and their creation has significantly increased its adoption. **They allow individuals to move out of our legacy financial system and into the new digital financial system.** If the on-ramps went away tomorrow, Bitcoin would remain a peer-to-peer system where people can pay each other for goods and services in bitcoins. Such an event would stifle Bitcoin's growth but not eliminate it. It's possible it could even benefit Bitcoin. The removal of exchanges from the equation would incentivize new groups to become miners and earn bitcoin as payment. This would further decentralize its adoption and security, strengthening its network in the long run.

In the words of the great prophet Kanye West, "*N-Now th-that that don't kill me, can only make me stronger.*"

***There are 4 primary ways of converting your fiat money into bitcoin. If exchanges are ever banned by governments, you can still earn it through mining or as payment.***

## The Bitcoin Network (Layer 1)

Once you have bitcoins, you are now a participant in the Bitcoin Network, and there are a variety of different things you can do with them. The Bitcoin network is referred to as "layer 1" because it is to act as the base monetary layer that other products and services (layer 2) can be built on top of.

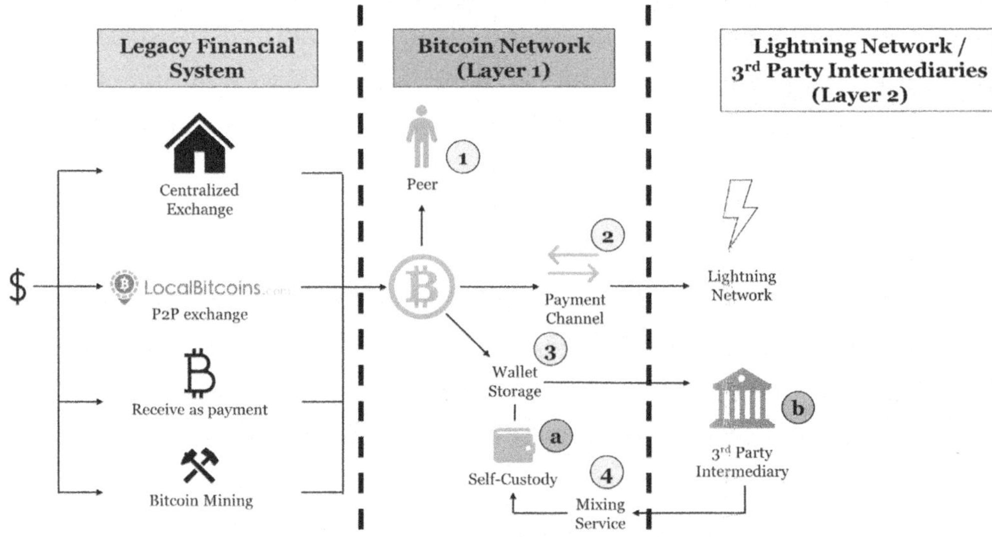


**Figure 101:** the Bitcoin Network (layer 1) and its interaction with layer 2 to systems

1. **You can send bitcoin to a peer in exchange for something.** This is the fundamental purpose of bitcoin. However, peer-to-peer transactions have become more and more expensive due to fees. While these fees are negligible for high value transactions like buying a car from a friend, they would be too expensive for splitting your $4 coffee shop bill. Small value payments will need to be supported by intermediaries and protocols, the topic of the next section.

2. **You can lock your bitcoins into a payment channel.** This allows you to post your bitcoins as collateral into a system that is outside the Bitcoin network. The details of these secondary (layer 2) systems will be explained later.
3. **You can store bitcoin in a wallet.** As an investor/saver of bitcoin, you may want to hold onto them yourself. There are 2 primary ways to do this but only 1 way without using an intermediary.
    a. **Self-Custody** – means holding your bitcoins yourself by using some form of wallet software. To do this properly you need to educate yourself so that you have a sophisticated process for doing so, especially if you have a material portion of your wealth in bitcoin. There are 2 primary ways of storing these that trade security for complexity:
        - **Hot Wallet** – downloading wallet software to your computer and keeping your bitcoin on it. The most standard form of this would be the Bitcoin Core software, but there are many service providers, such as Exodus. Some wallet services are better than others. Bitcoin Core is the best option for security, but its user experience is more complicated than others. These are called hot wallets because your computer is connected to the internet and is still susceptible to being hacked. If your computer can be hacked, then your private keys could be stolen and thus your bitcoin.
        - **Cold Wallet** – this is analogous to storing your bitcoins on a USB drive so they are not connected to the internet. Since it is not connected, no one can steal your bitcoins unless your computer is hacked before putting them on the USB drive. Companies like Trezor and Ledger make hard-

ware for this purpose. The idea is you put your private keys on one of those devices, put them in a waterproof case and throw that inside a fireproof safe. If nobody took your private keys before that process, nobody will ever be able to find them without physically stealing the hardware from you, which is also password protected. This is the least convenient and most secure form of storage.

b. **3rd Party Custody** – this option allows a 3rd party intermediary to control your funds for you. The most popular option for this type of custody is a web wallet, but institutions are beginning to emerge that provide sophisticated custodial services as well.

- **Web Wallet** – you can simply leave your bitcoins on the exchange you bought them from, which means you are dependent on that service provider's ability to keep them safe. If they are hacked and your private key is stolen, then they are gone forever. Many exchanges have cyber theft insurance, but why take the risk if you don't have to? This is the most convenient option with the least control and security.
- **Institutional Custody** – institutions are emerging that can store bitcoins safely for the long term. However, by giving your bitcoins to an institution, you are doing 2 things: (1) giving up your control (trust) and (2) centralizing control of the Bitcoin network. If everyone kept their bitcoins at institutions, then the government would have a small group to attack for confiscation. If you think this is not likely, recall the confiscation of gold during the Great Depression. As people flee

the fiat system for bitcoin, it is a likely risk. Of course, everyone has a tradeoff of convenience and security. It is up to the individual to make this decision for themselves.

- **Multi-signature addresses** – service providers are emerging for institutions that store bitcoins using **multi-sig**. These are addresses in Bitcoin you can create that require 2 of 3 private keys (or 3 of 5, 5 of 7, etc.) to unlock and send bitcoins, which removes a single point of failure if a key is stolen, increasing your security. A popular application that could emerge would be joint accounts – where the bitcoins are sent to a 2-of-3 address, 2 family members each hold 1 key, and a 3rd party holds the last key in case someone loses theirs. This increases security and allows you and your partner to spend bitcoins when you want without giving up custody to the provider who only has 1 key.

4. **Send bitcoin through a mixing service** – a key criticism of Bitcoin is that its blockchain is public. Bitcoin is pseudonymous, not anonymous. If someone can link your identity to your Bitcoin address, then there is a lot they could learn about your financial position. Effectively, you lose your privacy for all transactions – past, present, and future – associated with that address. This is not about hiding illegal activities but is a practical matter of everyday life. People do not want their wealth to be public and companies do not want their competitors to know who they are paying for goods and services. For example, if you run a company and send a payment of bitcoins for a large purchase from a supplier (who might be a peripheral competitor), they can link that address to your identity and follow all the transactions you

have made. Mixing services are a way to mix up transactions with other groups of transactions and send them out to new addresses like so:

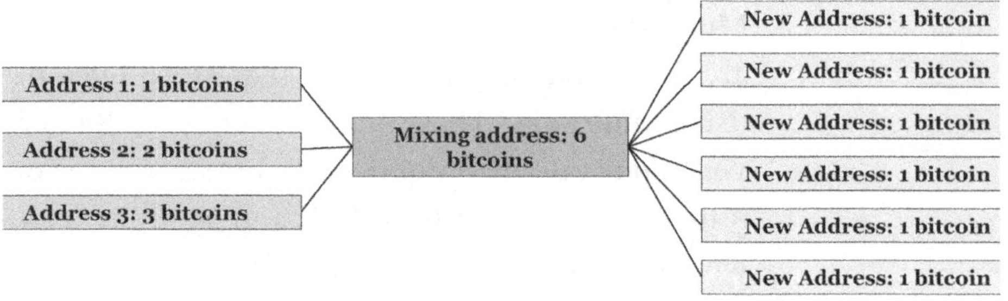


**Figure 102:** illustrative example of the mixing process

Anyone following this group of transactions can see what went in but does not know where it came out. This removes the link from your former Bitcoin address to the new one, as anyone looking at the blockchain will not be able to see which bitcoin was yours. However, you need to trust the mixing service provider and these types of services could become illegal. **There are also decentralized P2P protocols for mixing and even an alt-coin, Zcash, that provides the option to send anonymous transactions.** How does it do this when public verification is a requirement to send transactions on a blockchain? It uses something called zero-knowledge proofs, a powerful technology that is beyond the scope of this writing. In summary, privacy is a disadvantage unique to Bitcoin that layer 2 intermediaries will likely need to assist with. However, other layer 2 solutions, like the Lightning network, could also enable privacy.

***You can store bitcoins or spend bitcoins. 3rd Party intermediaries provide beneficial services that require a trade of trust for utility and convenience.***

## The Lightning Network / 3rd Party Intermediaries (Layer 2)

How bitcoin would be used to perform small transactions was a primary topic of debate in the early years of Bitcoin. The overarching vision was that banks would be needed as intermediaries to facilitate this function. A quote from one of the original Bitcoin contributors, Hal Finney, explains this well:

> *Actually there is a very good reason for bitcoin-backed banks to exist, issuing their own digital cash currency, redeemable for bitcoins. Bitcoin itself cannot scale to have every single financial transaction in the world be broadcast to everyone and included in the block chain. There needs to be a secondary level of payment systems which is lighter weight and more efficient. Likewise, the time needed for bitcoin transactions to finalize will be impractical for medium to large value purchases.*
>
> *Bitcoin backed banks will solve these problems. They can work like banks did before nationalization of currency. Different banks can have different policies, some more aggressive, some more conservative. Some would be fractional reserve while others may be 100% bitcoin backed. Interest rates may vary. Cash from some banks may trade at a discount to that from others.*
>
> *George Selgin has worked out the theory of competitive free banking in detail, and he argues that such a system would be stable, inflation resistant and self-regulating.*
>
> *I believe this will be the ultimate fate of bitcoin, to be the "high-powered money" that serves as a reserve currency for banks that issue their own digital cash. Most bitcoin transactions will occur between banks, to settle net transfers. Bitcoin transactions by private individuals will be as rare as... well, as bitcoin based purchases are today.* [1]

**Cash vs. Credit:** the difference between cash and credit is that cash is the physical settlement of money while credit is a promise to do so. As we have seen, paper cash is no longer backed by something with strong monetary properties and has itself become credit. For this discussion I refer to cash in its original meaning – the physical settlement of money. Cash payments do not require trust because the cash received has monetary value. Credit systems require trust, as they are promises that cash will be provided in the future (trading trust for efficiency). For example, when you send a payment on Venmo, the company updates its accounts to reduce the value in your account and add it to somebody else's. There is no cash changing hands internally at Venmo, they simply change the number in their computer. What matters to Venmo is when you send the payment to your bank account, because they must physically send cash from their accounts to your bank account (which settles in 1 to 3 days). Venmo is a credit system built on top of the banking system that provides ease of payments. Visa, Paypal, CashApp, etc. do the same thing. Venmo is quick for credit transactions but slow for cash transactions.

Bitcoin is a cash system that provides physical settlement of your bitcoins (it is all digital but economically the same as physical settlement in our current system). Note that this is the key innovation of Bitcoin; you cannot use the term physical settlement for its physical properties have been replicated in a digital system. The point is that the money is in your account, as opposed to a promise that it will be.

Comparing a cash system to a credit system is comparing apples to oranges – like when people compare Bitcoin to Visa. The Bitcoin network can handle a maximum of ~10 transactions per second while Visa can do ~1,700. All this tells us is a credit system is faster than a cash system. A proper comparison for Bitcoin would be our cash settlement banking system, which takes multiple days to process a transaction while Bitcoin takes 10 minutes. Likewise, comparing a credit system **built on top of Bitcoin** to Visa would be fair.

Systems built on top of bitcoin, meaning bitcoin is the underlying asset (collateral), are **layer 2 systems**. These systems are either intermediaries and/or applications that interact with the Bitcoin network. Analogously, Instagram has apps and service providers like Boomerang that interact with its network to provide additional functionality that Instagram itself does not provide. There are a variety of applications that exist in this partition of the ecosystem, but we will focus on the **Lightning network** and **3rd party intermediaries**.

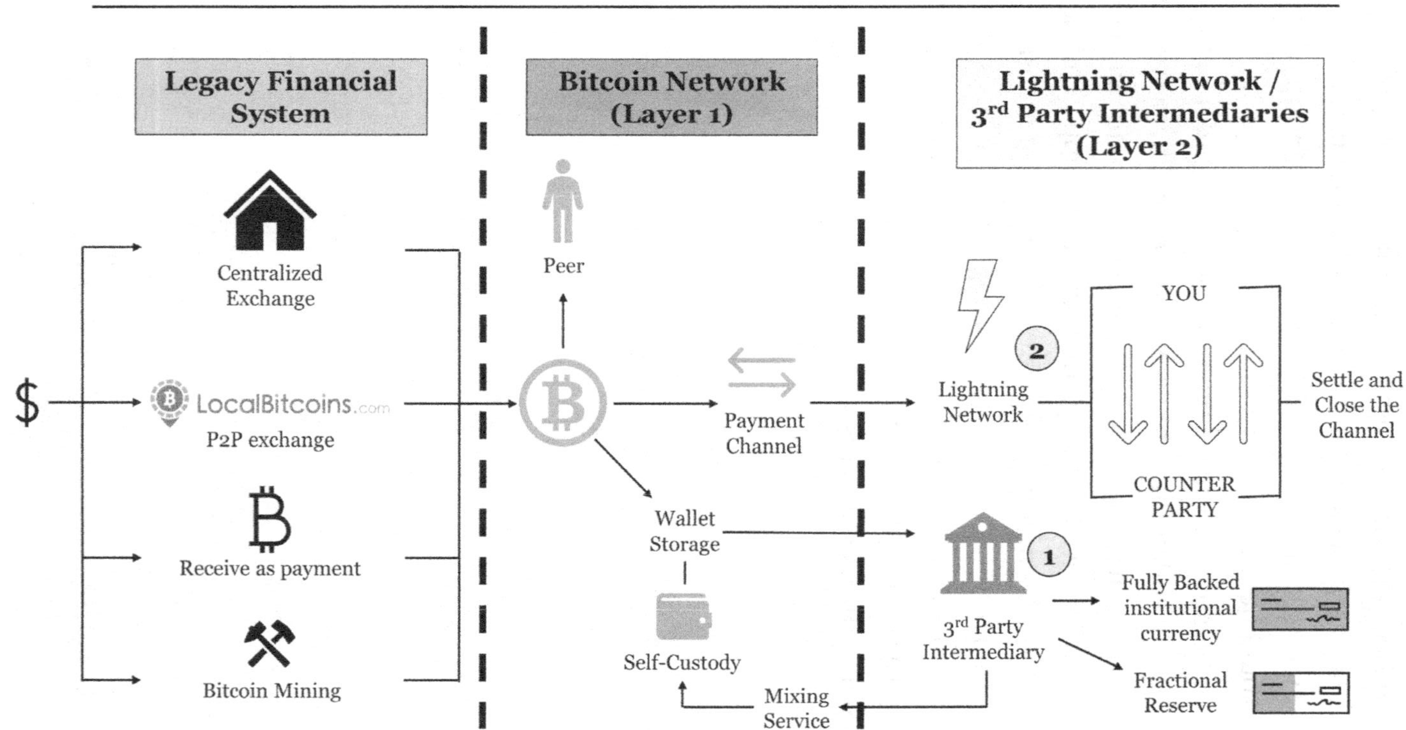


**Figure 103:** illustration of layer 2 systems including 3rd party intermediaries and the Lightning Network

1. **3rd Party Intermediaries** – Hal Finny's vision for payments. Operating in a competitive environment, 3rd party intermediaries (banks based upon bitcoin) can maintain full or fractional reserves and issue their own tradeable money on top of it. This would allow the market to decide and trade with whichever bank they are most confident in. Fractional reserve systems are not inherently evil, they just require a competitive environment and information transparency (not our nationalized currency and centralized banking system). When paired with a decentralized currency like bitcoin, people always have the option to hold bitcoins instead of bank credit (an option we do not have today for practical purposes). **Banks will have to compete with the invention of public blockchains; everyone in the world would be able to see precisely how much bitcoin they have in their reserves.** However, the total liabilities of a bank will still need to be presented and audited as the liabilities will not exist on the blockchain.
    a. These intermediaries will need to provide a variety of functions other than just payments. All the financial services that exist in our current system will need to be replicated in the bitcoin digital system, the details of which are beyond the scope of this writing. What is important is that **it will take time for the intermediaries to emerge, and until they do the legacy system will remain more desirable from a practical perspective.**
2. **The Lightning Network** – A decentralized alternative to Hal's vision and one that is currently being built. It is a layer 2 protocol that requires a degree of trust but will enable micro-transactions. Think of it as a decentralized credit system that is fully collateralized in bitcoin. It is based on the concept of **payment channels** in which bitcoins from 2 parties are sent to an address with a timer, meaning the bitcoins will be re-

turned once time is up. Within this time, the transaction can be repeatedly updated and the parties have the option to agree on extending the time period if they wish. By repeatedly updating, the transaction before broadcasting it on the Bitcoin network, the two parties can continually renegotiate how much of the funds one gives to the other party. This is economically equivalent to sending as many micro transactions as both parties wish, and faster than Visa transaction throughput. When both parties agree to close the channels, the final state of the payment channel balance can be broadcast to the Bitcoin network. So if you have 10 bitcoins, you can lock 1 into a payment channel and use lightning to pay for all of your minor, day-to-day transactions (if the merchants also have payment channels). The primary benefits of the lightning network are

a. **Scaling:** It reduces the number of transactions that need to be done on the Bitcoin network by moving them to the Lightning network.
b. **Fully collateralized transactions:** Because Lightning Network transactions are fully collateralized by code, this is remarkably similar to a cash system and is faster than any existing credit system.
c. **Privacy:** Transactions on lightning are not recorded on the blockchain and utilize onion routing. Meaning, **the privacy issues of bitcoin are materially reduced on Lightning.**

The Lightning Network is still in development and is not perfect. Its technical challenges are beyond the scope of this book, but it is worth digging into. What is important is that this is a viable option for a secondary payments layer, and even if it fails, 3rd party intermediaries could pick up the slack. However, there is a major hindrance to its adoption – taxation.

***3rd party intermediaries and layer 2 protocols will need to replicate the financial services of the traditional financial system into the new digital system.***

## Regulation

The regulatory environment of Bitcoin and its future is arguably the most controversial topic in the space. The moment I understood the capabilities of Bitcoin, my first thought was it was going to cause a financial war with incumbent institutions. However, as I have learned, I think there is a strong alternative argument for peaceful embracing of this emerging new financial system.

Currently the regulatory environment is a gray area under development. I will not dig deep into the specifics, as they will likely be far different soon after this writing is published. The goal here is to provide a framework for assessing this environment as it develops, starting with a quick overview of where we are at now.

Bitcoin is a new technology that does not fit neatly into any single regulatory category. Our current regulatory system was designed to regulate things as they were: money, property, commodities, securities, etc. Bitcoin, a decentralized P2P transaction technology, is the first of its kind. It exists as a confluence of multiple technologies and does not fit neatly into this framework. The result is that different regulatory bodies are defining it in different ways and often contradicting themselves. Bitcoin currently falls under the purview of the below regulatory bodies:

| Regulatory Body | Relevant Laws | Categorization of Bitcoin | Implications |
|---|---|---|---|
| **FinCEN** | Bank Secrecy Act – laws apply to "money transmitters" Anti Money Laundering (AML) | Bitcoin is a P2P network – not a money transmitter because it has no operator | FinCEN applies the law to participants in the Bitcoin ecosystem but cannot apply it to Bitcoin itself |
| **IRS** | Taxation | Property | Taxed as a capital asset – under this tax structure, using bitcoin or a derivative cryptocurrency product for payments is not feasible (every payment is a taxable event) |
| **CFTC** | Commodities Exchange Act (CEA) | Commodity | Regulations of the derivatives markets supporting bitcoin are to be regulated by this group |
| **OCC (part of FinCEN)** | Regulates national banks and thrifts | NA | Currently allows banks to act as a node on a decentralized network |

| Regulatory Body | Relevant Laws | Categorization of Bitcoin | Implications |
|---|---|---|---|
| SEC | Securities law | Money – Bitcoin is money and not a security | Security products tied to bitcoin will be regulated. Other crypto-currencies are determined to be securities on a case-by-case basis. |
| FINRA (overseen by SEC) | Know Your Customer (KYC) | Bitcoin businesses are subject to KYC compliance | 3rd parties that hold crypto-currency are subject to custody rules |
| CFPB | EFTA and consumer complaints | Bitcoin businesses may qualify as "financial institutions" | Notifies consumers of the risks of crypto-currencies |

**Figure 104:** relevant regulatory bodies of Bitcoin

There are a few points to note in the table:

1. Bitcoin, by its nature, is subject to a swath of regulatory bodies as it falls into a variety of categories in the legacy system's regulatory framework.
2. The IRS says bitcoin is property, CFTC says it is a commodity, and the SEC says its money. Coordination will be necessary among regulatory bodies to make any meaningful progress.
3. FinCEN realizes that Bitcoin itself cannot be regulated and thus focuses on regulating its enabling technologies/businesses in the ecosystem. I think this trend will continue as

regulators understand Bitcoin does not have a CEO. They will turn to participants in the ecosystem to exert force. Understand that Bitcoin can still exist without the ecosystem, although it would be materially hindered without it. As a last resort, regulators could attempt to attack the network itself. All the ways Bitcoin can theoretically be attacked will be discussed in the final chapter.

4. The IRS taxes bitcoin and other cryptocurrencies as property, and until that changes, payment technologies like Lightning will not be feasible. I think it is likely to change due to competition in the global economy. (More on this later.) Further, the IRS does not have a way of tracking individuals for taxes as it relies on compliance from the individuals themselves – this is not a sustainable way for the IRS to audit.
5. Regulations are materially hindering innovation in the space: *"Two of the best capitalized bitcoin businesses, Coinbase and Circle, report that it cost each company roughly $2 million in fees and compliance exercises and several years to attain license from only 25 US states"* [2]
6. Some aspects of bitcoin simply do not have a category in the current framework: *"It is not clear how the "maintaining custody or control" clause affects multisignature transactions wherein a bitcoin service might only control one of multiple private keys on behalf of a customer"* [2]

The current regulatory framework is inadequate, lacks continuity, and is slow to adopt change. This is not to bash regulators – their task is not easy– but to acknowledge the challenge that it is going to require some overarching group to take the lead. Many companies have had to move forward without guidance and have been put out of business by regulations (see the New York bitlicense).[3] On the bright side, some guidance has been given and the ecosystem continues to grow.

***Various governing bodies lack regulatory continuity because Bitcoin does not fit into the current regulatory framework.***

With this framework we can now discuss the incentives that will drive the evolution of the regulatory environment.

## What do governments want?

This depends on whether or not you have the world's reserve currency, but broadly speaking all governments want capital controls and taxes. Simply put, they want to know where money is going and have the ability to control or take it.

**Capital controls** are rules or laws designed to limit the flow of capital into or out of the country. Controlling financial institutions is the primary method of capital control. Untraceable digital cash, if it exists, defeats capital controls. While bitcoin is not quite an untraceable digital cash, with its ecosystem it could be. A government would likely try to defeat Bitcoin by disconnecting its ecosystem from the legacy fiat system. China has already done this to a degree.

**Taxes:** Governments want more control and more money. This power was expanded by FDR during the Great Depression with the creation of the welfare state.

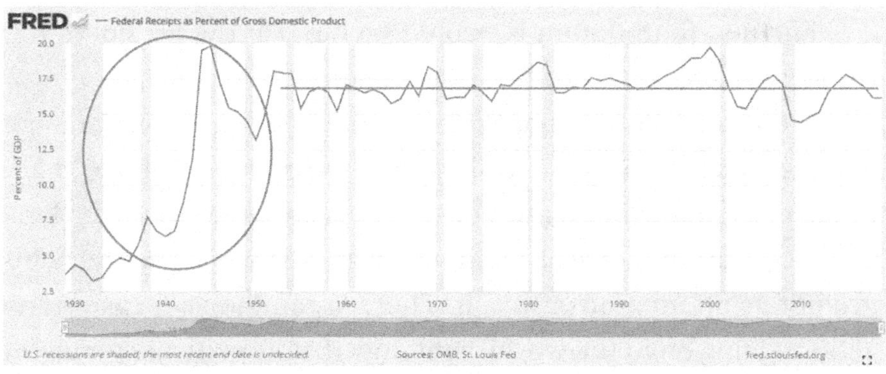


**Figure 105:** federal tax receipts as a percentage of GDP since 1930

In the latter half of the 20th century, cash was the primary medium of exchange. Cash is hard to trace outside of the banking system, and for centuries it was used for just that reason. All the while governments were implementing measures to collect tax revenues to capture some proportion of this cash. Anti-money laundering laws were not implemented until the 1970s, and KYC (Know Your Customer) laws were created as a part of the Patriot Act in 2001 to stop "terrorism." Together with the repeal of the gold standard in the '70s, these acts were a further intrusion into the financial privacy of the population. What is interesting is that governments were able to maintain tax revenue as a percentage of GDP both before these laws were created and after them. All that changed was privacy was lost and freedom was reduced.

The trend of government control is likely to continue with cryptocurrencies. Donald Trump tweeted this during while he was president:

> *I am not a fan of bitcoin and other Cryptocurrencies, which are not money, and whose value is highly volatile and based on thin air. Unregulated Crypto Assets can facilitate unlawful behavior, including drug trade and other illegal activity.*

Further, John Bolton is quoted saying that the president told the treasury secretary to "*Go after bitcoin.*"[4]

From a money laundering perspective, cash gets the job done, except moving it over large distances is hard. Bitcoin and other cryptocurrencies are borderless (can be moved over large distances autonomously), giving them an advantage over cash, **but are not as anonymous as cash**. There are millions of cash transactions going on in the world right now that nobody knows about. Bitcoin transactions are all visible on a public blockchain. If the government wants to track things, all transaction data is readily available. It is just a question of linkability – linking the personal identity to the address. The founder of Silk Road was ultimately caught by the FBI linking his identity to his online pseudonym. The point is that cryptocurrencies are not creating this new frontier of lawless money laundering as they are purported to be doing – they are allowing people to store their wealth over time. **The bad actors that already exist in our cash system are just used by officials as scapegoats to exert control over the bitcoin ecosystem by swaying public opinion.**

## What do people want?

People want to be wealthier. Every time the price of bitcoin goes up, more people get interested and learn about bitcoin. **No matter what the media says, people will continue to get rich from owning bitcoin, and this will continue to draw more people in.** As the price of bitcoins increases, its security increases, and it becomes more valuable. Bitcoin is creating a massive network effect that will soon be mathematically unstoppable. As this continues, people will continue to own it in whatever way they can.

More people will learn about bitcoin and decide if they want to be self-sovereign owners of their financial means or if they want to hire an intermediary to handle this for them. What consumers choose will be important as enough use of the same intermediaries could centralize the ownership of the system. There is a saying in the Bitcoin community – *not your keys, not your bitcoin* – meaning if someone else controls your private key, then the bitcoin is not yours. But some people do not want to spend the time to be their own custodians, and that is perfectly reasonable but potentially costly.

## How could this all play out?

From the perspective of a government, Pandora's box has been opened. A new decentralized savings technology has been created, and one way or another people are going to find a way to hold onto it. Governments can no longer steal from society with mechanisms like money printing and low interest rates.

There is a global competition beginning. Governments that restrict bitcoin's use or do not adopt it themselves will lose wealth. Those that adopt it early will gain a material amount of wealth. I think countries excluded from the USA's global banking will be the first to adopt bitcoin. Iran is already doing so and others will soon follow.[5] Hyperinflationary economies will likely be the next to adopt bitcoin, and the world will be watching. As all the emerging economies observe these early adopters rise, they will be forced to cut their losses and do the same. Countries excluded from the current global economic system have the greatest incentive to adopt bitcoin, while countries with the most ties to the global reserve currency, the dollar, have the least.

This will pose a dilemma for the USA, which will be at risk of losing its huge privilege of having the world's reserve currency. In a worst-case scenario, Executive Order 6102 (when the US government confiscated gold from citizens) could rise from the dead, but I don't think this is the most likely outcome. I believe our leaders will eventually gain the foresight to know what is good for them, though the wealth they extract from other countries will be hard to part with. There will likely be a battle between government and industry, and that will most likely be an attack on the ecosystem. However, I doubt any significant struggle will last long, as foreign countries will continue to grow rich by adopting the scarcest asset in the world as their new reserve currency.

## Conclusion

Bitcoin was designed to be the monetary base layer upon which a new financial system could be built. This contrasts with the current system in which our monetary base layer (the USD) has lost its monetary properties and is now purely credit (fiat). For Bitcoin to compete with the incumbent system, the incumbent's financial services will need to be replicated in bitcoin. Much of this is already happening, but there is still a long way to go. The current regulatory environment lacks continuity – significant change and guidance will be necessary to further build the ecosystem. Some governments have a strong incentive to adopt bitcoin, while others do not. This creates a global competitive environment and as bitcoin's adoption grows, battling the trend will become increasingly challenging. Countries furthest removed from the international system will likely adopt bitcoin first. If the USA is smart, it will not wait and be last. With this understanding, we can now look directly at the monetary properties of bitcoin and compare it to the antiquated forms of money that have existed throughout history.

## References

1. *Hal Finney Forum Post*, bitcointalk.org, December 30, 2010
2. *Bitcoin: A Primer for Policymakers*, Jerry Brito and Andrea Castillo, 48 – 50
3. https://en.wikipedia.org/wiki/BitLicense
4. https://micky.com.au/donald-trump-wanted-treasury-secretary-to-go-after-bitcoin-per-unpublished-book/
5. https://www.vice.com/en/article/qjppx3/iran-bitcoin-us-sanctions

# 13. THE PROPERTIES OF BITCOIN

*Would you believe in what you believe in if you were the only one who believed it?* – *Kanye West*

The first chapter defined the dimensions of money. Those dimensions are supported by monetary properties, without which a "good" will not fulfill monetary functions. With that understanding, we walked through the history and evolution of money, comparing the monetary properties with each evolutionary step. Bitcoin, or a decentralized form of money, is the next step in the world's monetary evolution.

How does bitcoin compare to other forms of money? To answer this question, we must first define what "bitcoin" means. There is the Bitcoin network (layer 1) and there is the Bitcoin ecosystem (layer 2) that enables it. Just as gold was enabled for payments over long distances by paper receipts, bitcoin is/will be enabled by layer 2 payments channels and $3^{rd}$ party intermediaries.

The layer 1 technology is most comparable to our current banking system, while the layer 2 technologies are most comparable to payment systems. Bitcoin's layer 2 systems are more theoretical than practical at this point, so a comparison is best done at the layer 1 level. From this perspective we can compare Bitcoin, property by property, to our fiat monetary system.

## Scarcity

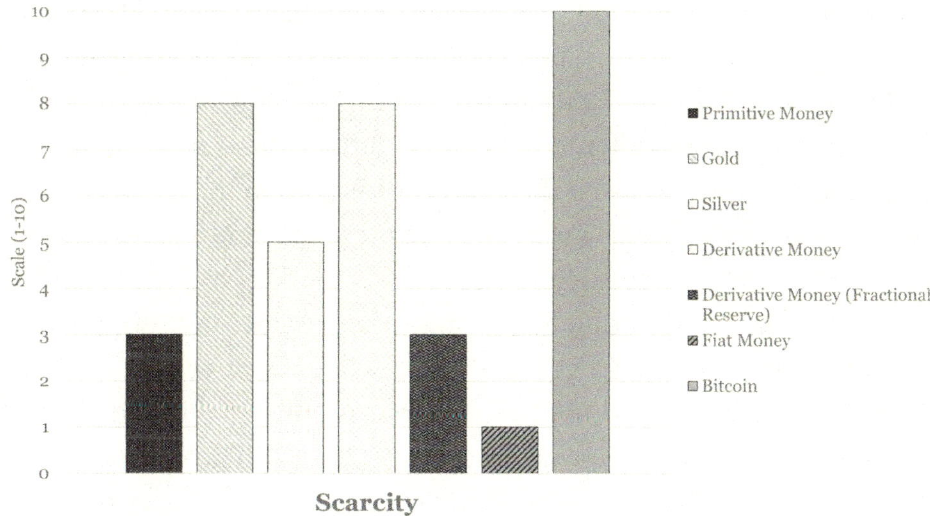


**Figure 106:** illustrative comparison of the property of scarcity by monetary medium

**Bitcoin is the scarcest monetary asset in the world.** There will only ever be 21 million in existence. Its current inflation rate is ~1.8%, on par with gold's, which ranges between 1.5% to 2.5%. Gold's inflation rate has existed in this range for centuries and likely will not decrease without a significant drop in its price. Bitcoin's inflation rate is guaranteed to halve every 4 years. While its inflation is near gold's today, its expected inflation is materially less. This is the most fundamental value proposition of bitcoin. If its ecosystem is shut down completely, it will still store value for people better than any other asset.

*Why can't someone else just create an even more scarce digital money than bitcoin?*

Somebody could copy the code of bitcoin right now and

adjust its supply schedule to produce an even more scarce cryptocurrency. However, this cryptocurrency would be without a supporting network and that person would have to bootstrap it.

Bootstrapping a cryptocurrency network is different today than it was in 2008 when Bitcoin began. Back then there was no competition, only Bitcoin. This gave Bitcoin time to grow in all the right ways. It allowed the community to encourage its use and let it blossom without the need for centralized control to outpace some form of competition.

Altcoins today do not have this luxury – the environment is highly competitive. To generate a network effect requires a full team with centralized control to support constant development changes, forks, and adoption/marketing efforts. **The competitive environment creates a need for centralized control just to combat the network effect of incumbents**.

There are altcoins with superior characteristics to bitcoin. For example, Zcash uses the same code as Bitcoin, with additions that allow users to completely anonymize their transactions. Zcash is controlled by two separate groups who support marketing and development efforts. They are also fighting against other cryptocurrency communities to control a narrative that incentivizes adoption. Meanwhile, more people are hearing about Bitcoin and it grows more decentralized.

If the government implemented measures of control, altcoins would be forced to abide. As much as any team might be against regulation, they are subject to the same regulatory consequences as everyone else. I am not certain if any altcoins are decentralized enough to thrive and compete with Bitcoin without more developments and marketing efforts from a financed team. Altcoins are not fully decentralized, and it's hard at this stage for them to become decentralized while also trying to grow. **If the government implements measures against Bitcoin, there is nothing they can do to the layer 1 protocol**. That is the major difference.

Is it possible altcoins could grow and earn market share? Yes, but possible is not the same as likely. The risk to reward ratios of any alternative is multiples greater than Bitcoin. Bitcoin is large enough and decentralized enough to be defensible. In the age of government control, centralized companies will likely be forced to comply with regulations, and that is major risk to their value proposition.

Most importantly, people buy bitcoin because they are certain its supply schedule will not change. The more the network grows, the more certain this is. Alternatives to bitcoin could easily change their supply schedules tomorrow without permission from their stakeholder groups.

For example, Ethereum (the 2nd largest cryptocurrency) is heavily influenced by its founder Vitalik Buterin. It was hacked in 2016, has undergone multiple hard forks, and there is disagreement in the community as regards to its total supply. The hack resulted in a hard fork that was created to give coins back to those who had lost them. Effectively, this was a change in the supply of ether, and if this happened to bitcoin, people would lose confidence in its scarcity. Bitcoin has no individual who could make changes to the protocol, has never had to create a hard fork (others have branched off but the main chain has not had to change), and everyone knows exactly what the supply is.

***Bitcoin is the scarcest asset in the world. Any other form of digital scarcity requires a network size comparable to bitcoin's to be competitive. Network size provides certainty that the supply schedule will not change, and therefore, bitcoin is incredibly hard to compete against.***

## Durability

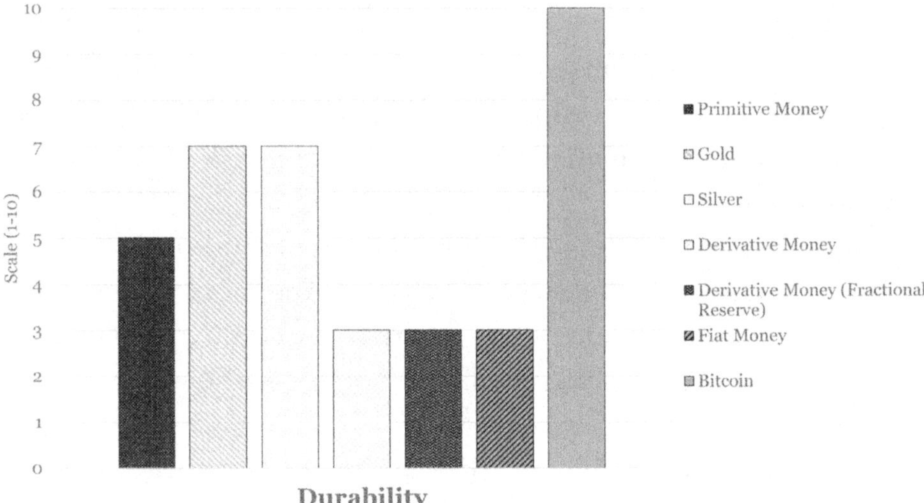


**Figure 107:** illustrative comparison of the property of durability by monetary medium

Bitcoin is purely digital and thus completely durable. Fiat money in this explanation is in reference its historical physical form (cash and coins), but much of it is obviously online now and maintains the same durability. An argument against its durability would be an argument against the internet – if the internet went down, then so would Bitcoin. If this ever occurred, Bitcoin would be the least of our problems. I would not bet on the internet "going down" because it is a resilient network. If it did, then all technologies supported by it would lose their value.

## Acceptability

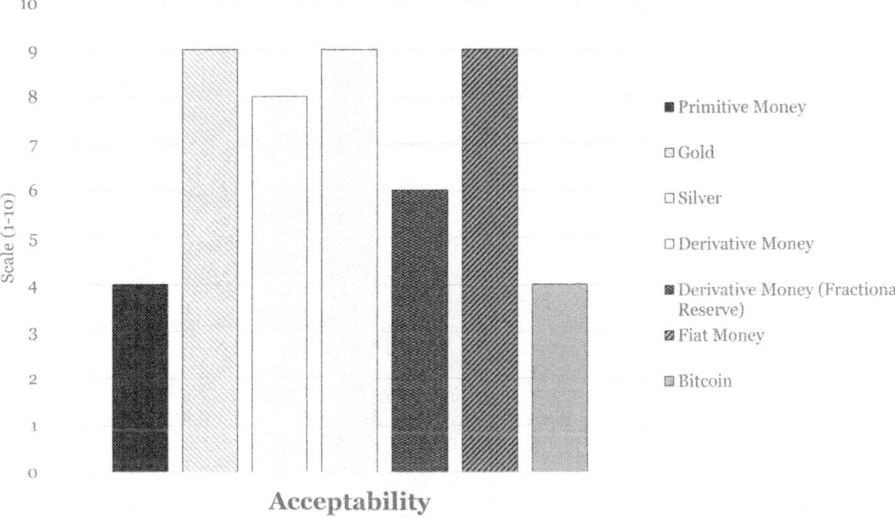


**Figure 108:** illustrative comparison of the property of acceptability by monetary medium

Currently, the acceptability of bitcoin is low. It is an emerging monetary system, and its growth will not happen overnight. Bitcoin's growth is driven by price appreciation. Continual price appreciation draws exponential growth in adoption with each market cycle. Only time will tell what happens to this property, but the trend in adoption is strong.

Bitcoin was built to be a monetary reserve asset – making its total addressable market, all the worlds assets (in theory), which is estimated to be around \$300 – \$400 trillion. Bitcoin is still in its infancy, with a current market value of \$1 trillion. Gold has a \$12 trillion market, and the current value of foreign currency reserves is also \$12 trillion. A \$24 trillion market is massive, and bitcoin has a long way to go before achieving a size even close to this. People who think bitcoin is too expensive do not understand its market size. If it were to consume these 2 markets, 1 bitcoin would be worth $1.1 million. Holding bitcoin for the long term is a good bet, even if it only consumes a small proportion of these markets.

## Portability

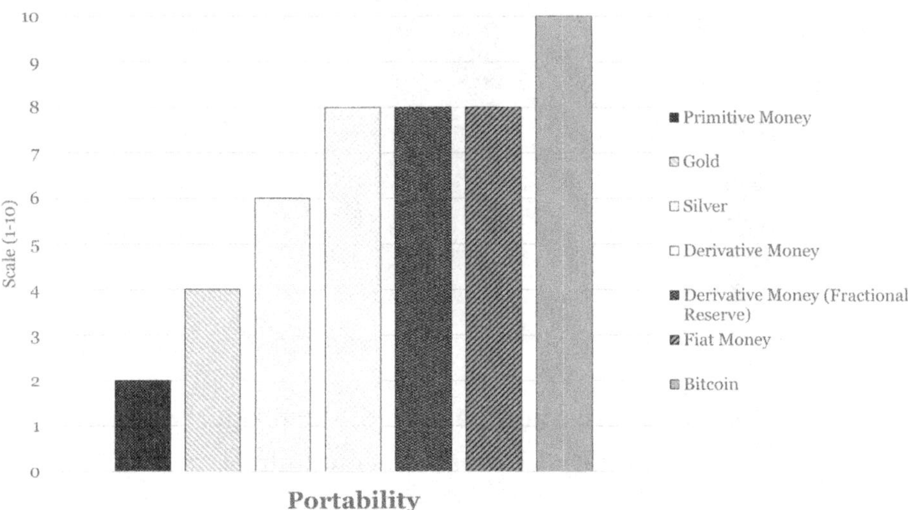


**Figure 109:** illustrative comparison of the property of portability by monetary medium

**Bitcoin is the most portable monetary asset in the world.** In April 2020 $1.1 billion was moved in a transaction in a matter of minutes and at a cost of 68 cents.[4] This transaction was done cheaply and efficiently without the transactors having to play by anybody's rules, reveal their identities, trust anyone with their information, or give anyone control over it. Someone moved $1.1 billion dollars for a cost of 68 cents, and there was nothing anybody could do about it. **No other payment system in the world can move that amount of value, for that price, in that amount of time, and completely autonomously.**

In our current system, 3rd party intermediaries require you to tell them who you are, follow their rules, trust they will keep your information safe, and give them control over your money. Bitcoin is the opposite of this system:

1. **Bitcoin requires responsibility.** You are responsible for your financial wellbeing. And bitcoin comes with benefits as well as responsibilities. With Bitcoin if you lose your private key, you have lost your bitcoin. Nobody can reverse the transaction for you; this is called **finality of settlement**. This is a cost of Bitcoin as being part of a centralized system does allow you to reverse transactions.
2. **Bitcoin is trustless.** It does not require trust in a 3rd party to hold your funds or move them. Systems like Paypal, Venmo, CashApp, etc. are controlled by centralized 3rd parties.
3. **Bitcoin is pseudonymous**. You do not have to give up all your most private information to participate in the Bitcoin network. While **linkability** is a major risk to privacy on the network, taking steps to remain private can be done on your own or with the help of 3rd party intermediaries. In our current system, you are "private" to everyone except your bank and the government. Your information also has a high risk of being hacked.
4. **Bitcoin is borderless.** It can be moved across the globe in a matter of minutes. To do the same in the fiat banking system takes days, if not weeks. Further, it requires you give up a substantial amount of your privacy and requires permission from your bank and regulators.
5. **Bitcoin is permission-less.** You can transact on the bitcoin network without any 3rd party constraints because it is peer-to-peer. As a participant in the Bitcoin network, you are completely sovereign.
6. **Bitcoin is a cash system.** Transacting in bitcoin means you have moved, in digital form, a monetary asset. **It is not credit**

such as Paypal, Venmo, and CashApp – to receive your cash from these systems requires multi-day settlement times that Bitcoin can do in minutes.

## Divisibility

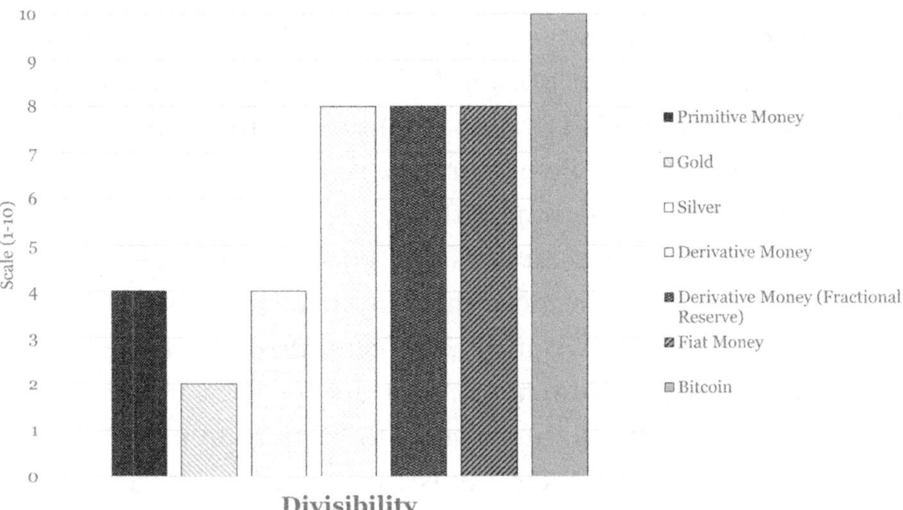


**Figure 110:** illustrative comparison of the property of divisibility by monetary medium

**Bitcoin is the most divisible monetary asset in the world.** It is so because it is digital. Fiat money can be divided down to the cent (.01). Bitcoin can be divided down to what is known as a satoshi or sat (.00000001). If 1 bitcoin were worth $1,000,000, then 1 satoshi would be worth $.01. There are proposals to change this system from sats to bits – which I think is likely to happen at some point. A bit is the basic unit of information in computing (1 or 0) and, coincidentally, used to be a US term meaning 12 ½ cents. It would make sense for digital money to return to this nomenclature to represent its most basic unit.

There is a popular argument that because bitcoin is so divisible, it is not scarce. I do not know who popularized this argument, but it is a non sequitur. If you have a bucket of water, then you can theoretically divide it down to the molecule or atom or whatever. This does not create new water – if we could create value through division, we would all be gods. There will only ever be 21 million bitcoins, and no matter how small you divide them, the total quantity remains the same. If anyone makes this argument to you, thank them for the information and then continue living your life. Keep a running list of all these people, and next time you are creating a pyramid scheme, give them all a call.

There is a related and more understandable argument against bitcoin's scarcity. It purports that hard forks create new currency, which continuously increases the supply of bitcoins or coins like it, and it is therefore not scarce. If you understand bitcoin, you immediately understand that its value is not defined by its software but primarily by its network. Bitcoin's functionality is one thing, but anyone can copy that code at any time and start their own currency. Bitcoin's network, however, cannot be copied. When a hard fork occurs, network participants can choose where to commit their computing power. Whichever network receives more mining power is the one that is more secure and more valuable. **Thus, while forks create new currency, they do not create new computing power, which is what VALUE is ultimately derived from.** In the long run, one currency's value will be consumed by the other. It is zero sum; the computing power remains scarce.

*The 7th Property*

# Fungibility

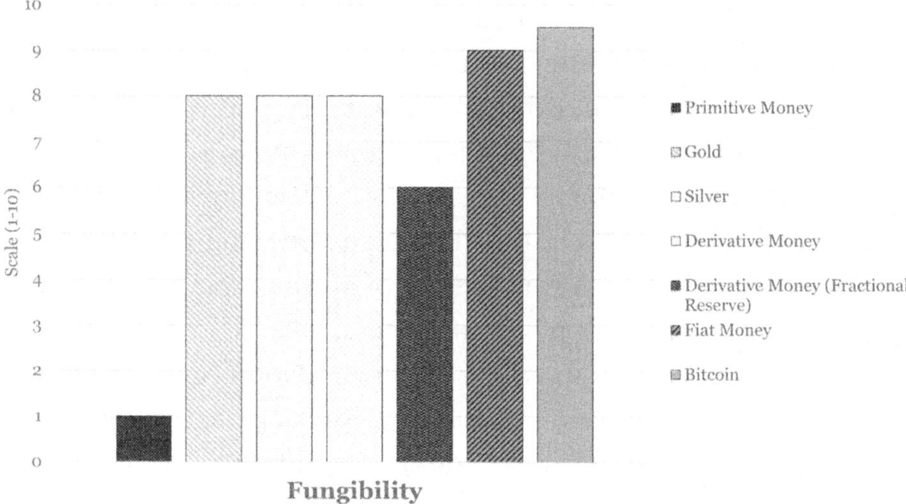


**Figure 111:** illustrative comparison of the property of fungibility by monetary medium

Fungibility means a good's individual unit is homogeneous and interchangeable, at least to some degree (i.e., 1 dollar bill is no different from another dollar bill). The US dollar is fungible, but not perfectly fungible. For example, a 2-dollar bill has some extra desirability because it is not frequently seen – people would give up two 1-dollar bills before giving up a single 2-dollar bill. Bills can also be tracked in some way, like bait money, making those bills harder to spend than others. Lastly, bills can be damaged and are less likely to be accepted once damaged.

Bitcoins are also fungible, but they are not perfectly fungible. Because you can trace ownership on the blockchain, every bitcoin has a history that anyone can view, tracing all the way back to its original coinbase transaction. This history can impact that coins fungibility in a variety of ways.

For example, **differing histories could impact the value of**

**coins** – just as coin collectors value coins above their monetary value for their historic or aesthetic value. In the first block ever mined (called the **genesis block**) by Satoshi, he added an extra piece of metadata which was the headline "*The Times 03/Jan/2009 Chancellor on brink of second bailout for banks,*" expressing his disdain for the English banking system socializing its losses and enabling moral hazard. I imagine any coin with lineage back to this block would be desirable to people in the future similar to the way historic art is desirable.

## Immutability

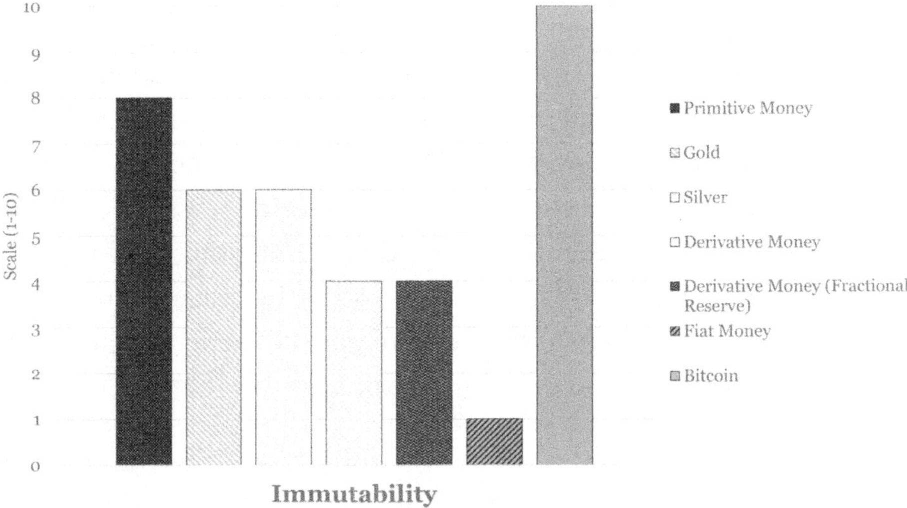


**Figure 112:** illustrative comparison of the property of immutability by monetary medium

In the 3rd chapter of this book, I appended a **7th property of immutability** (achieved by the decentralization of production and storage) to the 6 commonly accepted monetary properties. Given monetary history, immutability should be considered a property, as it is necessary to remove moral hazard from the monetary system.

Fiat money is produced by a central bank and multiplied in the banking system through fractional reserves. Fiat money is stored in banks, cannot be personally stored in digital form, and is impractical to store physically.

## Production

Bitcoin is produced in a decentralized manner through the efforts of thousands of individual mining nodes. However, there is a risk of centralization in this process through:

1. **Mining pools** – A previous chapter explained how miners form pools to increase their chance of earning a block reward, granting them more consistent cash flows. These mining pools follow rules and are controlled by managers. In figure 113 you can see that decentralized mining has been trending downward, and BitDeer – a mining pool – has taken a massive share of the total mining power. However, BitDeer is composed of 5 entities – AntPool, BTC.com, BTC.top, F2 Pool and ViaBTC. The future trend of increased centralization in mining pools is uncertain, but it is a considerable risk to decentralization of the network.

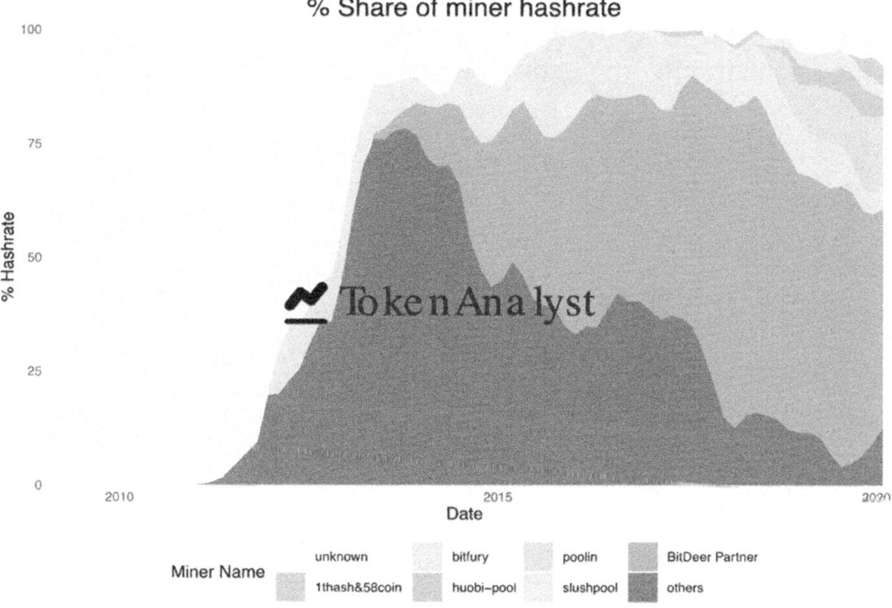


**Figure 113:** mining pools as a percentage of total hash rate as of January 2020 (Image source Token Analyst)[1]

2. **Industrial Mining** – Aside from mining pools, large companies are growing rapidly and searching for desirable environments in which to mine. Mining companies can economize on low electricity and fixed costs. Naturally, companies will want to grow larger, but the homogeneity of mining in a competitive environment should counter this tendency (i.e., mining is a commoditized business with low barriers to entry).
3. **Geographic concentration** – Companies are building large mining operations in low-cost energy environments. If enough miners concentrate in a single area, this could leave the Bitcoin network vulnerable to a state actor seizing the hardware of the miners. As of 2020, Chinese mining operations account for ~65% of the global hash rate.[5] However,

trends such as excess capacity mining are growing rapidly, and impede centralization. This development is an important stage in bitcoin's growth towards maturity.

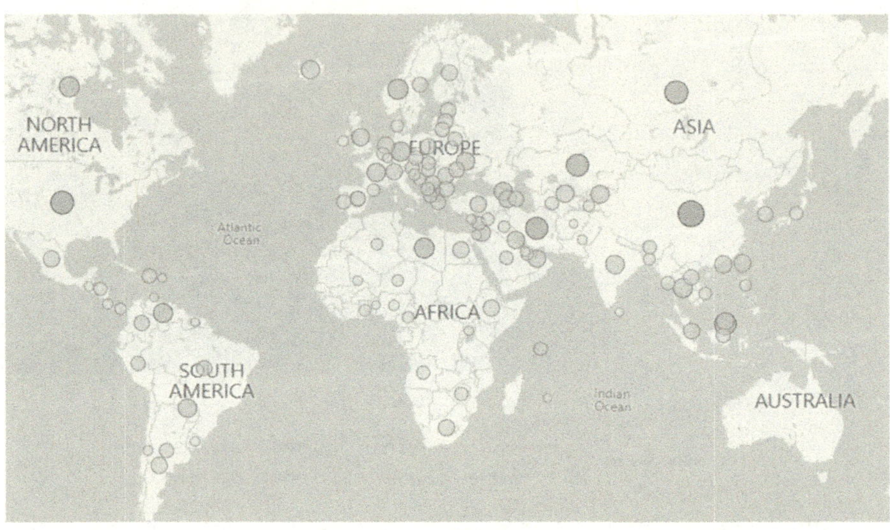


**Figure 114:** visualization of the Bitcoin mining hashrate by geography
(Image source Cambridge)[2]

4. **Mining Hardware** – In Bitcoin's early days, there were only a handful of mining hardware manufacturers. Since then, hardware manufacturers have diversified, but concentration still exists at the foundry level.

Most importantly, **the network is always protected from 51% attacks by incentives**. Those who accumulate a significant amount of hashing power have no reason to attack the network, as it pays more to play by the rules. The only exception would be an actor with malicious intent and a major interest in the legacy system, like a state actor.

Long-term decentralization is not yet an economic reality but is a technological possibility. Production is centralizing in some ways while decentralizing in others. This is important to the future of bitcoin as the value of the network is predicated on its decentralization.

## *Storage*

The decentralization of storage is important, not for network security but to ensure value remains in control of network participants. According to glassnode.com, the percentage of bitcoin held on exchanges increased from 4% in 2015 to 16% in 2020.[3]

As financial intermediaries emerge, participants will have to decide if they want to store their bitcoins themselves or with a 3rd party. Increased centralization of storage is likely, but the number of 3rd parties will remain decentralized to some degree. People will have to decide for themselves on the tradeoff between trust and efficiency. Further, as sovereigns begin to control and regulate intermediaries, self-custody will become more and more attractive. Operating in a "bankless" manner is not possible in our fiat system, but if it were, I personally would do it, even at a large inconvenience. As service providers continue to emerge in the Bitcoin ecosystem, self-custody becomes more and more feasible.

It is worth noting, however, that even if Bitcoin becomes "more centralized" it will only be centralized to a small extent compared to existing alternatives. On the spectrum of decentralized to centralized, it will likely always remain at the decentralized end. Our fiat system will always be centralized, and history shows that centralization is likely to increase. Bitcoin is the decentralized alternative to the moral hazard that results from centralization. **It is the only form of money that maintains the 7th monetary property of immutability**.

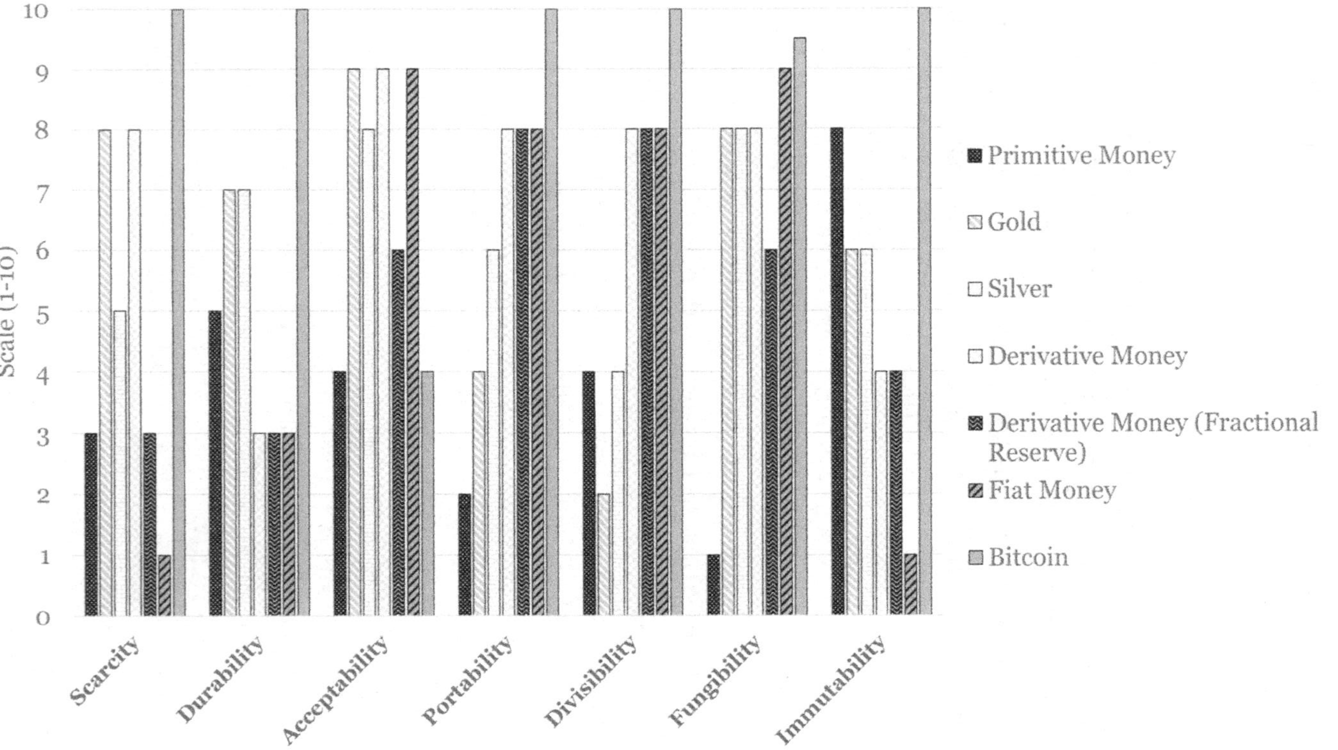


**Figure 115:** illustrative comparison of monetary properties by monetary medium

## Conclusion

Bitcoin is a peer-to-peer cash system. Its technological characteristics were designed to create superior monetary properties for the digital world. Through time, **its network has grown large enough that it is now the scarcest, most durable, most portable, most divisible, and most decentralized monetary asset in the world.**

All Bitcoin needs now is adoption. A thriving ecosystem and further adoption would eventually create a digital alternative to our current financial system. This new decentralized system would eliminate the moral hazard that ensues from centralized agents who are assumed to be acting in good faith.

Bitcoin is still in its infancy. It was built to be a global reserve asset, and it is still far away from achieving that scale. The trends and proportions of the ecosystem will likely change in a meaningful way over time. Using historical trends to predict future outcomes will likely have little value. There are structural and regime changes that have yet to happen while the network increases in scale. Even without an ecosystem, Bitcoin remains the best long-term savings technology in the world; but not enough people know it yet because its value proposition is counterintuitive and it takes a whole book to understand it.

This chapter covered some major criticisms of Bitcoin, but there are more. The goal of the next and final chapter in this book is to aggregate all major criticisms and discuss them. Read on to solidify your understanding of the value of Bitcoin.

## References

1. https://www.tokenanalyst.io/
2. https://cbeci.org/mining_map
3. https://studio.glassnode.com/metrics?a=BTC&category=Exchanges&m=distribution.BalanceExchangesRelative
4. https://www.cryptovantage.com/news/here-are-the-5-biggest-bitcoin-transactions-in-history/
5. https://news.bitcoin.com/65-of-global-bitcoin-hashrate-concentrated-in-china/

# 14. THE CRITICISMS OF BITCOIN

*I WILL SPARK A GENERATION OF THINKERS WHO WILL QUESTION TRADITIONAL THOUGHT UNTIL THEY FIND THE ABSOLUTE TRUTH* – *Kanye West*

Mainstream media, financial powers, and prominent economists have argued against Bitcoin for the past decade while it has grown to become a $1 trillion network.[5,6,7] Many of their arguments prove their lack of fundamental understanding of the technology and its implications. The same phenomenon occurred at the beginning of the internet. In fact, many high priests of media and business have been wrong about every transformational technology.[8] The controversy around Bitcoin shows just how transformational it really is, for there is a strong correlation between controversy and transformational technologies.

Few criticisms of Bitcoin are legitimate. Most criticisms are the result of misunderstanding the technology or ignoring its incentives. Of the legitimate criticisms, some have no current or potential answer, while others are a product of the fact that Bitcoin is still in its infancy. I've included a review of each major criticism I believe should be addressed in order to provide a complete picture of Bitcoin's opportunities and risks.

## How can Bitcoin be attacked?

Bitcoin can be attacked primarily in 3 ways:

1. **Attack the Bitcoin Network:** This would require a 51% attack discussed in depth in chapter 10. In short, if a group could gain most of the network's mining power, it could, with a strong probability, mine fraudulent blocks into existence. If a fraudulent block were mined, everyone on the network would realize that Bitcoin is no longer secure, and this would destroy its value. The group that ultimately mined these fraudulent blocks would consequently have a hard time selling their fraudulent bitcoins as they would have now publicly undermined the network's security, and the bitcoins would not have much value left. Today a 51% attack would cost tens of billions of dollars in hardware and energy costs to execute, and that cost is only rising as the network grows. The primary argument against the likelihood of this kind of attack occurring is that a group that had a lot of capital to invest **would find it much more profitable to play by the rules and earn bitcoin themselves** rather than destroying the value of the bitcoins they might be able to earn fraudulently. The only group that would likely be willing to allocate so many resources to destroying the value of bitcoin would be a group with a major interest in a competing (fiat) currency, most likely a government. However, attacking the Bitcoin network would likely be their last resort as attacking the Bitcoin ecosystem would be much more effective.
2. **Attack the Bitcoin ecosystem:** This method would be the most practical for a state actor. Regulations could be imposed upon various participants to force a desired behavior.
   a. The state could try to cut off the ability to acquire bitcoin by controlling or outlawing cryptocurrency exchanges.
   b. The state could outlaw the use of self-custody wallets and force cryptocurrency into the hands of 3rd parties, which they could in turn control. This could come as a

bait and switch strategy in which they create an attractive regulatory environment for 3rd party intermediaries and, once a significant amount of wealth has entered the system, implement a crackdown.

c. The state could attack the use of cryptocurrency for payments by either banning merchants from accepting it in any form or applying punitive taxation on transactions. Cryptocurrency payments are currently not feasible because of taxation, as each transaction is a taxable event.

d. All these methods would result in a global black markets being created. The internet is borderless, and cryptocurrency is a medium within it. National firewalls would have to be implemented to stop behavior like this, at which point our personal freedom would be a far greater concern than bitcoin (albeit bitcoin is an enabler of that freedom).

3. **Attack its underlying cryptography:** (Discussed in chapter 9.) Quantum computing is a risk to cryptography, but this argument is highly theoretical. If quantum computing is created to the extent that it can crack our modern cryptography systems, then all our security systems will be dismantled. This is a much broader threat to internet protocols in general. If this occurred, the fate of Bitcoin would be the least of our problems, as public-key cryptography itself would be undermined and practically everything would be insecure at that point. Further, quantum computing could also be used to increase the security of systems and to act defensively – perhaps to find larger primes for systems. Keep in mind, a trillion computers doing a trillion computations every trillionth of a second for a trillion years is not enough calculations to attack public-key cryptography today.

**When considering ways that a state could attack Bitcoin, it is important to understand that all these hypotheticals exist in a competitive global environment.** Every country wants to increase its power and wealth. When a new form of wealth storage is introduced to the world, countries will have a choice to use it to their advantage through adoption or attack it to defend the existing system. Countries that have the most to lose, like the USA as the country with the global reserve currency, will likely want to attack it. Countries that stand to gain the most, like those excluded from the international monetary system (e.g., Iran), will likely want to adopt it. As other countries watch the adopters gain material wealth relative to the fiat system, they will begin to transition to it as well. Once the dominos start to fall, Bitcoin will be hard to stop. The USA and other major developed countries will begin to lose their monetary dominance and will be forced to join the party or risk a further loss of power. If the US government is smart, it will start adopting bitcoin now, instead of trying to fight it. Once US officials understand the inevitability of decentralized money, it would be rational to skip the battle and just adopt bitcoin as a currency. That is the power of Bitcoin, which is now on the brink of becoming mathematically unstoppable. Machiavelli would disagree:

> *It must be remembered that there is nothing more difficult to plan, more doubtful of success, nor more dangerous to manage than a new system. For the initiator has the enmity of all who would profit by the preservation of the old institution and merely lukewarm defenders in those who gain by the new ones.* [1]

What Machiavelli missed is that this new system does not have lukewarm defenders – they are ardent and resolved. Admittedly, however, whatever change does come will likely not come easily.

## How can Bitcoin be hacked?

"Hacking" the Bitcoin network would mean successfully staging a 51% attack. What most people mean when they use the phrase "hacking" in relation to Bitcoin is that your *computer* can be hacked and your private keys stolen. This is the key risk to storing your bitcoin in hot wallets or in exchanges, and means that secure self-custody practices, like cold storage are incredibly important. Multi-signature addresses or 3rd party custody are other ways to protect your bitcoin. With this new financial system comes new responsibilities for those who want to either take self-custody of their wealth or place trust in 3rd parties. What is important is that this system gives people a choice in regard to this responsibility, while our current system, for all practical purposes, does not.

## Can another cryptocurrency eclipse bitcoin?

Not all cryptocurrencies attempt to compete against bitcoin as money (an explanation of this is beyond the scope of this writing). Of the cryptocurrencies that do attempt to compete with it, the most common reason why one of them might be better than bitcoin concerns better functionality. For example, alternative cryptocurrencies (altcoins) may claim to be faster, more-scalable, more-private, or more-malleable. Understand that **there is a trade-off between security and functionality**. Bitcoin was purposefully built to be as simple as possible with limited functionality.

Broadly speaking, **increasing Bitcoin's functionality, increases the risk of security threats.** If you update the software to do more things, this increases the risk that those new things can be used against it. For example, Bitcoin was purposefully built to use a language that cannot do iterative calculations. This was an intended security measure because software that does iterative calculations is at risk of a DDOS attack in which an attacker overloads the network to purposefully shut it down. The creators of Bitcoin decided that security was priority number 1 and achieved it through simplicity by creating decentralized money with rules that do not change. They believed that trying to reach for more functionality would undermine the security of the network. Bitcoin achieves security through simplicity.

Further, **to increase functionality and generate a network effect it requires increasing centralization** (explained in chapter 13). For alternative currencies to compete in the current environment, they must maintain control of the network and software for long periods of time. Most of them state that they plan to increase decentralization as they grow. It remains to be seen whether (1) they will do this and (2) if they will be able to do it in time. The more decentralized something is, the more resilient it is against attacks. I cannot speak about all altcoins – there are thousands of them – but very few of them represent legitimate **potential** value propositions, and of that group it is yet to be proven if any of them are, in fact, decentralized enough to require consensus.

**Bitcoin's resilience is unparalleled and has been achieved through simplicity.** Its simplicity necessitates a layer 2 ecosystem, which will take time to develop but is sustainable over the long term. **This ecosystem of centralized companies can provide further functionality and can fail repeatedly without hurting the underlying Bitcoin network.** By separating the Bitcoin network from layer 2 functionality, it enables experimentation in technology without sacrificing the underlying security of Bitcoin. Altcoins that claim to have new functionality are an experiment, and they must get it right the first time or else people will lose confidence in the network. Altcoin creators have had to stay centralized to keep changing and updating their protocols to deal with various issues. The

Bitcoin creators had the foresight to understand, that when it comes to a monetary medium, less is more.

If Bitcoin's network is not resilient enough to stand the test of time, then none of the other altcoins are either. This is not to say that **centralization could not be a survival advantage that would appeal to state actors**. In fact, altcoins could be adopted by states before bitcoin, because states know that they can influence the centralized altcoin networks, something they cannot do with Bitcoin. However, an altcoin controlled by the state would be no longer useful for the purpose of a private decentralized cryptocurrency.

To illustrate, let's briefly compare Bitcoin to the 2nd largest cryptocurrency network, Ethereum.

Ethereum was designed to have materially more functionality than bitcoin. Basically, Ethereum was built so that a layer 2 does not need to exist – it is supposed to be able to do layer 1 and layer 2 functions all within its network. This functionality is (1) incomplete and (2) came at the cost of security, as it was hacked in 2016 and forced to hard fork to give back coins to everyone who had lost them.[9] I am not saying Ethereum has no value; what I am saying is that it does not do what most people I talk to think it does.

Bitcoin's functionality is simple and limited, while Ethereum's is complex, with a wealth of applications. However, much more can be built on Ethereum, and we are watching Ethereum's ecosystem being built in real time. Bitcoin's ecosystem is building out less rapidly but could prove to have the security that most people desire.

Ether is the token that is needed to operate on the Ethereum platform, and its price increases (in part) as the demand to use the Ethereum platform increases. The problem with this token is that (1) it was hard forked due to the aforementioned hack (meaning its supply is centralized and malleable) and (2) there is uncertainty regarding its total supply. However, interesting things are being built on Ethereum that could create a new ecosystem of decentralized finance. There are legitimate forms of success (like decentralized exchanges) on Ethereum, but they are frequently hacked and are largely centralized despite being marketed as decentralized. However, these protocols have real world demand that in turn increases the demand for their native tokens.

Bitcoin's supply economics are its primary value proposition. People buy bitcoin because they are certain that its supply schedule will not change, and thus it will store wealth with more certainty than anything else. If Bitcoin's supply schedule were to change, that would materially undermine Bitcoin's value proposition, and this is likely why the community has never approved such an action. Changing Bitcoin is so hard because it is a truly decentralized community with the largest network. Today, the Ethereum community cannot claim to maintain this value proposition.

Ethereum will not be able to compete with bitcoin as money, but it has successfully generated a network effect for a variety of applications. The debate gets more complex from here, but when considering the risk/reward of each, Bitcoin amounts to a secure savings technology while Ethereum is an insecure financial services technology.

## Is bitcoin too volatile?

Yes. Most people do not want to purchase something so volatile. Understand that bitcoin, with a $1 trillion market value, is still in its infancy. Once its market value is in the multi-trillions, it will be much less volatile. In fact, its volatility has continued to decrease as it increases in scale. It was built to operate at a large scale, and its current size is still subject to the reality of large fluctuations from price discovery.

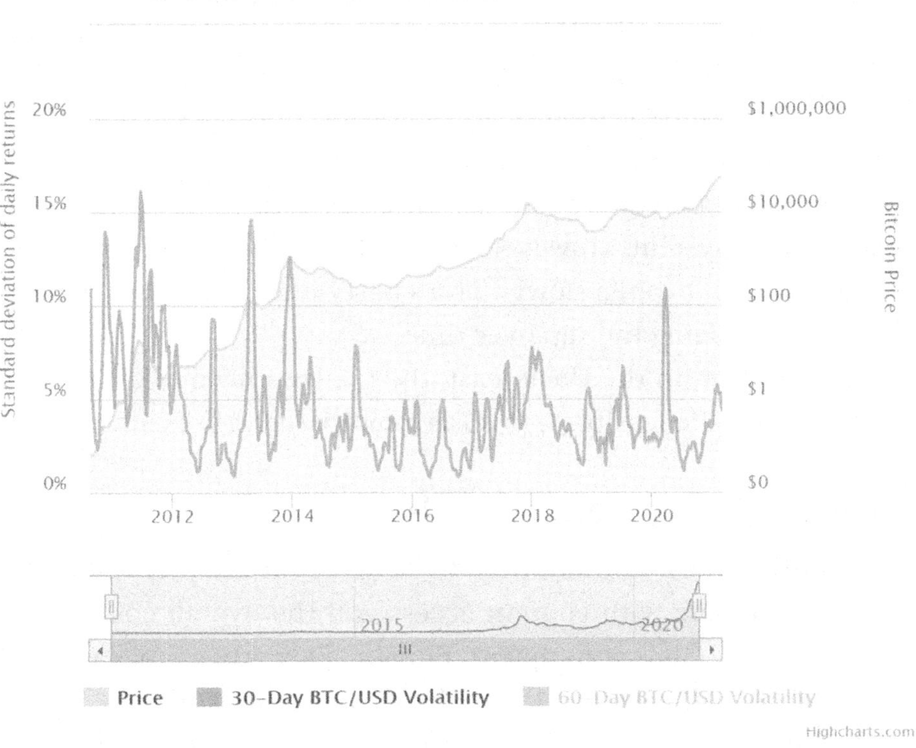


**Figure 116:** bitcoin price volatility declining as its price appreciates
(Image source buybitcoinworld.com)[3]

For those who want to own bitcoin without the volatility, using a 3rd party to assist you with hedging its downside risk could be appropriate. If you are putting a significant amount of wealth into bitcoin, paying to ensure it never falls below a certain threshold could be worth your while.

## Why would I want bitcoin if it cannot be used for payments?

The answer is to store value. Bitcoin is the best long-term

store of value that exists. Additionally, payments systems are coming, as was discussed in chapters 12 and 13.

In summary, payment systems will be built on top of Bitcoin. This could be through the Lightning Network or 3rd party intermediaries that issue their own paper backed by bitcoin. Using the Lightning Network, in my opinion, will be the future as it will be as fast as a credit system with the collateral benefits of a cash settlement system. However, this system will require time, and adoption will happen slowly. Third party intermediaries will play a role in bridging the gap over time.

However, in the US at least, the tax laws need to change for payments to be feasible – this is a major issue at present.

## Is Bitcoin too centralized?

- **Developers/community:** (Discussed in chapter 11.) The developers with commit access and the overall community work in tandem to update Bitcoin. This process has worked for over 12 years and is resilient to centralization.
- **Investors:** (Discussed in more depth in the next question.) A small group currently owns a large amount of the bitcoin supply. The risk is that all of them cooperate to sell their bitcoin, attacking its value. It is not fully understood how cooperative the members of this group are with each other (this group is thousands of addresses), but holding bitcoin seems to be the best strategy so far. Also, much of the supply held by this group is controlled at addresses (like Satoshi's address) that date from early in Bitcoin's development, and there are no signs of that changing. Some of these addresses have lost their private keys. The risk of a "pump-and-dump" is lowest in bitcoin relative to any other cryptocurrency, and the decision to do so would be irrational. It would be rational for this group to hold bitcoin and sell in small amounts over time to avoid putting downward pressure on the market.

- **Miners:** (Discussed in chapter 13.) There is a risk mining pools continue to increase centralization. How this trend continues is uncertain, but it's a risk to monitor in the network.

*Could big tech collude and shut down Bitcoin (a.k.a. is the network hardware too centralized)?*

Bitcoin does not get downloaded in an app store, can be found from any web browser, and only 6% of nodes utilize Amazon Web Services. To shut down the Bitcoin network through its hardware isn't feasible without nationalization of services or collusion outside of big tech. However, even if this happened, it would only prevent the use of Bitcoin in the USA – Bitcoin would continue to exist in other places with other services. Globally shutting down Bitcoin's network is unfeasible, as adoption has already spread too far.

## A small group of people own bitcoin – wouldn't this increase wealth inequality?

This is a legitimate criticism without a clear solution yet. Estimates currently show that 2% of bitcoin accounts own 95% of the outstanding supply.[10] Two points on this:

- Groups, like one ran by Jack Dorsey, are actively working to bring bitcoin to the underprivileged and unbanked.[11]
- The inequality of Bitcoin ownership will likely change significantly as it scales and users trade it.

If we consider a worst-case scenario where 1% owns 99% of bitcoins while the whole world is using it as a reserve, then the 1% could exert a significant amount of power over the rest of us. However, if significant power is being exerted by those who control the supply, those competing for the remaining supply will grow tired of what would amount to serfdom. Private cryptocurrency has low switching costs, and if the problem is bad enough, then the serfs could switch to using their own currency. In other words, in an environment of continuous currency competition, other groups could opt out of the bitcoin system and begin to use a competing currency. This competition could create multiple systems, using competition to defend each system from hoarders of the supply. I think this is a viable argument against the idea that only 1 cryptocurrency can exist. In fact, Carl Menger mentions that this phenomenon existed throughout history, and legal standards of currency were created to combat it:

> *The difficulties experienced in the commerce and modes of payment of any country* ***from the competing action of the several commodities serving as currency****, and further the circumstance, that concurrent standards induce a manifold insecurity in trade, and render necessary various conversions of the circulating media, have led to the legal recognition of certain commodities as money (to legal standards).* [2]

This statement supports the idea that at the beginning of private currency markets there was a natural emergence of competing monetary media (not be confused with bimetallism). I believe this natural emergence came about due to some combination of information opacity, sovereign coercion, and monetary utility tradeoffs (discussed in chapter 1). My speculation is that this competition was necessary to keep monopolization of a standard at bay.

This aside, I think there is value to be gained by bringing those excluded from the current system in quickly. In fact, bitcoin's growth should eventually attract poorer (but tech-enabled) people over time as they work to earn bitcoins instead of their inflating fiat currency. Bitcoin could be what is needed to bring developing economies back into the economic sphere of the developed world.

## What if I lose my bitcoins?

This is another legitimate criticism. This problem exists in 2 forms:

- **You lose your private key:** If you lose your private key, you can no longer access your bitcoins. This means that proper key management practices are incredibly important for self-custody. Professional services will likely be in high demand to reduce the probability of this occurring.
- **You send your bitcoins to the wrong address:** in bitcoin you have finality of settlement, meaning transactions cannot be reversed. This is a cost of using a decentralized system. In our current centralized system, transactions can often be reversed. With bitcoin, sending high value transactions should be done using best practices. Once again, professional services will be helpful in reducing this risk but are not a requirement.

***If bitcoin requires 3rd party intermediaries, aren't we right back where we started with the fiat system?***

This is discussed in chapter 12. Bitcoin was built to be the base monetary layer of a new financial system. That is, it will function as the US dollar does in our current system but bring back the monetary properties that the dollar once had. Bitcoin's **supply cannot be changed and thus provides superior wealth accumulation to the USD at the base layer of the financial system.**

People will have the option to use intermediaries if they wish (or even the dollar system, as none of this is being forced on anyone). Those intermediaries could create their own paper backed by bitcoin.

The risk is that fractional reserve practices will emerge and result in bank runs. **Bank runs existed because (1) centuries ago auditing banks was not easy, and (2) continuous government bailouts incentivized moral hazard** (i.e., banks took excessive risk because they expected and depended on bailouts from the taxpayers).

1. **Bitcoin solves the first problem via a public blockchain.** A bank can post its paper outstanding and its bitcoin reserves to be publicly verified. In fact, new technologies will allow them to prove their reserves without showing their address(es). This will create trust in the system, and if a bank wants to operate as a fractional reserve, people will be aware of the risk they are taking on. Of course, the banks' liabilities cannot be proven without audits (and even with audits, this is not certain). In a free market, banks will once again have reputations to protect, which is a strong but imperfect incentive.
2. **Bitcoin solves the 2nd problem by eliminating the government's ability to print money and bail out institutions.** They will no longer be able to tax through inflation, and this will change their behavior. The cozy relationship between banks and government will be eroded by this fact as the two will have much less to gain through partnership. Banks will have to operate under the assumption that if they fail, then they will fail, period.

**With bitcoin as the monetary base layer, the risk of moral hazard from financial intermediaries is reduced significantly.** This is not to say that risky practices will not occur, but they will no longer be structurally incentivized. Perhaps financial services could become a trusted industry once again. Last, bitcoin provides the option to use 3rd parties; it is not a practical requirement as in our current fiat system.

**A system with 3rd party intermediaries would not be the same thing as a gold standard.** Under a bitcoin-backed system of intermediaries, everyone has the choice of using an intermediary of their own bitcoin or self-custody of their own bitcoin, while under a gold standard system, self-custody is not feasible. If you don't believe me, try storing all of your wealth in gold and paying for everything with it.

## Is bitcoin mining bad for the environment?

Bitcoin mining consumes a lot of electricity, and this will only continue to increase as more miners are drawn in to secure the network. Is this bad for the environment?

First, the Bitcoin network consumes materially less than alternative systems. It is a deceiving argument that Bitcoin is worse for the environment than existing financial systems.

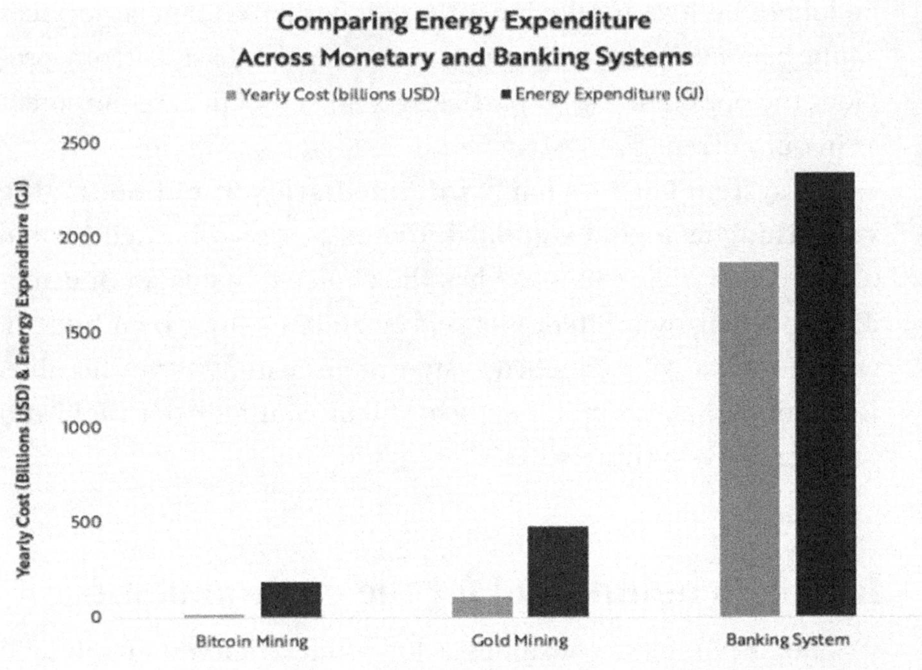


**Figure 117:** estimated comparison of electricity consumption across bitcoin, gold, and the banking system as of February 2020 (Image source Ark Investment Management)[4]

Next, let's understand energy. There are a variety of ways that energy is created: coal, oil and gas, nuclear, solar, wind, hydropower, etc. Producers of energy must deal with transmitting it to areas **where** it is needed and at times **when** it is needed. Transmitting energy from one place to another results in a loss of energy during transmission. Energy sources that are intermittent result in excess, and ultimately lost, energy. Said differently, these energy producer problems exist because energy sources are **intermittent and distributed**. If there were perfect methods of storing energy, the problem of intermittence would be solved. If there were perfect methods of transmitting energy, the problem of distribution would be solved. When too much energy is produced during times of too little or too distant demand, it is called excess energy and is ultimately never used.

Excess energy could be used if there existed **an energy buyer that always stands ready to buy energy and is nearest to where they can produce it**. Bitcoin is that buyer. Industrial bitcoin mining operations stand ready to consume **excess energy** right next to where the energy is being produced.

China is the primary source of bitcoin mining because the central planners of their economy have built large hydropower plants in remote areas. These plants produce a lot of excess energy that cannot always be transported economically. The result is that the excess energy is produced but not used because it does not make sense to transport it, at least not all the time. Bitcoin mining operations are built at these plants to consume the excess energy cheaply – cheaply because it would not be consumed otherwise. I surmise that going forward, production facilities will have bitcoin mining operations as a part of their business model because **economically it is the equivalent of storing that excess energy**. An example of this in the US is the industrial mining operations built in central Washington because of the large hydropower facilities on the Columbia River.

However, some energy sources produce more $C0^2$ emissions than others. Bitcoin, being focused on sources that are intermittent and distributed, fits naturally with renewable sources. However, bitcoin mining operations are also paired with oil & gas drilling sites. In these cases, if bitcoin miners were not consuming the excess natural gas, then it is flared into the atmosphere anyway.

Fundamentally, the argument that bitcoin energy consumption is bad for the environment presupposes that certain economies have a right to consume energy above others. Analyst Nic Carter succinctly summarizes this point:

> *This question relies on a kind of utilitarian logic about which industries should be entitled to consume energy. In practice, no one actually reasons like this. The bitcoin-energy supplicants are mum when it comes to the energy used to illuminate Christmas lights, to power the data centers behind Netflix or to distribute untold millions of single-serve meal kits. It's clear that because bitcoin's footprint is so easy to quantify — and an object of revulsion among the chattering classes — it is singled out for special treatment.*[12]

In summary, a large proportion of bitcoin mining consumes excess energy; it does not always demand that more energy be produced to power bitcoin mining (the energy is being produced anyway). Further, the nature of bitcoin complements qualities of renewable sources with a small carbon footprint, and the sources with a larger footprint would be burning gas whether or not bitcoin exists. Thus, the argument that bitcoin mining is bad for the environment is largely misconstrued, and **bitcoin is enabling the renewable energy industry by innovating energy storage economically**. Bitcoin makes renewable energy sources more viable.

## Isn't bitcoin disinflationary, and is that bad for the economy?

This answer could be a book itself, but I will summarize at the risk of oversimplification. I intend to write more on this in the future.

First, bitcoin is disinflationary because its supply is increasing at a decreasing rate. Increases in the bitcoin supply are considered **monetary inflation**. Monetary inflation is separate from its price in USD terms, which is its **price inflation**. This discussion will focus on monetary inflation, which does not consider bitcoin's price in USD terms.

Recall the discussion from chapter 7 where I presented the

**Producer's Trilemma** that results from central banks incentivizing people to overconsume or malinvest in risky assets because saving is not economically rational. Our economy is currently structured around this incentive scheme. If we were to have a disinflationary monetary reserve like bitcoin, this scheme would fundamentally change as savings would now be a more viable alternative to consumption or investing. Adoption of bitcoin would cause a structural shift in consumer behavior and thus a structural change in our economy. People would be spending less, investing less, and saving more.

Such a change would likely be bad for the economy in the short-term but good for it in the long-term. Bad, in that consumption and investment declines would hurt economic activity in the short-term. Because we have overconsumed and malinvested for so long, there will be a reversion to the mean. However, a healthy transition to an economy grounded in savings (as opposed to debt) would allow for capital accumulation at the individual level while reducing it at the institutional level.

It is hard to say precisely how an economy with a disinflationary currency would look as there isn't a directly comparable historical precedent to operate on (gold is inflationary). However, I believe the change in individual incentives will be beneficial. When someone can make money by simply holding bitcoin, their opportunity cost of capital changes. Every spending or investment decision is now subject to a maxim: "Since my bitcoin will gain significant purchasing power over time, I will only spend it on things I really want/need and invest it in ventures I think will outperform bitcoin." People will start to accumulate wealth without taking on undue risk, and living standards will rise.

A bitcoin system should increase personal responsibility and reduce dependency on institutions. Wealth accumulation through savings will reduce the demand for debt and people will be able to finance their lives how they see fit. The incentive to save will assist individuals in accumulating wealth in a sustainable manner.

In summary, the short-term costs of this structural shift will be painful but not permanent. Economic value would not disappear because we aren't investing or spending enough, it will be transferred to the future instead. People will spend and invest what makes sense today, and everything else can be saved for the future. This would be the opposite of our debt-ridden lifestyles today where we consume much of our future value in present. Bitcoin incentivizes long-term thinking.

However, a modern economy with a disinflationary currency is still an experiment. I'm not aware of an economy in history that is directly comparable. An economy with a disinflationary reserve currency would be a new world that likely empowers the individual through greater wealth. What we would choose to do with that wealth is uncertain.

## Isn't bitcoin used by criminals for money laundering and thus bad for society?

The answer to this was discussed in chapter 12. In summary, bitcoin can be laundered in a way similar to cash.

Ask yourself: If the government wants to end money laundering, why haven't they ended our ability to use cash?

An argument against bitcoin for money laundering is an argument against using cash as well. Remove bitcoin and the cash system still exists. Further, bitcoin is not nearly as anonymous as cash because bitcoin transactions are on a public blockchain.

This argument is a political tool to garner public support for regulating cryptocurrency. The same argument was used when the government tried to control public-key cryptography, which 2 federal judges ruled was in violation of the First Amendment. According to a study by Chainanalysis, 2% of bitcoin transactions are used for illicit activity.[13] The risk of criminal activity that already exists in our cash system is used as a scapegoat to sway public opinion toward justification of control over the cryptocurrency ecosystem. The fact that the government narrative focuses on this aspect of bitcoin, when only 2% of transactions are illicit, should tell you everything you need to know about their incentives. They do not want to lose control of their wealth extraction abilities; they do not care about criminals.

Practically every technology invented has enabled criminal activity, often in major ways. Consider all of the terrible things that have happened because of the internet. New technologies also provide better ways of defending against terrible things. There are new companies that analyze the blockchain full time to track transactions for the government (like Chainanalysis). The ability to analyze a public ledger of transactions is not possible in the current cash system.

## Isn't bitcoin's price too high now, and is it a bubble?

The value of bitcoin is based on monetary value, not market value. The monetary value of Bitcoin is assessed by qualitatively comparing its monetary properties to competing monetary mediums, as we have done. Bitcoin's monetary properties are far superior to fiat currency and gold. Its decentralized network provides certainty that these properties will not change.

The superior monetary properties of Bitcoin allow us to take a top-down approach to its valuation. Bitcoin's current market cap is ~$1 trillion. The market for gold is $12 trillion and for foreign reserves also $12 trillion. Those are just the two "reserve asset" market sizes. If bitcoin eventually became a global reserve, it could be much larger than that, representing all assets in the world. Bitcoin is still exceedingly small for its intended purpose.

As long as the network continues to grow, Bitcoins will continue to represent the value of goods and services in trade.

A common argument is to compare bitcoin to the famous Tulip Mania but bitcoin has 2 key distinctions.

- First is that bitcoin price appreciation draws in more miners, increasing network security, and thus increasing value. In other words, the more people that use bitcoin, the more valuable it becomes – in the same way as social media platforms. This growth in fundamental value by generating a network effect did not apply to tulips. People speculated that others would buy tulips from them, but the fact that many people were buying tulips did not create a sustainable network effect. Bitcoin has a growing and sustainable network effect.
- Second, bitcoin has been through 3 market cycles that each time have been called speculative bubbles by the mainstream financial media. With each cycle its price has rebounded from collapse and increased tenfold from its prior high. Tulip Mania was a speculative bubble because its price drastically increased and subsequently collapsed, never to return to its former highs again. Bitcoin has shown an exponential growth rate for 12 years. Its underlying fundamentals (i.e., network size, transaction count, number of addresses) all continue to increase. The Tulip Mania argument made a lot more sense in 2012 but it simply is no longer comparable.

Bitcoin has a consistent, albeit volatile, track record of long-term price appreciation that drives growth in its fundamentals, which is precisely the opposite of how a speculative bubble is defined. We are witnessing the birth of a new private monetary reserve asset. As with many transformational technologies, one can expect the road will be anything but straight.

## Why buy bitcoin when it is not "backed" by anything and/or isn't tangible?

If you read the first chapter, you know the answer to this question. For a good to be a monetary good, it needs to maintain monetary properties. To be "backed" by something means to have these monetary properties. By that terminology, bitcoin is backed by its inherent properties. Gold has these properties as well and is thus "backed" by them inherently. The US dollar does not have these properties, which is why it needed to be backed by gold (how the term "being backed" emerged). Once the gold standard was ended in 1971 under Nixon, the dollar was backed by the "full faith and credit" of the USA – meaning it is backed by the promise that it can always print more of it, in effect socializing the loss of wealth.

To maintain monetary properties a good does not need to be physical. It is self-evident that much of the value being created in modern times exists in a purely digital form. **These intangible things have value because they can create tangible consequences**. For example, if someone held your computer hostage and threatened to delete all its digital information, how much would you pay to stop them? Your answer describes how much value the sequences of digital bits that only exist in your computer have to you because if they go away, there are tangible consequences that will result.

The idea that gold is valuable as money because it is tangible is a non sequitur. Gold is valuable as a savings technology because it is scarce, which has tangible consequences. Scarcity can now be achieved digitally in bitcoin, making gold's monetary function obsolete.

## Is bitcoin scalable?

The answer to this is discussed in chapter 12. Bitcoin is scalable to a degree that is much faster than our current cash settlement systems (banking systems) today. Layer 2 payment systems (like Lightning or bitcoin banks) will be needed to compete with the credit settlement systems we have today, such as credit card companies. The creation of these systems will allow bitcoin to scale further.

## Is bitcoin not private enough to use?

This is a legitimate criticism discussed in chapter 12. Bitcoin is pseudonymous, and once your identity is linked to an address, all your transactions can be followed. Technologies exist to prevent this linking, such as mixing services that can create anonymity. However, these require technical ability. Privacy services will likely be a feature provided by 3rd party intermediaries in some form, and this is a huge area of development in bitcoin. Advancements currently underway in the Lightning Network will also significantly increase anonymity, but this will take time.

## Bitcoin can be forked infinitely, so how is it still scarce?

The answer to this is discussed in chapter 13. Forking a coin creates new coins but it does not create new nodes. Nodes will choose which network to participate in, and the network that most choose will win the fork. Forks of the bitcoin network result in a small amount of miners leaving bitcoin to instead mine the fork of bitcoin. So, the bitcoin network gets slightly smaller and a new small network with a new coin emerges. Eventually, prices adjust to represent the value of the underlying networks for each. The result is zero-sum.

## Bitcoin produces no cash flows so how is it a good investment?

This argument conflates the concept of market value with the concept of monetary value. Market value is determined by a good's utility for consumption, which is synonymous with the ability to generate future cash flows. Monetary value is determined by a good's utility for trade, which in turn is measured by the good's monetary properties.

**Bitcoin is an emerging monetary good, which is something that has not occurred for millennia.** It makes sense that people are confused about its value. We are witnessing the birth of a new monetary good which has a massive addressable market. Hopefully, this good will be used one day to trade all the goods and services which have market value.

**An investment in bitcoin is an investment in its monetary properties and network growth.** If it maintains its supply schedule and its decentralized stakeholder groups continue to grow, bitcoin will be the investment of a lifetime as its value could one day represent all other values. Even if you think this is unlikely, **the risk to reward is unmatched by any other investment opportunity**.

However, it is better in the long run to view it as savings technology. While it is still in its infancy it can be considered an investment; in the long run it will simply be used to save money. If you think about it as an investment, you will lose your hair from watching its volatility. **If you can successfully make the paradigm shift to understanding bitcoin as a long-term savings technology, you will likely accumulate material wealth stress-free (mostly).**

## Conclusion

I will quickly summarize the entirety of this book.

1. There are 6 monetary properties that define a good's utility for trade (as opposed to utility for consumption). The best of these emerge as monetary mediums.
2. Money emerged to facilitate trade and was produced and stored in a decentralized manner. Its production was later monopolized by sovereign institutions.
3. The centralization of the storage of money was the dawn of our modern banking systems. The resulting failures from the centralized production and storage of money demanded a 7th monetary property, immutability (achieved through decentralized production and storage).
4. Sovereigns responded to these failures not with decentralization but by further centralizing the banking system, creating the central bank. Their history of boom-and-bust cycles was tied to war and corruption.
5. The Federal Reserve is now the largest and most profitable company in the world. It determines the economic fate of a global monetary system through a politically appointed board of 7 members.
6. The Fed has led the world to the edge of a cliff on a mountain of debt, but for the first time in history, people have the option to opt-in to the new bitcoin monetary system.
7. Bitcoin was the result of 40 years of failed attempts to create digital money. The commitment to its achievement was driven by a movement of people who anticipated that governments would attempt to use the internet as a mechanism of control.
8. Bitcoin combines multiple technologies to allow individuals

to transact directly with one another pseudonymously. It is faster than any banking system existing today.

9. The technology is secured by a global decentralized network and clever incentive system.
10. The truly decentralized nature of the network provides certainty that its rules will not change extraneously and that it is resilient to attacks.
11. The Bitcoin network is the monetary base layer of a new financial ecosystem currently being built.
12. This monetary base layer is far superior to prior forms and is the logical next step in the world's monetary evolution.
13. Bitcoin is not perfect. There are many misconceptions about it but also many valid criticisms. None of the legitimate criticisms are fatal to its long-term value.

Hopefully, by now you see bitcoin not as a risky investment, but as a new monetary base layer that will store your wealth for generations and lead to the blossoming of a new era of personal freedom. If you're excited by this, I encourage you to opt out of fiat and into this new system. Bitcoin is being taken more and more seriously as it grows. Bitcoin is not yet a part of today's zeitgeist, but the resolve of the Bitcoin community may one day make it so.

*"The moral is to the physical as three is to one."* – Napoleon Bonaparte

# References


1. *The Prince*, Niccolo Machiavelli, chap. 6, 15
2. *The Origins of Money*, Carl Menger, 52
3. https://www.buybitcoinworldwide.com/volatility-index/
4. https://research.ark-invest.com/hubfs/1_Download_Files_ARK-Invest/White_Papers/Big%20Ideas%20 2020-Final_011020.pdf
5. https://www.vox.com/2018/4/24/17275202/bitcoin-scam-cryptocurrency-mining-pump-dump-fraud-ico-value
6. https://www.cnbc.com/2018/01/09/jamie-dimon-says-he-regrets-calling-bitcoin-a-fraud.html
7. https://www.investopedia.com/news/three-leading-economists-come-out-against-bitcoin/
8. https://www.forbes.com/sites/robertszczerba/2015/01/05/15-worst-tech-predictions-of-all-time/?sh=208184361299
9. https://en.wikipedia.org/wiki/The_DAO_(organization)
10. https://www.bloomberg.com/news/articles/2020-11-18/bitcoin-whales-ownership-concentration-is-rising-during-rally
11. https://www.forbes.com/sites/billybambrough/2019/12/01/jack-dorseys-future-defining-plan-to-bring-bitcoin-to-12-billion-people/?sh=734b1da24f6f
12. https://www.coindesk.com/the-last-word-on-bitcoins-energy-consumption
13. https://observer.com/2019/08/bitcoin-use-illegal-finance-mit-study-blockchain-ai/

# ACKNOWLEDGMENTS

Thanks to my editor Jon Harrison and designer Christine Keleny for all the hard work. Thanks to all those who spent considerable time providing honest feedback: Carl Jenkins, Brett Feeley, Raymond Au Yeung, Avinash Patel, Kyle Scholtz, Matt Serrao, Dan Guetig, Jesse Berger, and Heavy D. You all made this writing not only possible but enjoyable. Thanks to Annika Spetnagel for being my informal editor and for helping me filter my thoughts.

Lastly, thanks to my mother for everything and more.

# AUTHOR BIOGRAPHY

I'm passionate about:

- removing pretense
- showing how simple finance can be
- economic thought
- doubling down on your interests
- and Bitcoin

I graduated with a double major in finance & economics from Creighton University and 3 years later earned my CFA charter. I began my career at FTI Consulting in their Corporate Finance and Restructuring group for the TMT industry and then moved to Lion Equity Partners, a distressed buyout private equity fund.

All the while I intently followed Bitcoin, and its development eventually led me to jump into the industry. The world of traditional finance was a great place to begin my career, but I didn't find my passion there. I realized that my passion lay in finding ways to create and store value (through Bitcoin) rather than extract it.

I decided I wanted to be less professional and more real with people. I wanted to communicate transparently with others, as opposed to the opaque nature of financial institutions. My first step in this direction was writing this book – it is the resource I wish I had when I first discovered Bitcoin.

My website is yakes.io where you can subscribe to my thoughts about Bitcoin, crypto assets, finance, and economics.

My twitter is @ericyakes where you can follow me for my take on the world and the humor that gets better as you lower your expectations.

Made in the USA
Coppell, TX
19 January 2024